Culture, Secularization, and Democracy

Following the approach developed by Alexis de Tocqueville, this volume views democracy as a cultural phenomenon. It starts from the assumption that if we are to adequately address concerns about the current state and future of modern Western democracies, we need first to tackle the cultural preconditions necessary for the functioning of a democracy.

Since Tocqueville's time, the book takes the most crucial change in the West to be 'double secularisation'. Here, this concerns, first, the diminished influence of organised Christianity. Even though secularity was partly a product of Christianity, secularisation is highly significant in terms of the cultural underpinnings of Western democracy. Second, it involves a decreased interest in and knowledge of classical philosophy.

Chapters on secularity, family life, civic life, and public spirit focus on central elements of the changed cultural foundation of democracy, exploring issues such as identity politics, the public space, and the role of human rights and natural law in a pluralistic and resilient democracy. The volume concludes with a closer look at the implications of current presentism, that is, the view that only the present counts for the legitimacy and effectiveness of democratic systems. Finally, it asks if double secularisation can also offer fresh opportunities for promoting the conditions of a viable democracy.

The book will be of interest to academics and researchers working in the areas of law and religion, constitutional law, political science, history, and philosophy.

Sophie van Bijsterveld is Professor of Religion, Law, and Society at Radboud University, the Netherlands.

Hans-Martien ten Napel is Associate Professor of Constitutional and Administrative Law at Leiden University, the Netherlands.

ICLARS Series on Law and Religion

The *ICLARS Series on Law and Religion* is a new series designed to provide a forum for the rapidly expanding field of research in law and religion. The series is published in association with the International Consortium for Law and Religion Studies, an international network of scholars and experts of law and religion founded in 2007 with the aim of providing a place where information, data and opinions can easily be exchanged among members and made available to the broader scientific community. The series aims to become a primary source for students and scholars while presenting authors with a valuable means to reach a wide and growing readership.

Other titles in this series:

Law, State and Religion in Bosnia and Herzegovina
Nedim Begović and Emir Kovačević

The Church and Employment Law
A Comparative Analysis of The Legal Status of Clergy and Religious Workers
John Duddington

Business, Religion and the Law
Church and Business Autonomy in the Secular Economy
Matteo Corsalini

Religion, Human Rights, and the Workplace
Judicial balancing in the United States Federal Courts and the European Court of Human Rights
Gregory Mose

Religion and Contract Law in Islam
From Medieval Trade to Global Finance
Valentino Cattelan

Culture, Secularization, and Democracy
Lessons from Alexis de Tocqueville
Edited by Sophie van Bijsterveld and Hans-Martien ten Napel

For more information about this series, please visit: www.routledge.com/ICLARS-Series-on-Law-and-Religion/book-series/ICLARS

Culture, Secularization, and Democracy

Lessons from Alexis de Tocqueville

Edited by Sophie van Bijsterveld and Hans-Martien ten Napel

Routledge
Taylor & Francis Group
LONDON AND NEW YORK

First published 2024
by Routledge
4 Park Square, Milton Park, Abingdon, Oxon OX14 4RN

and by Routledge
605 Third Avenue, New York, NY 10158

Routledge is an imprint of the Taylor & Francis Group, an informa business

British Library Cataloguing-in-Publication Data
A catalogue record for this book is available from the British Library

ISBN: 978-1-032-61855-5 (hbk)
ISBN: 978-1-032-64097-6 (pbk)
ISBN: 978-1-032-64104-1 (ebk)

DOI: 10.4324/9781032641041

Typeset in Galliard
by Deanta Global Publishing Services, Chennai, India

The Open Access version of the Chapter 4 was Fundación Ciudadanía y Valores (FUNCIVA).

Contents

Contributors

Sophie van Bijsterveld is Professor of Religion, Law, and Society at Radboud University Nijmegen, the Netherlands. She publishes on the topics of religion, law, and democracy. Monographs include *The Empty Throne. Democracy and the Rule of Law in Transition* (2002) and *State and Religion. Re-assessing a Mutual Relationship* (2018). From 2007–2019 she was a member of the Senate for the Christian Democratic Party.

Jonathan Chaplin, Wesley House, Cambridge, UK. He is Political Theologian and Fellow of Wesley House, where he works with the Centre for Faith in Public Life. He is a Research Fellow of the Canadian think tank Cardus. His recent books include *Faith in Democracy* (2021) and *Beyond Establishment* (2022).

Trey Dimsdale is Executive Director of the Center for Religion, Culture, and Democracy in Plano, Texas, USA, an initiative of First Liberty Institute, and is Fellow at the Oxford-based Centre for Enterprise, Markets, and Ethics. He completed his legal education at the University of Missouri-Kansas City and holds degrees in theological ethics.

Carinne Elion-Valter teaches legal theory and methodology at Erasmus School of Law, Rotterdam, the Netherlands. Her research is focused on a critical analysis of legal thought, legitimacy, and the rule of law using literary theory and history of ideas. Topics she recently dealt with are the social contract as a relationship of reciprocity, and Tocqueville's travel companion Gustave de Beaumont's novel about slavery in the United States.

Stacey Hibbs is Senior Lecturer in the Honors Program at Baylor University, Waco, Texas, USA. She completed her MA and her PhD at Boston College, Chestnut Hill, USA. Her dissertation focused on Tocqueville's 'new science of politics'. Hibbs has led seminars and discussion groups on political philosophy, the importance of rational discourse, and civic friendship.

Hans-Martien ten Napel is Associate Professor of Constitutional and Administrative Law at Leiden University, the Netherlands, and Senior Fellow at the Center for Religion, Culture, and Democracy in Plano,

Texas, USA. As the fruit of an earlier Research Fellowship at the Center of Theological Inquiry in Princeton, New Jersey, USA, he published the monograph *Constitutionalism, Democracy and Religious Freedom. To Be Fully Human* (2017).

David Thunder is Researcher in Political and Social Philosophy at the University of Navarra's Institute for Culture and Society in Spain. His research focuses on the social and institutional conditions under which people can pursue free and flourishing lives. David's writings include *Citizenship and the Pursuit of the Worthy Life* (2014), *The Ethics of Citizenship in the 21st Century* (2017), and numerous articles in peer-reviewed journals.

Sarah J. Wilford is Professor and Researcher at Centro Signos, Universidad de los Andes in Santiago, Chile. She received her PhD in Politics from King's College London. She studies the political thought of Alexis de Tocqueville, especially regarding family, women, and the maintenance of liberty in democratic societies.

John D. Wilsey is Associate Professor of Church History and Philosophy and Chair of the Church History Department at The Southern Baptist Theological Seminary in Louisville, Kentucky and Research Fellow at the Center for Religion, Culture, and Democracy in Plano, Texas, USA. His most recent book is *God's Cold Warrior: The Life and Faith of John Foster Dulles* (2021).

1 Introduction

A new political science

Sophie van Bijsterveld and Hans-Martien ten Napel

1.1 Introduction

'A new political science is needed for a world altogether new', the French thinker, politician, and nobleman Alexis de Tocqueville (1805–1859) wrote in his magnificent book *Democracy in America* (Tocqueville 2000, 'Author's Introduction', 7). The book caused an immediate sensation in France when its first volume appeared in 1835. The book described, sharply analysed, and explained the new political formula that Tocqueville discovered in America: Democracy. The book stands out because it does not equate democracy with rules and procedures. Tocqueville places democracy in a broader social, cultural, and religious context. In his view, democracy is more than a technique; it is, first of all, a way of living together, a culture. He believes that a democratic system presupposes social, cultural, and religious circumstances to be sustainable and to flourish. In line with this perspective, Tocqueville directs his attention to constitutional arrangements, but also to democratic society and even democratic man.

About 100 years after the introduction of universal suffrage, we have become so familiar with democracy in the West that some of us have come to see the realisation of democracy more and more as a mission for the whole world. Just as the modern nation-state has become the organising model for political communities worldwide, for many, democracy is the only remaining defensible model for organising public decision-making. The ultimate confirmation of this conviction was the triumphalist-sounding assertion of the American writer Francis Fukuyama (1992), who stated that with the establishment of democracy and the rule of law – liberal democracy – the 'end of history' had been achieved. Just as some nation-states may have fundamental defects – failed states – not all democracies function flawlessly. For Fukuyama, this reality was not decisive. The system itself was superior.

Western familiarity with, and widespread belief in, democracy have pushed the significance of the 'cultural factor' that Tocqueville emphasised much to the background of our collective consciousness. However, the fact that democracy as a system cannot simply be transplanted to any random society was strikingly demonstrated by the Western interventions in Afghanistan and

DOI: 10.4324/9781032641041-1

Iraq that took place after the terrorist attacks in New York and Washington DC on September 11, 2001, as well as by the developments in Afghanistan after the withdrawal of American and other Western troops in 2021. In societies where the actual structures of power run along tribal lines, and theocracy is the stake of the leaders of the dominant faith, neither democracy nor the rule of law is truly viable. The British philosopher John Gray even sees the unquestioning belief in exporting democracy as a cultural good, expressing dangerous wishful thinking.[1] The vicissitudes of the Western presence in establishing a stable democracy and constitutional state in countries such as Afghanistan and Iraq have made us more sensitive to democracy as a cultural good, even in the West.

Indeed, it is now almost impossible to find a scholar who is optimistic about the state of democracy. Thus, according to the Economist Intelligence Unit's Democracy Index 2022 (2023), there are currently only 24 'full democracies' in the world, where a mere 8% of the world's population lives. Even within these 'full democracies', widespread support for democracy is no longer self-evident, especially among younger generations (Foa & Mounk 2016). Even those who do not wish to question the viability of modern mass democracy in a fundamental way must nonetheless face the question of whether democratic systems as they function today can still produce viable policies for the pressing problems that face the West today, such as the environment, migration, and social cohesion. That is partly due to the faltering of the post-Second World War international liberal order to successfully recognise, address, or take on these issues (Ikenberry 2018). In other words, not only the legitimacy of democratic decision-making, but also, increasingly, its effectiveness, have come under pressure.

These problems can be observed across Western democracies, regardless of whether democracy is embedded in a presidential, parliamentary, or hybrid form of government; regardless also of whether there is a tradition of a two-party or a multi-party system; regardless of whether the electoral system is based on the first-past-the-post principle or proportional representation; and regardless of whether referendums are possible or not. Current democratic dysfunctions and discontent, therefore, are not tied to the technicalities of the constitutional system. Consequently, viable perspectives on today's foundational issues in public life cannot limit themselves exclusively to issues of institutional design. Despite this obvious fact, that is still the dominant approach to improving democratic legitimacy and effectiveness in the literature (Graber, Levinson & Tushnet 2018). Discussions of these topics are kept 'technical' to fall within the traditional boundaries of parliamentary history, political science,

1 Television interview, 'In Gesprek Met John Gray', *Tegenlicht, VPRO,* 28 April 2008, https://www.vpro.nl/programmas/tegenlicht/kijk/afleveringen/2007-2008/in-gesprek-met-john-gray.html (accessed 14 August 2023).

and public law. Advisory committees or state-sponsored think tanks also typically consist of representatives of these disciplines.

In contrast, the current volume approaches democracy as a cultural phenomenon, a cultural achievement. It starts from the assumption that if we are to adequately address concerns about the current state and future of modern Western democracies, we need to tackle the cultural preconditions necessary for the functioning of a democracy first. Of course, this does not preclude subsequent recommendations on constitutional change, but the cultural question must come first. This approach to democracy aligns with that developed by the 19th-century French political thinker Alexis de Tocqueville, undoubtedly one of the most important theorists of modern democracy. In *Democracy in America* (1835 and 1840), Tocqueville approaches democracy as a cultural phenomenon and analyses, in turn, the effects of democracy on culture. His mission is to search for the conditions under which a viable, freedom-orientated democracy is possible.

The current volume aims to continue Tocqueville's quest, albeit under the radically changed circumstances of today's democracies. That implies that the project is not a study in Tocqueville; nor is it an exercise of merely transplanting Tocqueville's ideas to our current time. Tocqueville himself would have already warned against such a method in his day; if his warning applied to his contemporaries, it should apply even more to those of us writing two centuries later. Mindful of the cultural approach, the most crucial change is the 'double secularisation' since Tocqueville's time. This double secularisation concerns, first, the diminished influence of organised Christianity. Even though the secular state was partly a product of Christianity (Ferrari 2014), secularisation is highly significant in terms of the cultural underpinnings of Western democracy. Second, it involves a decreased interest in and knowledge of classical philosophy. This development, which has accelerated since the 1960s, is, as has been rightly noted, one of world-historical significance (Kinneging 2020: 13). The numerous detailed studies making up the dominant approach to improving democratic legitimacy and effectiveness in the literature risk obscuring this.

The combined effect of the two secularisations is a cultural 'outlook' less rooted in history than before. Of relevance in the context of the proposed volume is the changed view of human flourishing. Human flourishing is, after all, the goal of any 'good' political order. In classical philosophy and Christianity, visions of the good life in general, and liberty, were 'objective' in character, whereas nowadays, they are commonly represented as defined by predominantly subjective traits. In connection with this, the individual pursuit of happiness now seems to take pride of place in visions of the good life. Tocqueville, too, was explicitly aware of the emerging individualism. However, if individualism turns into narcissism, that has irrevocable consequences for both family and associational life, which, according to the same Tocqueville, are essential for a well-functioning democracy. The state's increased role in social life also reinforces the trend of individualisation, as was equally foreseen in *Democracy in America*.

Chapters on secularity, family life, civic life, and 'public spirit' deal with central elements of the cultural foundation of democracy with the aim of exploring how the consequences of the cultural shifts in these areas affect the functioning of democracy and also to seek viable ways to address these. How can Tocqueville's notion of 'self-interest well-understood' counter the narrow self-interest of identity politics? Attention then shifts to the more visible superstructure. Under conditions of secularity, how can maximum public space still be created to express both religious and other opinions within democratic bodies? What contribution can human rights and natural law (continue to) make to a pluralistic and resilient democracy? Does the double secularisation perhaps also offer fresh opportunities for promoting the conditions of a viable, liberty-orientated democracy? The volume concludes with a closer look at the implications of current presentism, i.e., the view that only the present counts for the legitimacy and effectiveness of democratic systems.

Just as Tocqueville did not want to turn back the clock, nor does this volume. However, it maintains that a solid solution is inconceivable without re-evaluating democracy's cultural preconditions first. Too often, democracy is only looked at from the outside. It is certainly important to look at its institutional aspects, which is done throughout the volume. Ultimately, however, the 'inner workings' of democracy keep it running. It is to this that Tocqueville called attention in his day. The 'inner workings' of democracy, the ethos without which it becomes an empty shell, are now widely recognised to be in disrepair. Consequently, constitutional engineering will only make sense when considered in conjunction with the cultural basis of democracy and the ideas of flourishing and character embedded within it.

Concern for the functioning of our democratic society should not only be essential for legal scholars and political philosophers. It is ultimately about the democratic system being experienced as democratic, corresponding to citizens' real-world experiences and values. It must also generate real solutions to real problems with authority. With the above developments in mind, a 'new political science' seems necessary again in our time. For Tocqueville, the new – democratic – era was heralded by the irreversible social equality that marked the end of the aristocratic class society. For us, the present state of democracy implies an assignment to rethink the 'political formula' of our democratic system.

The great political theorists of the 17th and 18th centuries, such as Locke, Hobbes, and Rousseau, laid the philosophical foundations for what would develop into our modern democratic constitutional states. They rethought the nature of the relationship between state and citizen and the nature of society, each in their own way and building on their particular views of man. They expressed their ideas in the form of a social contract as the basis for the organisation of society and public decision-making. Their ideas resonate in the modern constitutional states that evolved over the last two centuries. Their common core was an idea of liberation by defining government in terms of its service to the citizen and society, assuring the citizen's influence in the law's development, and limiting the state's power. What have we overlooked when this idea of liberation is no longer experienced this way? Where did we go wrong? Do we need to adjust our perspectives?

Dutch Minister of State, Herman Tjeenk Willink, with his longstanding and in-depth theoretical and practical expertise in the public domain, wonders whether we are 'not thinking much too simply about the government and the possibilities of maintaining the democratic rule of law'. At the same time, he observes that this democratic legal order 'is probably our only remaining common foundation' (Tjeenk Willink 2019: 18, 15–16). When read together, these statements seem to produce an almost unbridgeable field of tension. When the functioning of our system raises issues that are both fundamental and urgent, it is not enough to simply analyse our current predicament. It is necessary to use our constitutional imagination and to develop future-orientated perspectives. This book aims to contribute to the latter by examining a number of crucial concepts with a view to the future of democratic society. As mentioned above, these are secularity, family life, civic life, public spirit, personhood, public space, natural rights, natural law, and legitimacy. As also indicated, each of the contributions to this book takes its starting point from Tocqueville's ideas.

1.2 Why Tocqueville?

Tocqueville is one of the greatest thinkers of modern democracy, if not *the* greatest. With America as his living example, he understood democracy in all its facets. He himself expressed his commitment thus:

> I confess that in America I saw more than America; I sought there an image of democracy itself, of its penchants, its character, its prejudices, its passions.
>
> (Tocqueville 2000, 'Author's Introduction', 13)

In that search, Tocqueville broached all the major themes of democratic constitution, democratic culture, and democratic man. The result is a unique starting point for thinking through the questions of democracy in our time (Atanassow 2022).

Tocqueville's interest is broad. He describes the customs and morals of Americans in all areas, from the arts to male-female relationships, from the nature of scientific practice to the role of money in society, from the inexorable drive for innovation to social association life. This broad interest also characterises his approach to democracy. Democracy is influenced by daily living conditions and habits and, in turn, it exerts influence on these. In this approach, Tocqueville distinguishes himself from the 17th and 18th-century contract philosophers referred to above who chose the imaginary starting position of a 'state of nature' and drew conclusions from this via an abstract, deductive line of reasoning about the nature of government authority and the relationship to the citizen. Tocqueville chooses reality as his starting point; the reality that has been shaped historically and that presents itself concretely. This leaves room in his analysis for observations and reflections that would remain out of the picture in a strictly disciplinary approach.

The central idea that runs through Tocqueville's work is that of the social equality that characterises modernity. Equality changes everything, from the way individuals perceive themselves to the way they view others and behave in society. Equality defines the character of society and leads to a democratic form of government. In all these respects, a democratic era is the radical opposite of an aristocratic one.

Tocqueville saw the advent of equality as the result of a historical development occurring over centuries and therefore as an inevitable, irreversible fact. The essence of personal identity, the nature of citizenship, and economic dynamics all change profoundly through equality in comparison with the class society of the aristocracy. This change affects the nature of politics and the organisation of the state. Indeed, it reshapes the way power and authority are seen and thus transforms the character of the state itself. The insights Tocqueville developed on this subject were, and still, are unique.

After the fall of Napoleon in 1815, a constitutional monarchy came into being in France. The post-Napoleonic state inherited the highly centralised state apparatus that had already been formed before the Revolution. The bureaucratic power machine that the state had become remained, even though it now had formal democratic legitimacy. Was this democratic freedom? Was this real democracy? Was a democratic system ultimately about changing only the external label of the exercise of power, but leaving its nature untouched? Who or what could counterbalance excessive centralisation now that the nobility and the old intermediary organisations could no longer fulfil that role? Was the concentration of power through centralisation in a democracy as inevitable as the end of the aristocracy? These were questions with which Tocqueville turned his gaze to America for an alternative.

In his younger years, Tocqueville had already analysed the development of the English and French state institutions. He had already come to the conclusion that England could not be a model for France because of a different historical development. France traditionally had a strong nobility and a weak monarchy. The nobility was an effective counterweight to royal authority. As a result, the monarchy looked for an ally in the people and vice versa. This fact gradually led to centralisation. After the Revolution, the centralised state machinery remained in place. England, on the other hand, had a strong monarchy. In order to form an effective counterweight to this, the nobility gradually sought allies against the monarchy among the prominent representatives of the people who emerged from the masses. The sovereignty of Parliament meant in practice something quite different from the sovereignty of the French state bureaucracy. For Montesquieu, who, with the separation of powers, aimed at spreading power within the national level of government,

England could offer an example. Tocqueville's questions extended further. In America, he could study democracy in an almost archetypal form. American democracy did not carry the burden of history that the developing European democracies did. From the point of view of guarding the balance between the different levels of government, federalism was particularly interesting to Tocqueville.

In the townships of New England, Tocqueville found an ideal image of modern democracy. They were characterised by their local, small-scale character and by the lively involvement of the – well-informed – population in public affairs. The deliberations concerned issues that directly affected the people. Democratically elected officials had limited terms of office. They were primarily accountable to the people rather than to a higher level of government. Tocqueville saw a citizenship among equals, driven by their involvement and own initiative. These observations also led Tocqueville to question the geographical scale on which true democracy could be exercised.

Democracy makes the individual human being powerless, both towards other people who are, after all, equals and towards the state. In their own well-understood self-interest, democratic people join together to achieve common goals. This leads to a lively associative life, in which people also gain personal experience in the promotion of issues that transcend individual interests and in government, and develop a feeling for public affairs in the broader sense. Tocqueville considered the recognition of classical fundamental rights for limiting government power alone too meagre. He was an advocate of societal democracy, that is a democratic society rather than a mere political democracy.

Tocqueville considers radical decentralisation that keeps citizens involved in decision-making about their daily living environment and that cultivates personal experience in the practice of democracy to be a precondition for democracy. This includes a well-informed citizenry. Tocqueville expresses his admiration for the lively daily press and the many different newspapers, which were also read in the furthest corners of what was then inhabited America. The third precondition is Christianity. He considers its significance so great that he calls religion the 'most important political institution', even though church and state are strictly separated. Faith, writes Tocqueville, teaches Americans the art of being 'free'. The spiritual orientation of religion provided a foundation on which democracy could thrive. We could say that the societal democracy of associational life and the social significance of faith and the church helped to prevent the absolutization of politics.

Radical decentralisation, a well-informed citizenry, and religion are, in Tocqueville's eyes, critical success factors for a democracy. Democracy, however, was not a peaceful possession in Tocqueville's eyes. Democracy could also turn into its opposite. Ultimately, Tocqueville would distinguish three forms of this: Tyranny of the majority, 'mild' despotism, and 'democratic despotism'.

In Tocqueville's view, popular sovereignty was the ideological foundation for democracy. That same popular sovereignty also harboured the seeds of a tyranny of the majority. Nothing, in Tocqueville's view, was so irresistible as a 'tyrannical power' of the majority as it can act effectively and coercively, being 'vested with the moral power that belongs to the will of the greatest number' (Tocqueville 2000, 1:2; 5.212). Socially, tyranny of the majority finds its equivalent in a disproportionate coercion of public opinion.

Similarly, social equality, the prerequisite for democracy, harbours a threat to democracy. It essentially casts every human being back upon himself. Democratic people see themselves as individuals rather than as links in the chain between the generations and rather than as part of their social class. The individual's life takes place in the here and now and in a small circle of housemates and friends; the people outside are strangers to him. Everyone has the same social status, but the socio-economic position must always be fought for. That is what democratic people do. Democratic living conditions lead to individualism and materialism. As a result, public affairs are increasingly left to others.

These are favourable conditions for the state to emerge as a 'supergovernor' and to assume exclusive responsibility for the welfare of its citizens. It takes control of society and smothers personal initiative 'with a network of small, complicated, painstaking, uniform rules through which the most original minds and the most vigorous souls cannot clear a way to surpass the crowd'. Thus it 'reduces each nation to being nothing more than a herd of timid and industrious animals of which the government is the shepherd' (Tocqueville 2000, 2:4; 4.663 (both instances)). This is the 'mild' despotism that can manifest itself as a new form of tyranny in a democracy. 'Democratic despotism', finally, was a formally democratically legitimised autocratic rule.

The almost unstoppable centralisation that we are witnessing, the power and at the same time the powerlessness of the state to address important issues and move them forward, the coercion of public opinion, and the withdrawal of people into the seclusion of their living environment are therefore not innocent phenomena from Tocqueville's perspective. The same applies to secularisation and the accompanying task for every individual to construct their own philosophical project and 'give meaning' to their existence. Tocqueville would abhor a citizenship constructed by the government or a citizenship that is no more than a result of public policy.

Tocqueville's ideas – his approach to democracy, his analysis of its conditions of existence and risks to it – are an excellent source of inspiration for thinking through political and social issues in our time and, in dialogue with them, developing perspectives on our state, society, and democratic man.

1.3 Tocqueville in his time

Alexis de Tocqueville lived on the threshold of a new era. Although he was yet to be born when it took place, the French Revolution was of great significance in his life. His father and mother narrowly escaped the guillotine, but other family members were not so fortunate. In his family and social circles, the Revolution was seen as a catastrophe and there was a desire to restore the old regime. This was the spiritual-political atmosphere in which Tocqueville grew up (Siedentop 1994).

In his relatively short life, Tocqueville experienced political extremes. The Napoleonic era in which he was born was followed by the restoration of the Bourbon monarchy in 1815 with Louis XVIII as constitutional king, initially with a moderate-liberal parliamentary majority. After 1820, the parliament was dominated by ultra-royalists who sought the restoration of the Ancien Régime and, after 1824, with Louis XVIII's royalist younger brother, Charles X, on the throne, gained the upper hand.

It was the time when Alexis de Tocqueville mastered the major themes of the political-state debate, the debate between ultra-royalists and liberals. With his good friend Gustave de Beaumont, with whom he would travel to America a few years later, he attended lectures at the Sorbonne by François Guizot, one of the leading figures of the moderate liberals, also known as the Doctrinaires. Tocqueville himself had come to realise at an early age that the restoration of pre-revolutionary relations was an illusion and that the democracy that came in the wake of the Revolution was not transient. Tocqueville and Beaumont were attracted to this moderate-liberal movement.

Three themes dominated the debate. The first was the nature of the relationship between culture and the organisation of the state, and by extension, the question of the interpretation of French history. According to the moderate liberals, in order to be successful, the state and political institutions had to be modelled on social reality and not the other way round, as was the position of the ultra-royalists. It was also important to show that, given changes in society, a return to the Ancien Régime could be pursued for a short time but was ultimately doomed to failure. At the same time, it had to be argued to radical liberals that the unsatisfactory state of democracy was not the inevitable result of unchangeable circumstances.

The second theme was the meaning of church and Christianity. For the ultra-royalists, church and faith were pillars of authority and were thus intertwined. When the Ancien Régime was overthrown, they therefore naturally fell into disfavour. As Tocqueville wrote, the radicals' aversion to it was mainly a political statement. What was the relationship between church, religion, and democracy for the moderate liberals?

The third theme was the basis of state authority and thus the idea of the state itself. The ultra-royalists could only see this in hierarchical terms. They found the moderates, with their acceptance of democracy, facing a horizontal legitimisation of authority. But, again, when the old intermediary structures are destroyed, society 'atomises' and the state only has loose individuals facing it, is unbridled power of the state the undesirable result? These main themes recur in Tocqueville's work.

With the July Revolution of 1830, the Bourbon monarchy was overthrown. The politically progressive citizen-king Louis Philippe of the House of Orléans, a branch of the Bourbons, came to power. It marked the self-selected end of Tocqueville's father's administrative career. Alexis had just accepted his first job as auditor of the court and had to swear an oath of allegiance to the new king. In his own circles, he was frowned upon for this. The new regime regarded him with suspicion because of his origins. Although he later thought that this king was not democratic enough, he realised that his prospects were not good.

The idea of a trip to America took shape. It was immediately an opportunity to escape the impasse. He and Beaumont succeeded in getting a government contract to study the prison system in America, a hot topic in France. It offered Tocqueville the opportunity in America to search for answers to his profound questions about democracy and, with a bit of luck, to advance in career terms afterwards. In 1831, he boarded a sailing ship with Beaumont for the New World. There, the friends would travel around for nine months. The letters that Tocqueville and Beaumont each wrote from America show how much they shared the same thoughts. Tocqueville's findings were published in *Democracy in America*. Beaumont wrote the novel *Marie*.

The publication of the first part of the book *Democracy in America* in 1835 had the desired societal effect for Tocqueville. It paved the way for his career in politics. After an unsuccessful attempt in 1837, Tocqueville was elected as a Member of Parliament in 1839. Part two of the book was published the following year. Although his aim was a career in active politics, he lacked the natural talent for it. The concrete political circumstances that needed to be promoted were not in the area of his constitutional interest either. He did find that interest in the aftermath of the February Revolution of 1848, after which he was re-elected. He served on the committee that had to draft a new Constitution. On the basis of that Constitution, Louis Napoleon was elected president. This president appointed Tocqueville as Minister of Foreign Affairs in 1849. A few months later, the cabinet resigned and Tocqueville became a parliamentarian again.

From an early age, Tocqueville took the possibility into account of an outbreak of civil war and of imprisonment. Civil war did not break out, although he did experience short revolutions and a coup d'état. He was, however, imprisoned. Louis Napoleon seized power in 1851 and established the French Second Republic. Tocqueville was then imprisoned for a night with other parliamentarians. Louis Napoleon's coup was democratically legitimised by a referendum. Tocqueville wanted nothing to do with democratic despotism and he decided to leave politics. His Memoirs of the 1848 revolution appeared posthumously in 1893.

In his later work *The Ancien Régime and the Revolution* (1856), he examined the undercurrents in French society and French public administration that paved the way for the Revolution. Tocqueville did not get around to writing a follow-up on the Revolution and the rule of Napoleon. His health, already frail, deserted him, and he died in 1859 at the age of 53. His ambition had always been to play a role in public administration. His lasting significance lies in his ideas on democracy.

1.4 Tocqueville today

The interest in Tocqueville's thought has proven to be enduring in a number of Western countries, such as America; in others, the interest in Tocqueville's thought is undergoing a revival. His name regularly appears in academic circles, in politics, and in newspapers.

His prophetic gifts continue to fascinate. In a way, he predicted the 'disposable society' (Tocqueville 2000, 2:1; 8.426–428). He also realised that while the 'old' Europe continued to regard itself as the centre of the world, on both sides of it new superpowers were developing, based on mutually radically differing world views. Thus, a century in advance, he already foreshadowed the arrival of a Cold War (Tocqueville 2000, 1:2; 10.395–396). Tocqueville explains why people in a democratic society are sensitive to the misery that befalls on others: As equals in equal circumstances, they are prone to such misery themselves as well. The 'mild despotism' of the modern regulatory state that tries to control society and human life in every detail as well as the pressure of public opinion are all too familiar to us today, even after the retreat of the state in certain domains of the classic Western European welfare states.

The issues that Tocqueville raised in relation to the cultural dimensions of democracy continue to be our issues today: The role of religion and world views in shaping our societies, and, therefore, influencing democracy; the relationship between family structures and democracy; the significance of civic engagement; the alignment of self-interest with public spirit; the notion of personhood in democratic societies; the way of dealing with pluralism; and the nature of law and its changeability – these remain current fundamental issues. The contributions to this volume take up these issues and, starting from the perspective formulated by Tocqueville, reconsider them in relation to contemporary Western democracy.

Sophie van Bijsterveld discusses which features of Christianity Tocqueville discerned as having a sustaining influence on democracy. She shows how the themes Tocqueville addresses in this respect emerge in concerns about Western democracy and democratic societies today. She argues that, transposed to contemporary times, the intuitions Tocqueville attributed to Christianity have the potential for mediating between opposing states of mind that are marked by either hubris or apathy towards the public domain. From this perspective, she asserts that the cultivation of these Christian intuitions remains essential, even if Christianity can no longer fully fulfil the role of being their primary carrier.

Recognising both the equalising and transformative influence of democracy on family life, while maintaining aspects of authority and normative moral production, the family in Tocqueville's account was important to the flourishing of democratic societies. Using the analysis of the 20th-century social critic Lasch as a bridge between Tocqueville's times and ours, Sarah Wilford discusses the major issues surrounding modern family life, notably the advance of outside experts into the family. She offers suggestions from Tocqueville and

Lasch that can serve as an inspiration to enable the modern 21st-century family to live up to the public significance it potentially possesses.

Alexis de Tocqueville understood the critical importance of associational life for a free and prosperous democratic nation, as well as any modern thinker. David Thunder shows how the right to associate with one's peers in pursuit of purposes not established or tightly regulated by the state exists in permanent tension with the prerogatives of the 'people', which seem to press ever more aggressively for complete sovereignty over social life. After considering various mechanisms to check this drift towards democratic despotism, he suggests a hybrid form of federalism, incorporating non-territorial associations into the territorial pact.

According to John Wilsey, Tocqueville's conservative articulation of the doctrine of self-interest rightly understood is essential for our current democratic societies. Complemented by religion, expressed through voluntary associations, informed by the mores and customs of morality, and animated by public spirit, it brings people together starting at the local level. It combats the tendency of indifference towards others and assists in the 'apprenticeship of freedom'. The Tocquevillian notion of self-interest, therefore, deserves renewed attention.

Today, alarms that are raised about 'identity politics' point out the ways in which viewing a particular identifier as the wellspring of non-negotiable views rends our social fabric. What can Tocqueville teach us about identity and identity politics in a democratic society? Stacey Hibbs reminds us that Tocqueville does not deny identity. He acknowledges that both mutable and immutable characteristics shape us. How can we value liberty, yet maintain community? The clue to this question lies in correcting the narrow self-interest of identity politics by recognising that an individual's personal well-being is connected to the well-being of his or her community.

Jonathan Chaplin explores how – even in conditions of pervasive secularity, now jostling with ever-deeper moral, cultural, and religious diversity – public religion can still supply uniquely valuable civic resources that can help sustain, and perhaps even renew, the increasingly fragile, fragmented, and tribalised democracies of our day. Lending an 'agonistic' twist to Tocqueville, he argues for a model of constitutional democratic pluralism in which maximal political and legal space is facilitated to express contending faith-based political visions. He proposes that the welcoming to democratic fora of political visions that allow citizens and their associations to express their deepest faith-based identities (both religious and secular) would both deepen the moral seriousness of democratic debate and enable a more sustainable consensus, than a system that denied, marginalised, or de-legitimised such faith-based offerings would do.

Classical jurisprudence defines rights with respect to just action. Every rights claim, then, implicitly involves a moral claim that is only intelligible by reference to a referent external to the individual. The rise of the 'unlimited sovereignty of the individual', as Manent calls it, in liberal democracies forecloses the possibility, however, that an external referent to morality, justice, goodness, or truth can demand an individual's action or the uniformity of any group.

Tocqueville addressed the collision of these two incompatible conceptions of rights in his 'Speech to the Constituent Assembly on the proposed constitution, concerning the right to work' on September 12, 1848, as he warned that by departing from a classical conception of rights, the result would be to abandon the ideal of 'equality in liberty' for the reality of 'equality in bondage'. Ultimately, a concrete example of Tocqueville's prediction has been borne out in the evolution of French constitutional history, Trey Dimsdale asserts, as the present Constitution incoherently articulates the virtuous ends of the Republic (*liberté, égalité, fraternité*) while simultaneously codifying a radical secularism (*laïcité*) that has unmoored those virtuous ends from any context that can make them intelligible.

Hans-Martien ten Napel observes that, until recently, modern democracy has revolved around the triad of truth, unity, and plurality. Truth is the concept best associated with natural law in constitutional studies. When awareness of natural law was still widespread, at least in theory, there was a high degree of unity in the field of 'mores' and consequently relatively little plurality. These were the conditions under which so-called 'natural law liberalism' could thrive. These were also the conditions that prevailed when Tocqueville travelled across America. The cultural revolution of the 1960s, in which the element of 'truth' was pushed into the background, led at first glance to an increase in pluralism. That comes at the expense of unity. However, on closer inspection, Ten Napel sees that a new kind of unity seems to be growing, precisely at the expense of pluralism. Thus, paradoxically, the situation is beginning to resemble the premodern era. After all, value relativism grows into a new kind of truth, albeit opposite in content to the traditional concept of truth.

Carinne Elion-Valter focuses on the temporal dimension of democracy; that is, its relation to past, present, and future. Tocqueville trusted the legal mind or the *esprit des légistes* to counter democracy's temporal fragility. According to Tocqueville, democracy might fall prey to a rush to the future, in fact, a one-way ticket to despair, or, due to extended welfare regulation, turn into a certain form of statis, or immobilism emptied of hope or enthusiasm. To counter these temporal risks, Tocqueville presented the legal spirit of lawyers and the judiciary, whose business it is to connect the present with the past and with the future. They are experts in thinking transhistorically. Contemporary democracy and regulatory practices curtail these aspects of legal thinking, resulting in a democracy without a (legal) story and without hope. The chapter explores how legal thinking today might again counterbalance contemporary democracy and provide it with a sense of hope.

Tocqueville himself already warned against simply transplanting constitutional and social structures and mechanisms that worked for the America he visited to his native France. This warning concerns us all the more, across a time span of almost 200 years. This volume is perfectly aware of this. However, to reflect on the urgent issues of our contemporary Western democracies,

Tocqueville's thought provides an excellent starting point and a source of inspiration.

The chapters of this volume provide a wealth of ideas to critically reassess the state of our contemporary Western democracies, in relation to culture and secularisation, in line with Tocqueville's approach.

References

Atanassow, Ewa (2022), *Tocqueville's Dilemmas and Ours*, Princeton & Oxford: Princeton University Press.

Economist Intelligence Unit (2023), *Democracy Index 2022: Frontline Democracy and the Battle for Ukraine*, Economist Intelligence Unit. *https://www.eiu.com/topic/democracy-index.*

Ferrari, Silvio (2014), 'The Christian Roots of the Secular State', in Rene Provost (ed.), *Mapping the Legal Boundaries of Belonging: Religion and Multiculturalism from Israel to Canada*, Oxford: Oxford University Press, 25–40.

Foa, Roberto Stefan & Yascha Mounk (2016), 'The Democratic Disconnect', *Journal of Democracy* 27(3): 5–17.

Fukuyama, Francis (1992), *The End of History and the Last Man*, New York: The Free Press.

Graber, Mark A., Sanford Levinson & Mark Tushnet (eds.) (2018), *Constitutional Democracy in Crisis?* Oxford: Oxford University Press.

Ikenberry, G. John (2018), 'The End of the International Liberal Order?', *International Affairs* 94(1), January: 7–23.

Kinneging, Andreas (2020), *De onzichtbare Maat. Archeologie van goed en kwaad*, Amsterdam: Prometheus.

Siedentop, Larry (1994), *Tocqueville*, Oxford & New York: Oxford University Press.

Tjeenk Willink, Herman (2019), *Groter denken, kleiner doen. Een oproep*, 8th ed., Amsterdam: Prometeus.

Tocqueville, Alexis de (2000; original, French edition 1835, 1840), *Democracy in America* (Translated, edited, and introduced by Harvey C. Mansfield & Delba Winthrop), Chicago & London: University Press of Chicago.

2 Secular democracy and the public significance of religion

Sophie van Bijsterveld

2.1 Introduction

Alexis de Tocqueville (1805–1859) regarded *mores,* 'the whole moral and intellectual state of a people' (Tocqueville 2000, 1:2; 9.275), as one of the great sustaining forces of the thriving democracy he witnessed in America, next to its laws and the politico-geographical position of the country (Tocqueville 2000, 1:2; 9.265). Democracy, the inevitable political translation of a society built on the premise of social equality, needed sustaining forces. It could not sustain itself. As he elaborated specifically in the second volume of *Democracy in America* (1840), democracies as formal constitutional systems may have a high degree of stability, but as cultural phenomena, they do not. Not only do democratic cultures differ, but they are open to development, also for the worse. Tocqueville's quest was to explore the forces that sustain democracy, that is, a *particular kind* of democracy: A democracy as the expression of liberty – liberty seen as the virtue of self-government. Participation in public decision-making is, in Tocqueville's view, a key element of democracy and an expression of liberty.

Among the *mores* that Tocqueville identified, religion was a crucial factor. Prior to his travels to America, Tocqueville was already concerned with the role of religion in democratic society. In America, he experienced a society in which religious faith was embedded in the soul of the people, where it permeated society and provided spiritual nourishment for the informal constitution of public life. Tocqueville even went so far as to call Christianity the 'first of … [the American] political institutions' (Tocqueville 2000, 1:2; 9.280). Christian faith taught Americans, in Tocqueville's words, 'the art of being free' (Tocqueville 2000, 1:2; 9.278).

What exactly was it in religion – more specifically, in Christianity – that Tocqueville regarded as indispensable for a well-functioning democracy? In line with many current discussions about the state of Western liberal societies and liberal democracies, one may think first and foremost of 'Christian values' or equivalents to this expression. Indeed, Tocqueville did point at the moral dimension of religion. It would be a mistake, however, to equate his analysis of the public significance of religion with current controversies over

DOI: 10.4324/9781032641041-2

particular values and norms, promoted or combatted in the name of a religious faith. First, and contrary to many current debates, Tocqueville did not venture into the promotion of very specific values and norms that should or should not be upheld in society or by law – morality, narrowly defined. This may be explained by the fact that such values could, by and large, be regarded as self-evident (see Chapter 9). Second, his analysis of the public significance of religion reaches beyond the moral dimension of religion.

Profound concerns over the functioning of contemporary democratic systems across the wide spectrum of the specifics of constitutional design confront us once again with the question of their cultural underpinnings (see Chapter 1). Tocqueville's analysis of modern democracy and democratic culture presents a challenging guide in this respect. For our secularised societies, especially his views on the public significance of religion provide valuable insights.

This chapter explores the relevance of Tocqueville's views on the public significance of religion, in particular, Christianity, for democracy in today's highly secularised Western societies. After examining what Tocqueville's stakes were in the issue of religion, the chapter discusses which features of Christianity Tocqueville discerned in *Democracy in America* as having a sustaining influence on democracy. Three such features are considered: apart from its engagement with morality, Christianity cultivates an openness towards the future, and stimulates an orientation towards the common good. The chapter explores how in contemporary concerns about the state of Western democracy, and Western democratic societies, these themes implicitly or explicitly emerge and how, transposed to contemporary times, the Christian intuitions that Tocqueville discerned are significant to the functioning of contemporary democratic societies as well. It argues that these features of Christianity have the potential for mediating between opposing impulses or states of mind that are marked by either hubris or apathy towards the public domain. From this perspective, the chapter asserts that secularity is not a matter of indifference. Cultivation of these Christian intuitions remains essential, even if Christianity can no longer fully fulfil the role of being their primary carrier and alternatives may only partially be able to contribute in this sense.

2.2 Post-revolutionary stakes in religion

Arriving on American shores, Tocqueville's fascination with the religious nature of the country was immediately triggered. 'On my arrival in the United States', Tocqueville wrote, 'it was the religious aspect of the country that first struck my eye. As I prolonged my stay, I perceived the great political consequences that flowed from these new facts' (Tocqueville 2000, 1:2; 9.282).

Tocqueville's upbringing in a traditional Roman Catholic family tradition that bemoaned the French Revolution and the fate of the church in its slipstream, the education he received from the family priest, well into his teens, and his personal struggles with dogmatic faith, had no doubt played a role in developing a sensitivity for religion. More importantly, with his keen intellectual interest in religion, high political stakes were involved that directly concerned the functioning of the state and its new system of government, that of democracy.

At the constitutional and institutional levels, the position of the Church and the place of religion in the public domain were matters of profound controversy in Tocqueville's France. The ultra-royalists, who sought a reestablishment of the times of the *Ancien Régime*, believed in the institutional connection between throne and altar that characterised pre-Revolutionary France. They could not come to terms with the change in public status of their church and religion. The revolutionaries, on the other hand, did not believe that religion – read: the Catholic Church – was able to play any role in the new post-Revolutionary democracy; indeed, they doubted whether Catholicism was even compatible with democracy.

Tocqueville rejected a role for the Church as in former times. He regarded the Church's fall in the wake of the Revolution as an almost inevitable consequence of its pre-Revolutionary political position, rather than as an aversion to faith itself, although faith and the Church were often lumped together in the heat of the debates. Against the revolutionaries, he did see a crucial role for religious belief in a democracy, not as a pillar or legitimiser of power, but in its operation at the level of individuals and, through individuals, of society.

Tocqueville recognised a basic congruence between democracy, grounded as it is in the acceptance of social equality, and Christianity, with its tenet of equality of every man in the eyes of God. 'Christianity', Tocqueville wrote, 'which has rendered all men equal before God, will not be loath to see all citizens equal before the law', adding that in France, at the time, nevertheless 'religion' resisted 'democracy' and vice versa (Tocqueville 2000, 'Author's Introduction', 11). Tocqueville saw the impact of Christian religion on American democracy also beyond this basic congruence.

Kahan demonstrates how Tocqueville's anthropology is influenced in particular by themes of the 17th-century Christian moralists Nicole and Pascal: opposing impulses of self-interest versus charity of man, and of man's material versus immaterial inclinations. Tocqueville recognised these impulses, without disqualifying self-interest and material desires per se. Democratic societies encouraged these impulses, which meant that they should be channelled in the right direction and, to avoid excess, be counterbalanced by their opposites. In particular, the 18th-century political thinkers Montesquieu and Rousseau stimulated Tocqueville to relate the theme of human nature to religion, culture, and politics, modifying their views and applying them to the new democratic era (Kahan 2015: 16 ff.). Personal ambition, the impulse of striving for perfection, striving for social equality, and the desire to achieve higher standards of material well-being, phenomena that Tocqueville dealt with, were not in his eyes to be approached per se with suspicion or disapproved in a democratic society. They needed to be channelled in the right direction and placed in the right perspective (Kahan 2015: 10 ff.; 31 ff.). It is in these respects that Tocqueville, parallel to secular checks, also saw a role for religion.

2.3 Tocqueville and Christianity's public significance

Throughout *Democracy in America*, Tocqueville repeatedly addresses church and state relationships, the potential of Christianity in shaping social mores, and its governance of individual souls. Tocqueville, however, does not present a systematic analysis of the Christian faith or its public significance. Tocqueville unfolds his views on Christianity as a spiritual basis for a well-functioning democratic society and democratic political system through his observations on the democratic system in America, his reflections on its underpinnings, and speculations about possible directions democratic systems may take. Only occasionally are religion, religions, or the Christian faith discussed more extensively.

Tocqueville observed that in America, church and state were not only separated institutionally. He also witnessed that the clergy voluntarily kept their distance from day-to-day politics and did so with a sense of professional pride (Tocqueville 2000, 1:2; 9.283). This apparent abandonment of influence was ultimately its strength: it increased its 'real power' (Tocqueville 2000, 1:2; 9.283). 'The powers of society are all more or less fugitive', Tocqueville wrote (Tocqueville 2000, 1:2; 9.284). In a democracy, the political opinions of the majority are in constant flux. Keeping a distance from this dynamic protects the credibility and authority of the church and its faith. Acting otherwise, it would run the risk of discrediting itself when majority opinions change. Left to its own domain, religion's influence 'is more lasting' (Tocqueville 2000, 1:2; 9.286).

Christianity's moral influence is its most obvious public significance. Tocqueville remarks that Christianity meshes well with the democratic mind. Focusing on the fundamentals of Christian morality, Tocqueville observes that its central tenets are open enough to social change: the love of one's neighbour as oneself and the love of God above all else. In this regard, Tocqueville compares Christianity and Islam. His conclusion is striking. In his view, the elaborate and detailed legal prescriptions contained in the Koran are harder to reconcile with the democratic mind.

The prime impact of Christian morality in a democratic society according to Tocqueville then lies beyond moral specificities. Christianity's moral significance lies in the consciousness that not everything possible is good or morally defensible. The love of God implies the cultivation of a healthy self-restraint, of an inner civilisation. In Tocqueville's words:

> So, therefore, at the same time that the law permits the American people to do everything, religion prevents them from conceiving everything and forbids them to dare everything.
>
> (Tocqueville 2000, 1:2; 9.280)

The large number of different religious groups in America was a revelation to a Frenchman raised in the Catholic faith. Tocqueville discovered that the way in which the various religious denominations thought about morality was similar. They only differed in 'the worship one must render to the Creator' (Tocqueville 2000, 1:2; 9.278).

A second defining factor of Christianity's impact on democracy that we can identify in Tocqueville's work was its openness towards the future. Tocqueville saw in religion what he called 'a particular form of hope' (Tocqueville 2000, 1:2; 9.284). Christian faith is a faith in progress, it preaches confidence in the future. It combines a belief in a yet unfulfilled future with the awareness of an imperfect reality. Precisely this combination prevents a flight into utopias while ensuring that people do not become trapped in the limitations of immanent reality. It encourages a particular kind of resilience that is essential for democracy. Tocqueville may have had this feature of Christianity in mind when he wrote:

> Despotism can do without faith, but freedom cannot.
> (Tocqueville 2000, 1:2; 9.283)

The belief in a transcendent reality that is implied in religion as a special form of hope instils the understanding that there is 'something bigger than me'. It prevents an excessive focus on the self and the idolising of other phenomena, such as the nation (Atanassow 2022: 167 ff.).

Surprisingly perhaps for a work on democracy, Tocqueville also discusses the role of dogma in religion; he does so from a cultural point of view. It is obvious that in order to function in society, all people need to accept a certain body of knowledge that is presented to them as authoritative, without being able to verify its substance on their own. Tocqueville applies this to religious dogma as well. For most people, it would simply absorb too much of their energies to be fully occupied with probing religious dogma, so acceptance of what is handed over is the most obvious route. It frees people from the responsibility and anxieties to carve out the meaning of life on their own.

As a third defining factor, Tocqueville saw that Christianity was a force in motivating people to be orientated towards the common good. In a democratic society, man is thrown back on his own resources. In a society where everyone is each other's equal, everyone is powerless to achieve anything significant on his own. People seek each other out and participate in society in order to achieve common goals. Well-understood self-interest propels them in that direction (see Chapter 5). Tocqueville was struck with the energy with which Americans formed associations for any purpose. And as an individual, democratic man is also powerless against the state. Uniting for a common cause also helps keep the state at bay.

Christianity encourages and underpins cooperation and social engagement out of a spiritual responsibility: The love for one's neighbour. It prevents people from being isolated and frees them from living within the limited horizon of their own individual self. A democracy orientated towards maintaining liberty and human greatness is well-served by the spirit of cooperation for the common good.

Today's debates on democracy and democratic society show concerns that reverberate with the issues to which Tocqueville was convinced Christian intuitions provided a crucial contribution.

2.4 Democratic concerns today (I): Morality – between autonomy and heteronomy

For Tocqueville, democracy equalled political liberty. Liberty, for Tocqueville, was essentially a political category. This was a classic approach to liberty. It reached back to ancient Greek thought and was revived by the early modern political theorists (De Dijn 2021: 8 ff.; Atanassow 2022: 20 ff.).

Our political-constitutional understanding of liberty no longer is that of Tocqueville's. As De Dijn maps out in detail, the dominant perception of liberty is not that of self-governance, but one that can be framed in terms of fundamental rights – a liberty of a private sphere with which the state should not interfere (De Dijn 2021: 9 ff.). The dominant shift from an understanding of liberty in terms of *participation in* public decision-making to a *no-entry zone for* public decision-making took place in the course of the 19th and 20th centuries. It was triggered by the American and French Revolutions. According to De Dijn, this shift was the result of a deliberate attempt by political thinkers to create a protection *against* the democratically governed state; as a bulwark against democracy, against popular participation. As a result, constitutional liberty came to mean the liberty of the private individual vis-à-vis the state.

The dominant cultural understanding of liberty has also undergone a profound transformation compared to the understanding of liberty informed by Christianity such as was Tocqueville's. Atanassow writes: 'Freedom, for Tocqueville, requires trust in a moral universe, supportive of human endeavor' (Atanassow 2022: 14). Parallel to the individual turn of political-constitutional liberty, the cultural interpretation of liberty is also defined from the perspective of the individual. It is furthermore orientated towards the – preferably instant – fulfilment of individual desires. Kinneging attributes this shift to the cultural influences of Enlightenment and of Romantic thought respectively. He traces consumerist mentality back to Enlightenment's unbridled belief in progress, with technology and the market as driving forces (Kinneging 2020: 20 ff.). Romantic thought with its preoccupation with 'authenticity', then, is the fertile ground for the development of excessive individualism. This individualism stresses personal identity and, ultimately, places a burden on individuals to live up to their true individual identity (Kinneging 2020: notably 28–29). The parallel with Tocqueville's concerns about the direction in which democratic societies might develop is striking. Tocqueville feared that the dynamics of democratic societies, in which no person was certain of his socio-economic position, would become focused on this, inclining individuals to overvalue material goods and to be predominantly occupied with themselves. This, in turn, would lead to neglect of their civic responsibilities, enabling a mildly despotic state to step in (Kinneging 2020: 13 ff., 49 ff.).

According to Tocqueville, Christianity's morality provided a cultural underpinning for democracy in the sense that it cultivated an inner condition and attitude towards life that were instrumental to sustaining the 'right' kind of democracy. Healthy self-restraint in one's behaviour, love of one's neighbour, and a sense of interdependency in social relations were the kinds of moral orientations that mattered to Tocqueville in this respect. Such moral orientations provided a substructure for the exercise of liberty. Christian morality seen in this way, helped mediate between the extremes of radical autonomy and submission to external control.

The combined political and cultural shift in our understanding of liberty is well characterised by an attitude to regard liberty as the freedom to do whatever one wishes as long as it is not prohibited by law.[1] To a certain extent, this makes sense, i.e., from the viewpoint of positive law. From a cultural perspective, such an understanding of liberty when actually practised would lead to an inhospitable, even unliveable society. Postliberals, among others, are vocal criticists of a self-centred and self-gratifying notion of liberty and its potential 'borderlessness'. Some postliberals tend to attribute the misguided notion of liberty to liberal democracy as such (Deneen 2018).

In various ways, the effects of the combined transformation of the dominant understanding of liberty are manifest in contemporary concerns over and debates on the functioning of democracy and democratic society. The first way in which the transformation of the notion of liberty is apparent is in the persistent belief in the power to shape society through law and in the dependency on the state for regulation of social life.

Individualism stimulates etatism. With the erosion of intermediate social structures – associational life – that is socially legitimised, the buffer they form between the individual and the state disappears. Lack of internal conditioning – in the Tocquevillian sense informed by Christian intuitions of morality – invites external conditioning by the state. The problem with external conditioning, especially in its appearance as a combination of detailed administrative regulation sanctioned by criminal law, however, is that it is intrinsically unable to cover all situations, that it usually lags behind, and that it often limits ordinary social life while providing ample loopholes for those who deliberately want to avoid it. Examples can easily be found in measures in the sphere of financial and fiscal regulation, in the sphere of preventive measures as requirements of certificates of conduct, or camera surveillance.

1 The Dutch Government defines liberty thus in *Kernwaarden van de Nederlandse samenleving*, Uitgave van het Ministerie van Sociale Zaken en Werkgelegenheid, 20 February 2014, p. 6; see < https://www.rijksoverheid.nl/documenten/brochures/2014/05/21/kernwaarden-nederland> (accessed 26 June 2023).

Changes in what is regarded as socially acceptable certainly do not always originate within the political domain; nor are they always a prompt political reaction to social incidents (the 'rule-regulation reflex') (cmp. Boutellier 2019). However, even when they are driven by developments outside the political domain (such as concerning sexuality, gender, and '#MeToo'), they often find their way to the political domain and result in regulation, rather than continue to rely on informal *mores*.

A second way in which the combined transformation of the notion of liberty is apparent is in debates on the desirability of a 'Leitkultur'. This German concept literally translates as 'leading culture'. It echoes in discussions on 'values and norms' or even in phenomena such as 'culture wars', at least in as far as they rely on state endorsement or state intervention. These debates do not primarily concern individual behaviour but rather the social acceptance of a dominant culture within society. They are a reaction to increasing religious and secular pluralism in Western societies. Although the idea of a 'Leitkultur' itself is controversial, Western states increasingly seem to take on 'soft' issues in the value sphere but leave matters that are traditionally state responsibilities to the market. These 'soft' issues are often more substantial than the broader intuitions Tocqueville had in mind. Examples are value-laden citizenship education in schools or integration programmes for immigrants, especially non-Western immigrants. These 'soft' issues are notoriously hard for the state to address successfully. Moreover, they trigger controversy over the nature of the values that the state desires to instil in its citizens or over the questions of whether such values are part and parcel of liberal democracy as such, as witnessed, among other things, in debates over the interpretation of human rights, the mutual relations between various human rights, and the proliferation of human rights (also Chapter 8). This, in turn, carries the risk of disconnection of parts of the citizenry from the state and the democratic system.

A third way in which the double transformation of the notion of liberty becomes manifest is in the dominant approach to personal success. The opportunities that democratic societies provide in the socio-economic and immaterial sphere to make something of one's life are potentially liberating: One's birth does not determine one's social and economic position or one's set of beliefs. The perception that only oneself is ultimately individually responsible for material and immaterial happiness, however, also places a burden on the individual's shoulders. Not only being successful, then, is one's own achievement, but being unsuccessful is to blame on one's personal shortcomings. For the successful, success provides a feeling of entitlement. For the unsuccessful, there is no excuse.

These implications are being criticised and challenged from various sides. Political philosopher Sandel has made it a point to expose the idea that success is merely a personal achievement. He has powerfully warned against the 'tyranny of merit' and its effects on democratic society – the idea of being represented in the public domain, the idea of fairness, and of basic trust within a society, all necessary preconditions for a well-functioning democracy risk being eroded. He reminds his readers that success is often a result of circumstances that are 'given' to one, even if one personally has the disposition to succeed (Sandel 2020). In the immaterial domain, 'superstar' psychiatrists, practically 'secular theologians', criticise contemporary dominant cultural expectations of the self as the ultimate source for achieving personal happiness.

Personal liberty, in the sense of a large degree of choice in all areas of life, cannot be redressed in modern Western societies, nor should it be. The wisdom of the Christian attitude to life and its experience with the human condition, however, can provide a mediating force between the twin tendencies of materialism and individualism (autonomy), and etatism (heteronomy), tendencies inherent to democratic societies. Its view of man as a relational being, the acceptance of man's interdependency, the belief in man's flourishing in and through his relationships with others, and its view of life itself as a gift are moral orientations conducive to this. It also implies that worldly success comes with responsibilities. The role Tocqueville attributed to religious dogma, sublimised in a cultural understanding potentially relativises the hazardous search for meaning as an individual life project.

2.5 Democratic concerns today (II): Hope – between fatalism and utopianism

Tocqueville was fully alive to the fact that democratic societies were intrinsically dynamic. During his travels in America, he saw dynamics at work in all areas of life. He witnessed these in technical innovations, economics, family relationships, and political convictions. In a democratic society, characterised by equal conditions, man had no fixed place in society, but was continuously involved in making a living, earning his income, and carving out a career. Economic dynamics were a consequence of this. Economic growth, innovation in all areas of life, and better living conditions and welfare for all were a result. The ideas of unlimited progress and controllability of our environment and society have become deeply ingrained in society and our subconsciousness.

In a secularised version, the belief in progress is strongly ingrained in politics. Democratic politics live off the idea of progress. Political parties and politicians promise to improve living conditions and are elected on that basis. Although the idea of controllability of society through politics is widely recognised to be an illusion, political dynamics and the relationship between the electorate and politics continue to be driven by the combined ideas of progress and controllability.

In the international sphere, the attempts to bring Western-style democracy to countries like Afghanistan and Iraq show how strongly these ideas are rooted in politics – and to what consequences they may lead. In a less dramatic way, the idea of universal human rights is a powerful vehicle for imagining and shaping 'a better world' and an expression of the belief in progress and controllability, both in the international sphere and at home.[2] Similarly, the ideas of progress and controllability find an inexhaustible ally in the aspiration to achieve equality in ever greater detail in ever more areas of life.

The downside to this is that temporary or structural flaws in the realisation of progress and control are readily perceived as a 'crisis'. In recent decades, the number of 'crises' that are proclaimed in a wide variety of areas is telling. In many cases, the crises were quite readily predictable (such as in the sphere of migration, climate change, or the international financial system) or, at least in part, part and parcel of ongoing political challenges (such as in the field of the well-functioning of the labour or the housing market). The proliferation of crises bears witness on the one hand to the pervasiveness of the belief in progress and controllability and on the other hand shows the deep deception when progress and control are not achieved. This, then, easily results in a loss of perceived legitimacy of the democratic system. Cumulatively, the result of the democratic system is often to put in even more effort to achieve control. The usual reaction to incidents and wrongs is to turn to stricter rules and to set more mechanisms of control in place – known as the 'risk-regulation reflex'.

The idea of progress is a deeply Christian theme. Precisely for that reason, Gray labels modern utopian thinking as 'another chapter in the history of religion' (Gray 2008). In his view, modern secular utopian ideologies, including those we have seen with devastating effect in the 20th century, have built on the ground pattern of the Christian idea of progress. At a personal level, the idea of progress gives meaning to people's lives, according to Gray, such that people easily fall into despair when their belief proves to be false. The crucial difference with religious belief is that modern secular belief in progress is combined with an overoptimistic view of mankind. Religions, certainly Christianity, have a realistic view of mankind. Thus, a religiously informed belief in progress can mediate fatalism and utopianism.

Like the idea of progress, the aspiration to cultivate the world is a profoundly Christian theme. Controllability is connected to cultivation but is not identical to this. Indeed, belief in controllability in Christian thought is considered hubris. The biblical story of the Babylonian tower is exemplary. Christian belief not only avoids the trap of belief in full controllability, it also provides spiritual resources to deal with the downsides of the uncontrollable. In its encouragement to cultivate the world, Christian belief thus mediates between fatalism and controllability. It reconciles the hope for a better world with the consciousness of living in an imperfect world.

Controllability of one's personal or professional life and of society is an illusion. Rosa, who distinguishes between various dimensions of controllability (to render visible what used to be invisible, to bring something within reach and to make it accessible, to conquer something, and to utilise and

2 Marcel Gauchet sees in the retreat of transcendence a cause for human rights becoming a secular doctrine of salvation, see Martin Sommer 2019: 78 ff.

instrumentalize something) criticises the omnipresent impulse of controllability (Rosa 2020).

In our democratic society, the impulse of controllability takes many shapes. The stress on optimisation and output is one manifestation. Another is the expansion of regulation in all fields of life – the principle of equal treatment drives ever more detailed regulation to determine everyone's specific claims to access any facility or good. In connection with this, the demand for transparency and accountability increases. This leads in the public domain to consumerism and juridification. Rosa contrasts these dynamics with the experience of joy and happiness which flow from the encounter with the unexpected and the uncontrollable. Transplanted to the public domain, the over-reliance on and belief in controllability, which can never be fully satisfied, leads to frustration.

If Christian belief can fulfil a mediating role between fatalism and utopianism, this implies that it provides resources to deal with ambiguity; ambiguity that is encountered in the personal, but also in the social and public sphere. The loss of tolerance to ambiguity and the loss of our ability to deal with ambiguity is characteristic of our times, according to Bauer (Bauer 2011). This is related to modern dynamics in all fields of life, from the biological to the psychological and public domains, towards unambiguousness and against genuine diversity. Rosa sees the church, especially the Catholic Church, as an institution, as exemplary for ambiguity. Religious scriptures are full of ambiguity too. Christianity does not have a monopoly as a resource for tolerance towards ambiguity. Genuine expressions of culture have such potential too.

Rather than a development towards stimulating the ability to deal with ambiguity, Rosa sees a rise in pressure to be 'authentic'. This pressure makes itself felt in the personal sphere but can be recognised in the cultural, social, and political domains as well. To be 'authentic' is to be identical to oneself; it is the negation of culture. Seen from this perspective, the political manifestation of 'authenticity' and the loss of tolerance towards ambiguity can be witnessed in the growth of fundamentalism in politics and the aversion of the willingness to reach political compromises, an essential feature of classic democratic politics. According to Bauer, democratic politics rely heavily on the ability to deal with ambiguity on the side of politicians, and on the tolerance for ambiguity on the side of the electorate. Thus, the loss of cultural resources to strengthen the art of dealing with ambiguity, including that of Christian belief, is an impoverishment for democracy and democratic society.

2.6 Democratic concerns today (III): Participation – between indifference and self-idolatry

As a drive for individuals in a democratic society to join efforts in order to achieve common goals, Tocqueville regarded self-interest as well understood. Individuals living in a democratic society realise that it is in their own interest to sacrifice some of their liberty and independence to work together for the common good. Itself not a virtuous inclination, self-interest well understood eventually leads to virtuous conduct and is therefore to be applauded. In a democratic society, joining forces in civic associations of whatever kind prevents individuals from standing powerless vis-à-vis the state and helps to limit the state's inclination towards ever stronger expansion (see Chapter 4). In that sense, political participation at the municipal level fulfils the same role. In Tocqueville's thought, Christianity spiritually undergirds civic and political participation. The congregational nature of religious practice and the important tenet of love of one's neighbour are cases in point. Putnam's credit of religion as a source of social capital, the social infrastructure of relationships between individuals, creating mutual trust and reciprocity, reiterates this vision.[3]

Despite the self-evident character of participation for a well-functioning democracy, participation, and furthermore, the *right kind* of participation, is not self-evident. Tocqueville's apparitions of democracy in one way or another suffer from a lack of democratic participation. Individualism and materialism, in particular – tendencies to which, in his eyes, democracies by their very nature are prone – induce people to abandon public life and relish in their own cocoons. A periodical tribute to the ballot box does not equal democratic participation and even such tribute is often not deemed worth the effort. A democratic political system, meanwhile, requires a democratic society.

One of the causes of the widespread discontent with democratic politics is a breakdown in the communication lines between the electorate, on the one hand, and political parties and democratic politics, on the other. Such communication channels, traditionally activated by active political participation, civic associations with real social legitimacy, and decentralised public decision-making, are eroding. In some cases, notably that of the European Parliament and decision-making in the European Union, such communication channels never actually existed. The risk is that the direction of democratic politics is not in alignment with the undercurrent of the will of large parts of the populace, at least in certain areas. This manifests itself, among other things, through artificial majorities in coalition governments with tight coalition agreements or by the fact that the ambit of democratic decision-making is significantly restricted through centralised legislation or judicial decision-making. In the Tocquevillian sense, we could say that democracy should resonate with the 'mores' of a society, an implicit understanding of the social and political expectations of society (Sommer 2019: 24 ff.). So-called anti-establishment political movements can, at least in part, be seen as a response to the erosion of these communication channels; and because populist parties cannot deliver the desired results either, they also fall prey to disillusion.

The shift towards pragmatism in democratic politics, the abandonment of the 'grand narratives' in politics, has been pointed at as another cause of discontent. Again, the decision-making in the EU is exemplary for this style of political decision-making. As a result, it is hard to relate to the decision-making process, with the risk of leading people to indifference or turning away

3 See Putnam and Campbell (2020) for religion as a source of division.

from democratic politics to their own 'cocoons'. The 'high absorption capacity' of pragmatic politics has also been referred to as making it harder to criticise, leading to more extreme forms of criticism and contributing to a climate in which anti-establishment politics thrive (Boutellier 2019).

Destructive political polarisation, the apparent difficulty of relating political ambitions to grander narratives of a 'common good', and the elusiveness of democratic control also lead to a mismatch between how many people actually experience and live out their values and what they see represented in the political domain. In other words, existing civic engagement does not always find representation in the public sphere, and, therefore, seems non-existent (Van den Brink 2012: 509). Instead of carving out contemporary visions of narratives of the common good, identity politics are making their way into the public domain. Identity politics cater to what could be called 'micro goods', politics tailored to please specific groups in society who are preoccupied with themselves, often on the basis of real or perceived injustices or discrimination. Lilla strikingly showed that the official website of the American Democratic Party had sections for 17 (!) different identity groups, 17 'bubbles', in which it told 17 different stories of what the Democratic Party stood for (Lilla 2018: 11–12). It is not surprising that Lilla calls for a reorientation towards the common good.

Christian belief and participation in congregational practice encourage attitudes towards oneself, society, and the public domain that avoid the abovementioned traps. Religions are a source of social capital. They stimulate participation in social and public life in a way that exceeds individual short-term interests and calls one to practise care for one's neighbour. Religious communities thus also appeal to the idea of a common good. Dealing with ambiguities and difficulties that arise in practice equips citizens for participation in wider society and for political participation.

In contributing to creating a genuine social fabric, religions provide a sense of belonging and community. Religious communities may be the very few places left where people from all different walks of life have the opportunity to meet each other, irrespective of background or social position. In that sense, they also fulfil an integrating function as few other institutions or practices do. Whatever differences may keep people apart in other domains of society or politics, religious communities accept each other as 'children of God' as equals; a 'cancel culture' is not part of their vocabulary.

The idea of transcendence embodied within the Christian faith has social and political significance in this respect. The very idea of transcendence tears down the glorification of any other human institution, of oneself, one's identity, one's material well-being, one's social group, one's country (De Kesel 2010). It does not ridicule these notions or dispute their value but prevents idolising them. In this way, it forces one to be self-critical, a pre-condition for a genuine dialogue.[4]

4 See Adrianus van Luyn, 'Authentieke Dialoog' *(blog)*, 5 November 2021, on: Authentieke dialoog – Tocqueville (ru.nl) (accessed 10 August 2023).

For the Western European continent, a political equivalent to civic engagement developed with the rise of the party political system in the 19th century, which came to its full fruition in the century thereafter. These parties played a part in the social emancipation of segments of society that until then had little or no political voice, organising a constituency and integrating them at the same time into wider political society. In the post-World War II period, such political parties played a central role in Western European politics. In some countries, specifically in the Netherlands, they were part of the famous system of pillarization, but always integrating at the top. In that sense, they filled both the role of bonding and bridging at the level of national politics and society. They were not single-issue parties. In current debates on controversies over religion and democracy, it is important to realise that Christian democratic parties often stood at the cradle of the development of modern democracies and played a formative role in this, together with their non-denominational counterparts (Casanova 2010). As with civic organisations, the total of the pillarized organisations provided spiritual engagement, a communal religious or non-religious political orientation, social integration, and vertical communication lines. They were strong social organisations, with a genuine social legitimation. Many of these parties played a role in keeping the state at a distance, which could substantiate the role that was defined for them under the promoted principles of sovereignty in one's own sphere and subsidiarity.

In this context, finally, it is worthwhile casting a glance at conceptions of the state. In Christian thought, various theories have been developed to stress the nature and the limited ambit of the state. In Catholic theory, the principle of subsidiary holds that social and public responsibilities should be carried out at the level as nearest to people as possible, from families to civic associations to municipalities, up to the state and beyond. Calvinist thought developed the idea of spheres of sovereignty, claiming that each sphere is characterised by the specifics of that sphere and should, therefore, have the sovereignty within that sphere. Only in situations of conflict between spheres or for the overarching common good, the state should be responsible. In Anglican thought, the idea of the state as a 'community of communities' has been proposed (Williams 2012: 37 ff.).

Limitation of the ambit of the state in a liberal democracy is a central tenet as well. It is underpinned by the rule of law, especially by fundamental liberties. It remains the question of whether fundamental liberties alone are capable of securing the state's limited ambit, as various analyses have shown a shift in the approach towards such liberties in terms of liberty in service of the state's particular liberal ideology (Ten Napel 2017).

2.7 Prospects: Religion, secularity

The ideal-typical significance Tocqueville attributed to Christianity with respect to democracy and democratic society continues to bear significance today. Does this significance manifest itself necessarily in any democratic Western society? Tocqueville would be the first to caution against such a conclusion. What he witnessed in America starkly contrasted with the situation in France. The French Catholic Church and French Christian religion did not and could not fulfil the role Tocqueville attributed to the churches and Christianity in America. Tocqueville was very well aware of the importance of a contextual approach. This was not only true for the cultural role of Christianity but for constitutional mechanisms as such. Tocqueville would have warned of uncritically assuming that features of a particular society or constitutional system could be transplanted to different times.

From this perspective, a few difficult questions need to be addressed. The first question is: Have our contemporary Western democracies and actual living conditions developed in such a way that the complexity of social and political issues, the centralisation and enlargement of scale, and the excessive production of regulation are impossible to turn back? After all, factors like these run counter not only to Tocqueville's ideal of democracy, they are also a cause of frustration with the public domain for many. Perhaps the answer must be – at least in part – affirmative. But that does not discharge us from the fact of contemplating these current conditions and sounding out cultural energies that might induce change.

Another question is whether the Christian religion and the social and cultural vehicles for manifesting itself in society are energetic enough to fulfil the roles with regard to a democratic society as discussed earlier. After all, an important reason for the fact that Christianity could fulfil these roles in Tocqueville's America was because its social presence was pervasive. Although its cultural achievements in many ways continue to have an effect, in secularised societies it remains to be seen whether precisely in the areas we have discussed, the influence of Christianity endures or can be retrieved. This influence is a by-product, a consequence of Christian faith; it is not the other way around. Its beneficial role for democratic societies does not stimulate people to become religious.

Furthermore, Christianity itself is affected by a number of cultural developments of which we asserted it could provide a mitigating role. That is on the one hand indifference and on the other hand fanaticism. The cultural demand for instant accessibility and the inability to deal with ambiguity also affect religion itself.

A third question is whether other institutions can fulfil these roles, if only complementary. This is a question Tocqueville is also aware of (Kahan 2015: 94 ff). Indeed, in a number of ways, at least in part, the answer must be affirmative. Sport, for example, can fulfil a role in the participatory area, at least to a certain extent. Its strength is that it constitutes a social practice; unlike religion, however, it is not embedded in a spiritual or intellectual tradition. Various art forms can be considered as well. Literature and poetry, theatre and film, whether supported by (mass) media and education or not, for example, have the potential to thematise the issues we discussed, as does intellectual thought. Apart from education perhaps, their weakness is that they are not necessarily embedded in or supported by social practice. In that sense, none of these alternatives, it must be feared, are able to fulfil the roles with respect to democratic society in such an integral way as religion can. Besides, they, too, like religion, are not fully able to resist the cultural tendencies to which they could be an antidote. That does not mean, of course, that they should be neglected in this respect.

2.8 Conclusion

Currently, religion has once again become a topic that cannot be politically ignored (Van Bijsterveld 2018). This in itself makes religion relevant to democracy. One of the reasons for this is that we have once again become aware of the cultural dimension of religion and the social consequences of spiritual life and theological stances. Ferrari, for example, points out that even the idea of the secular state itself has Christian roots (Ferrari 2014). And, although the dogmatic position of religion as a mere private matter continues to be professed, the interest that Western states take in religion shows that it is the collective and public dimension of religion that prompts this interest. This is mostly visible when real or perceived negative effects are feared, which, these days, is especially connected to the presence of Islam in Western societies. The focus of this chapter was on religion's positive impact on democracy.

This chapter has argued that, translated to contemporary times, the ground patterns that Tocqueville recognised in Christianity's positive role vis-à-vis democracy are as relevant as they were in Tocqueville's time. Contemporary discussions on the state of Western democracy point to fundamental cultural conditions that contribute to an ill-functioning democracy – ill-functioning in current understandings of democracy as well as in that of Tocqueville. These causes can be seen as taking to extreme natural tendencies within democratic societies. Christian intuitions concerning the nature of man and the attitude towards human behaviour and towards what it means to be part of a society can fulfil a mediating role between the extremes. Even if Christianity cannot fully fulfil this role today, it is important to recognise the significance of these insights. Although alternatives can only be expected to step in partially, their potential deserves to be explored rather than ignored.

References

Atanassow, Ewa (2022), *Tocqueville's Dilemmas and Ours. Sovereignty, Nationalism, Globalisation*, Princeton & Oxford: Princeton University Press.

Bauer, Tomas (2011), *Die Vereindeutigung der Welt. Über den Verlust and Mehrdeutighekit und Vielfalt*, Stuttgart: Reclam.

Bijsterveld, Sophie van (2018), *State and Religion. Re-assessing a Mutual Relationship*, Portland: Eleven Publishing.

Boutellier, Hans (2019), *Het seculiere experiment; over westerse waarden in radicale tijden (herziene versie)*, Den Haag: Boom.

Brink, Gabriël van den (ed.) (2012), *De Lage Landen en het hogere. De betekenis van geestelijke beginselen in het moderne bestaan*, Amsterdam: Amsterdam University Press.

Casanova, Jose (2010), 'Religion Challenging the Myth of Secular Democracy', in Lisbet Christoffersen et al. (eds.), *Religion in the 21st Century: Challenges and Transformations*, London and New York: Routledge.

Deneen, Patrick (2018), *Why Liberalism Failed*, Yale: Yale University Press.

Dijn, Annelien de (2021), *Vrijheid. Een woelige geschiedenis*, Uitgever: Alfabet.

Ferrari, Silvio (2014) 'The Christian Roots of the Secular State', in Rene Provost (ed.), *Mapping the Legal Boundaries of Belonging: Religion and Multiculturalism from Israel to Canada*, Oxford: Oxford University Press, 25–40.

Gray, John (2008), *Zwarte mis. Apocalyptische religie en de moderne utopieën*, Amsterdam: Ambo.

Kahan, Alan S. (2015), *Tocqueville, Democracy, and Religion. Checks and Balances for Democratic Souls*, Oxford: Oxford University Press.

Kesel, Marc de (2010), *Goden breken. Essays over monotheïsme*, Amsterdam: Boom.

Kinneging, Andreas (2020), *De onzichtbare maat. Archeologie van goed en kwaad*, Amsterdam: Prometheus.

Lilla, Mark (2018), *The Once and Future Liberal. After identity Politics*, London: Hurst and Company.

Napel, Hans-Martien ten (2017), 'Geloof in de liberale democratie', *Tijdschrift voor Religie, Recht en Beleid* 8(3): 5–19.

Putnam, Robert D. & David D. Campbell (2020), *American Grace: How Religion Divides and Unites Us*, New York: Simon and Schuster.

Rosa, Hartmut (2020), *Unverfügbarkeit, Salzburg*: Suhrkamp.

Sandel, Michael (2020), *De tirannie van verdienste. Over de toekomst van de democratie*, Utrecht: Ten Have.

Sommer, Martin (2019), *De kleine Tocqueville,* Amsterdam & Antwerpen: Atlas Contact.

Tocqueville, Alexis de (2000; original, French edition 1835, 1840), *Democracy in America* (Translated, edited, and introduced by Harvey C. Mansfield & Delba Winthrop), Chicago & London: University Press of Chicago.

Williams, Rowan (2012), *Faith in the Public Square*, London: Bloomsbury.

3 Family tensions in Tocqueville and Lasch

Two perspectives on the domestic sphere and democratic life

Sarah J. Wilford

3.1 Introduction

In the 19th century, the democratic theorist Alexis de Tocqueville (1805–1859) provided a formulation of family life that both accepted democracy's equalising and transformative power while maintaining the aspects of authority and normative moral production that served democratic life. Tocqueville offered a broad theoretical framework that was aspirational. In the 20th century, the social critic Christopher Lasch was preoccupied with a similar tension and moral concern, and observing a more advanced American democracy, his treatment of the subject was scathing.

While Tocqueville described an ideal and Lasch critiqued a reality, their discussions are similar, connoting that the family is at risk in modern societies and is also fundamentally important to the flourishing of modern societies. Today, in the 21st century, we continue to confront the same tension and continue to witness a withdrawal from public life. Lasch serves as a bridge between Tocqueville's time and our own. Though Tocqueville often seems relatable, his thought on domestic life is one area in which his discussion can appear distant and possibly irrelevant. Aspects of Tocqueville's portrait have aged, such as the exclusion of women from the public sphere typical of the 19th century and his own optimism that family unity could be maintained in the face of individualism. Therefore, Lasch serves as a more recent touchstone for insights similar to those of Tocqueville.[1] Lasch's critique updates our terms for this important conversation. For example, a connection is drawn between Tocqueville's understanding of 'individualism' and Lasch's updated term 'narcissism', and Tocqueville's earlier concept of the 'tutelary

1 To justify bringing these thinkers together, this chapter reflects the precedents in Tocqueville scholarship of this form of comparative study: Dana Villa (2005), 'Hegel, Tocqueville, and "Individualism"', *The Review of Politics* 67: 659–86; Eileen Hunt Botting (2009), 'A Family Resemblance: Tocqueville and Wollstonecraftian Protofeminism', in Jill Locke and Eileen Hunt Botting (eds.), *Feminist Interpretations of Alexis de Tocqueville*, University Park: Pennsylvania State University Press, 99–124; James L. Nolan (2016), *What They Saw in America*, Cambridge University Press.

DOI: 10.4324/9781032641041-3

state' is made concrete in the army of 'trained experts' that Lasch identified. Additionally, Lasch's sociological summary reviews the transformation of the family since the 19th century. The purpose of this comparative study is twofold: (1) To update our terms for conceptualising the tensions of family life and (2) to emphasise the connection between family authority and the cultural norms that sustain a democratic society. Proponents of democracy, many of us Tocqueville acolytes, benefit from this updated (and more urgent) approach to family life, and we are prompted to consider how to best preserve family to serve democratic culture.

This chapter provides two discussions of the same social and moral problem in parallel, drawing on Tocqueville's *Democracy in America* and Lasch's *Haven in a Heartless World* and *The Culture of Narcissism*. The exegeses provided in this chapter are an introduction to an understudied yet important aspect of each thinker's work. This chapter also demonstrates how the family relates to the more familiar, well-trod themes of each (i.e., individualism, for Tocqueville, and narcissism, for Lasch), and thereby, this chapter highlights the importance of the family in their corpora. Then, the nexus of equality, freedom, and family is discussed. Conversely, authority, religion, and family are then examined. The conclusion compares Tocqueville's hope and Lasch's despair for the family and draws these themes into the current moment. The principal insight offered by these thinkers is that there is a profound connection between authority within the family and the cultural reproduction that can support a democratic society. Additionally, Lasch's updated critique urgently reminds us to consider how we maintain the scope for authority within families in the face of encroaching expert authority.

3.2 Tocqueville on the modern family and individualism

To begin with, Tocqueville highlighted how democratic norms altered courtship and marriage. He noted that American girls are afforded a wide education that prepares them to choose their husbands carefully. They 'marry only when their reason is trained and developed' (Tocqueville 2010, 2:3; 10.1049). Tocqueville also suggested that the 'equality of conditions' brought by democracy supports norms of chastity before marriage. Without the barriers of class and social hierarchy, marriages are made freely, negating the need for 'clandestine unions' and enabling women to preside over sexual mores (Tocqueville 2010, 2:3; 11.1054). Tocqueville argued that in free societies, it is difficult to seduce a woman, or convince her of love, when she knows the suitor 'is perfectly free to marry her' (Tocqueville 2010, 2:3; 11.1054). Marriage itself, according to Tocqueville, is made perhaps more practical and austere by democracy. The education of democratic girls fosters 'honest and cold women rather than tender wives and amiable companions' (Tocqueville 2010, 2:3; 9.1045). Though perhaps generating less passion, democracy does allow spouses to come together based on 'similarity of tastes and ideas' (Tocqueville 2010, 2:3; 11.1056). Notably, Tocqueville praised that the Americans had not made the error of introducing full equality between the husband and wife. While the 19th century in fact saw great changes to the position of women in the United States, Tocqueville insisted that 'the natural head of the conjugal association was the man' (Tocqueville 2010, 2:3; 12.1064).

Beyond this, Tocqueville's presentation of the democratic family is shaped by strict gender roles. After enjoying a free and liberal childhood, Tocqueville's democratic woman 'lives in the house of her husband as in a cloister', serving her family in the private sphere to the ultimate benefit of the public sphere as the maker of social mores (Tocqueville 2010, 2:3; 10.1048). She chooses 'an abnegation of herself and a continual sacrifice of her pleasures to her business' (Tocqueville 2010, 2:3; 10.1049). Tocqueville's democratic family life is governed by intimacy and women's self-sacrifice.

Another principal feature of Tocqueville's democratic family was the changing relationship between father and son. According to Tocqueville, 'filial obedience' wanes quickly in democratic families, and 'adolescence' is short-lived as young men establish 'independence' and their 'own path' readily (Tocqueville 2010, 2:3; 8.1033). Tocqueville stated that this maturation is not a product of 'domestic struggle', and fathers are disposed to let their sons pursue their independence. Tocqueville added that the division of property among children in democracies also greatly affects the nature of family relations. Large 'patrimonies' of the aristocratic era are more infrequent, and most families pursue middling fortunes in democracies. For Tocqueville, fathers with 'little property' often work with their sons, 'busy together with the same work' (Tocqueville 2010, 2:3; 8.1036). Tocqueville thought the daily proximity of fathers and sons led to 'familial intimacy' and softening of 'authority' (Tocqueville 2010, 2:3; 8.1037). Tocqueville was inspired by this in the democratic family, thinking that though perhaps 'society loses with this change', 'the individual gains' from these 'intimate and milder' relations between fathers and sons (Tocqueville 2010, 2:3; 8.1037). According to Tocqueville, 'rule and authority' decline, while 'confidence and affection' increase, making 'the natural bond' more secure as 'the social bond loosens' (Tocqueville 2010, 2:3; 8.1037).

The father's position within the democratic family related to larger social transformations brought by democracy, in Tocqueville's estimation. He considered that in democratic societies, 'the arm of the government goes to find each man', and 'the intermediary' role that fathers played in aristocratic societies is no longer essential (Tocqueville 2010, 2:3; 8.1035). In aristocracies, 'power never addresses itself directly to the whole of the governed', and amid the interdependent structures of aristocracy, power addresses the 'head' of groups and 'associations' (Tocqueville 2010, 2:3; 8.1035). Society and government relate to 'sons only by the hands of the father' (Tocqueville 2010, 2:3; 8.1035). In aristocracies, this gave the father 'a political right to command' his children, in addition to 'a natural right' (Tocqueville 2010, 2:3; 8.1035). The aristocratic father was, according to Tocqueville, the 'magistrate' of the family (Tocqueville 2010, 2:3; 8.1035). The democratic father, conversely, is just another 'citizen older and richer than his sons' (Tocqueville 2010, 2:3; 8.1035). In addition to examining how power reached the people in aristocratic times, Tocqueville also connected the authority of the aristocratic father to his role in sharing knowledge and norms. Tocqueville thought that in an aristocratic society, a preoccupation with the past prevails, and people are interested in 'what their ancestors thought' rather than 'trying to think for themselves' (Tocqueville 2010, 2:3; 8.1036). In this context, the father linked the 'the past and the present', which meant that not only did he govern, he was also 'the organ of traditions, the interpreter of customs, the arbiter of mores' (Tocqueville 2010, 2:3; 8.1036). In democracies, the father is no longer the 'arbiter of mores', and 'the power of opinion' in his family is diminished because democratic citizens think for themselves, referring to 'ancient beliefs as information and not as a rule' (Tocqueville 2010, 2:3; 8.1036). Tocqueville illustrated the democratic family with these references to the aristocratic family, saying that the paternal roles of 'master and magistrate' of the aristocratic father 'have disappeared', and 'the father remains' (Tocqueville 2010, 2:3; 8.1037). The democratic family offers 'sweet pleasure' and 'something free, familiar, and tender' (Tocqueville 2010, 2:3; 8.1038-9). Unlike aristocratic families, the democratic family is shaped by 'filial love and fraternal tenderness' (Tocqueville 2010, 2:3; 8.1039).

Importantly, Tocqueville's democratic family is not bereft of all moral direction without the authoritative aristocratic father. Elsewhere, Tocqueville wrote of the important role of women in making social mores. We may think of the democratic wife described by Tocqueville as an 'arbiter of mores', but it is not in the same sense as the aristocratic father who linked past and present while holding political authority. In Tocqueville's illustration, the democratic woman is not powerful in that sense, but nevertheless, she is considered to be the provider of mores. In his chapter on the education of girls, he stated that women were of 'political interest' to him because 'it is that woman who molds the morals' (Tocqueville 2010, 2:3; 9.1041). In the first volume of *Democracy*, he also stated that 'it is the woman who shapes the mores' (Tocqueville 2010, 1:2; 9.473). Here, Tocqueville also wrote that religion 'rules with sovereign power over the soul of the woman', and her role as the maker of mores allows religion to influence men through marriage and the home (Tocqueville 2010, 1:2; 9.473).

Apart from the political exclusion of women, there is much to be admired in Tocqueville's portrait of family life as virtuous, but, curiously, the family also features at the centre of his discussion of individualism, the defining democratic problem. Tocqueville described individualism as a 'peaceful sentiment that disposes each citizen to isolate himself from the mass of his fellows and to withdraw to the side with his family and his friends' (Tocqueville 2010, 2:2; 2.882). The family unit becomes the democratic man's retreat to 'small society', forgoing responsibilities in 'large society' (Tocqueville 2010, 2:2; 2.882).

In order to define individualism, Tocqueville described 'egoism', 'a vice as old as the world' that does not belong to one time or place (Tocqueville 2010, 2:2; 2.882). Egoism is a 'passionate' and instinctive feeling that destroys 'all virtues', whereas individualism is a more gentle phenomenon – a result of 'erroneous judgement' – that damages 'public virtues' first before undermining other virtues and being 'absorbed into egoism' (Tocqueville 2010, 2:2; 2.882). Individualism is less obvious and more insidious than egoism, and Tocqueville considered individualism to be a problem unique to the democratic era.

Tocqueville believed that the links of hierarchy that kept people 'placed in fixed positions' meant that people were 'always tied in a close way to something that is located outside of themselves' (Tocqueville 2010, 2:2; 2.883). This is not the case in democracies, where 'duties' and 'devotions' are reshaped by equality (Tocqueville 2010, 2:2; 2.884). Tocqueville thought that as the fortunes of families rise and fall and the links between generations weaken, democratic citizens naturally 'forget those who preceded' them and do not think of 'those who will follow' (Tocqueville 2010, 2:2; 2.884). This leaves democratic citizens interested in only their most proximate relations and companions (Tocqueville 2010, 2:2; 2.884). Where aristocracy established 'a long chain that went from the peasant up to the king', 'democracy breaks the chain and sets each link apart' (Tocqueville 2010, 2:2; 2.884). Amid these conditions of disconnectedness brought about by equality, many citizens emerge with 'enough enlightenment and wealth' to look after themselves, but not enough to 'influence' others (Tocqueville 2010, 2:2; 2.884). These people 'owe nothing' and 'expect nothing', and they operate independently, 'consider themselves in isolation', and believe themselves masters of 'their entire destiny' (Tocqueville 2010, 2:2; 2. 884). In addition to obscuring connections to 'ancestors' and 'descendants', democracy also detaches 'contemporaries' (Tocqueville 2010, 2:2; 2.884). The independence afforded by democracy makes for inward-looking citizens according to Tocqueville. Democracy guides the citizen 'back toward himself alone and threatens finally to enclose him entirely within the solitude of his own heart' (Tocqueville 2010, 2:2; 2.884). Tocqueville worried the conditions of modern democracy made for individualistic attitudes that, though not aggressive, would encourage a retreat from public life and ultimately threaten the fragile liberty of democracies. In Tocqueville's view, individualism was a self-undermining feature of democracies that could exacerbate the threat of democratic despotism and the 'tutelary power' of the state (Tocqueville 2010, 2:4; 6.1250).

Tocqueville's anxiety that individualism encourages democratic man to think only of himself was bound up with his hopes for the family. In Tocqueville's estimation, the family, supported by women's exemplary self-abnegation, needed to bolster democracy by encouraging the mores that counter individualism, while ensuring the family itself does not become a mode for the expression of individualism.

3.3 Lasch on the modern family and narcissism

Formulated in the 1970s, Lasch's presentation of the modern family in *Haven in a Heartless World* was deeply cynical. He valued the family as a central mode of moral and cultural instruction, much like Tocqueville had in the previous century. For Lasch, culture must 'be embedded in personality' (Lasch 1995: 4). He wrote that '[s]ocialization makes the individual want to do what he has to do; the family is the agency to which society entrusts this complex and delicate task' (Lasch 1995: 4). The habituation of moral duties and responsibilities happens at home, so the breakdown of family life is a social problem, not just a personal tragedy.

For Lasch, the family's situation was the product of a century of breakdown (Lasch 1995: xx). According to Lasch, the bourgeois family of previous centuries fostered an 'inner-directed, self-reliant personality', which contributed to a competitive, individualistic, rational, material 'market society' (Lasch 1995: 4). This personality type, though made by the family *for* the market, was protected by the family *from* the market. Lasch noted that the family was supported in the 19th century by a pervasive ideal of 'domestic life as an emotional refuge', 'a haven in a heartless world' (Lasch 1995: 7). As work became merely a means to finance 'consolations outside of work', family life became central to a highly exalted private life (Lasch 1995: 7). The alienation from work, the competitive marketplace, and the spiritual suffering of modern life were ameliorated at home, but the great irony, Lasch noted, was that the same 'conditions' that necessitated this retreat also increasingly undermined any hope 'for the family to serve in that capacity' (Lasch 1995: 8).

The haven that sheltered 'children and adolescents from the full impact of the market' in the 19th century was failing by the 1970s, according to Lasch (Lasch 1995: xxiii, 6). Far from sheltering children, this modern family, void of 'emotional intensity', initiated children 'into the easygoing, lowkeyed encounters that predominate in the outside world as well' (Lasch 1995: xxiii). Lasch blamed the pressures of the marketplace as well as the large-scale socialisation of the work of family life for this transformation. His greatest criticism was reserved for the experts and social scientists who sought to remake the family.

Beginning with the end of the 19th century, Lasch recounts how both conservative defenders of family and radical progressives increasingly conceptualised and justified family life in terms that ultimately yielded a great invasion of private family life. Thinkers on all sides of the discourse disappointed Lasch by laying the groundwork for outside experts to subsume the authority for a professionalised parenthood and for external agencies to compete with the services provided by the family. As an early historical example, Lasch pointed to the reaction to feminism at the turn of the century. He noted that 'critics of feminism' tried to establish 'motherhood and housewifery' as 'satisfying "careers," which required special training in "homemaking," "domestic science," and "home economics"', but by professionalising housework, this way of thinking made 'the housewife more dependent than ever on the help of outside experts', those who taught the sciences of the home (Lasch 1995: 10). Lasch considered this invasion of expertise where it was intentional, too. He noted how the family 'was deliberately transformed by the interventions of planners and policymakers' allied with '[e]ducators and social reformers' who sought to eliminate impediments to 'social progress' – chief among these the 'separatist religious traditions, alien languages and dialects, local lore, and other traditions' maintained within families that threatened reformers' ideas of 'the political community and the national state' (Lasch 1995: 13). Lasch detailed the progression of thinkers, scholars, and intellectuals who contributed to the outsourcing of family life, even among their own pleas for the importance of private family life.

The family and many of its 'functions' were annexed by wider society, which was supported in this endeavour by the increase in the 'helping professions' that occurred in the early part of the 20th century (Lasch 1995: 18). Lasch noted the inherently expansionist tendency of this 'new ideology of social welfare'; as parents were convinced they must depend on external expertise, the family became less capable of fulfilling the 'functions' for which it was so lauded, which ultimately 'justified the continuing expansion of health, education, and welfare services' (Lasch 1995: 18). Additionally, once the real value of the family was established as 'emotional', the other purposes of the family could be easily subsumed by an urbanising world where the nuclear family was increasingly isolated yet open to coordinate with anonymous services and agencies of both the marketplace and the state (Lasch 1995: 37).

Further, the precious value placed on emotional functions within the family gave way to a throng of professionals equipped to perfect and advise on these essential functions. Lasch saw this process, '[t]he socialization of reproduction', as a continuation of 'the process begun by the socialization of production itself – that is, by industrialization' (Lasch 1995: 18–19). According to Lasch, industrialists commandeered the 'technical knowledge' of workers, which they improved upon via 'scientific management' in order to further specialise labour while withholding 'knowledge' of the larger operation (Lasch 1995: 18). In turn, this knowledge demanded 'a vastly enlarged managerial apparatus' (Lasch 1995: 18–19). The encroachment of mass society on the family reflects this. As the material functions of the family shifted radically, all functions and purposes of the family became subject to review and management. With increasing importance placed on certain functions, an 'apparatus' of sociologists, scientists, therapists, teachers, and reformers emerged to direct these functions.

For Lasch, the recommendations of experts further exacerbated the 'deadly chill' of the modern American family (Lasch 1995: 157). Lasch understood the recommendations of experts and concomitant cultural changes as unfolding across every decade of the 20th century, not simply as hallmarks of the counterculture movements of his own era (Lasch 1995: 105). Even though, as Lasch remarked, 'current folklore' deems the 1950s, 'the heyday of the "traditional" family', the domestic norms of the 1950s were already subject to expert orthodoxy, centring friendship over 'romantic love', 'undemanding and non possessive' interpersonal relations, and parental permissiveness (Lasch 1995: xx, 105–106). The expert 'consensus' was established by the 1950s that 'parents who had absorbed the ideology of mental health' were best suited to raise successful children, and this consensus denounced 'unenlightened sexual attitudes', 'religious dogmas', and 'possessiveness', all of which was potentially damaging to mental well-being (Lasch 1995: 109).

This consensus continued into Lasch's own era, and he observed the changed relationship between parents and children. He thought this 'invasion of the family' had 'created an ideal of perfect parenthood while destroying parents' confidence in their ability to perform the most elementary functions of childrearing (Lasch 1991: 169). According to Lasch, modern parents try to provide 'a refuge', but they lack confidence and therefore cannot endow their children 'with a sense of security' (Lasch 1991: 176).

Lasch criticised many interpretations of family life for misunderstanding the psychological components and 'unconscious mental life' of children's maturation; and by not valuing these features of family dynamics, commentators overlooked the worst effect of 'the invasion of the family by the marketplace and the street' and outside expertise – lack of maturation (Lasch 1995: 156, 166). Lasch believed children are affected positively by being exposed to 'the union of love and discipline' in parents, which encourages them to control 'rage' and better understand their relationship to authority (Lasch 1995: 123). The undermining of 'the psychic mechanism whereby the young internalize their parents' was the crux of the problems suffered by the modern family (Lasch 1995: 123).

Lasch noted that in societies where the production of goods remained within the family, or where the family 'at least hands down useful knowledge', 'fathers' educate 'sons', but the real value of their 'daily contact' lies in how the overwhelming authority of the father figure is moderated and 'the father establishes himself in his son's affections by his mastery of the skills and techniques the son also needs to master' (Lasch 1995: 123). The conditions of modern society undermined this sharing of both productive and practical knowledge, as the father's mastery 'become technologically obsolete in his own lifetime' (Lasch 1995: 124). Lasch considered adolescence to be in decline, not because children grow up fast, but because they favour their peers and readily discard the previous generation as 'out-of-date' and 'superfluous' (Lasch 1995: 74–75). For Lasch, children do not seek to replace fathers but rather aim 'to enjoy life' free from parental authority (Lasch 1995: 124). Anxious to be free of authority, children do not mature but develop inflated ideas of an oppressive authority that they cannot relate to or see as valid (Lasch 1995: 124–1255).

Lasch also believed that the conditions of modern commercial societies affected the maternal role in psychological development. Because strong parental bonds are so damaged in modern society, children are left with 'early impressions of the mother' as dominant in their formation, in place of ongoing parental authority and mutual respect. This immature relationship with maternal figures exaggerated phobias of 'maternal abandonment', leading to a preoccupation with the pursuit of mental health, rather than the formation of character or virtue (Lasch 1995: 165). The mother is anxious, which supports her powerful position within the domestic circle. Here, contrary to Tocqueville's hopeful model, the wife and mother of Lasch's despairing portrait is the ruler in her family by virtue of the 'imposition of her own madness on everyone else' (Lasch 1995: 156). Far from 'her effective management of the household', her role as 'the principal disciplinarian', or anything akin to the moral exemplarity of Tocqueville's democratic woman, her capriciousness is what holds her family in thrall (Lasch 1995: 156). This does not make for meaningful authority either.

With absent fathers, anxious mothers, immature children, and 'a growing gap between discipline and affection', Lasch thought that the modern family 'clings to a flimsy equilibrium by attempting to exclude everything that might disturb it' (Lasch 1995: 157, 174). Lasch found the modern family severely damaged. A self-centred pursuit of mental health and psychological well-being had superseded 'intimacy and parental guidance' as the primary purpose of family life (Lasch 1995: 157). Norms of 'nonbinding commitments' and friendship have replaced passionate romantic love (Lasch 1995: 157). Passive and anxious, parents lack authority over their children, while 'the spirit of economic rationality' further penetrates the family, leaving children unprotected from the demoralising impact of a harsh, competitive world (Lasch 1995: 36). The haven in a heartless world was soon overcome by the very forces that had necessitated it in the first place (Lasch 1995: 168–169). The 19th-century 'work ethic' fostered within the family that equipped children for the marketplace and civic life yielded to 'an ethic of survival and immediate gratification', and Lasch concluded that the narcissist emerged as the product of the modern family (Lasch 1995: xxiv, 156).

In *The Culture of Narcissism,* Lasch referred to the family again as the originator of the 'patterns' of narcissism reflected in modern American culture (Lasch 1991: 176). He summarised that parental withdrawal from children accompanied by efforts to flatter children was a good recipe for 'a narcissistic personality structure' (Lasch 1991: 50). In turn of course, the prevailing narcissism in society erodes the family (Lasch 1991: 50). Like Tocqueville's individualism, Lasch's description of narcissism relates to a sense of historical disconnectedness (Lasch 1991: xviii). Society was 'losing the sense of historical continuity, the sense of belonging to a succession of generations originating in the past and stretching into the future' (Lasch 1991: 5). While Lasch acknowledged the daunting uncertainty of the future in the modern world, he associated our modern narcissism with the failure to understand ourselves in relation to our ancestors or contextualise ourselves as 'part of a historical stream' (Lasch 1991: 51; see also Chapter 10). Instead, individuals 'live for the moment' for themselves (Lasch 1991: 5).

While historically dislocated, the narcissist, in Lasch's reading, is still highly dependent 'on others to validate his self-esteem' and requires 'an admiring audience' (Lasch 1991: 10). Free 'from family ties and institutional constraints', narcissists are not happily liberated, but rather in their 'insecurity' they anxiously seek validation in others (Lasch 1991: 10). Lasch considered 'anxiety, depression, vague discontents, a sense of inner emptiness' to all be features of the modern psychological condition. This condition leads us, not to pursue achievement or enlightenment, but simply 'peace of mind' (Lasch 1991: 13). This pursuit is supported by 'the therapeutic sensibility' of our time, which discredits ideas of 'self-sacrifice' and 'submission' and offers freedom from 'outmoded ideas of love and duty' that threaten individual well-being (Lasch 1991: 13). Lasch criticised that, for many, 'mental health' amounted to 'the overthrow of inhibitions and the immediate gratification of every impulse' (Lasch 1991: 13). Though Lasch acknowledged that narcissism may be a practical answer to 'the tensions and anxieties of modern life', this grasping for well-being leaves the narcissist frustrated and the family broken (Lasch 1991: 50).

Lasch is most famous for his discussion of narcissism, but his portrait of the modern American family is essential to understanding this self-centred culture that destroys the hope for a common democratic life. He did not merely bemoan divorce and parental permissiveness; he offered a historical explanation for how the family lost its former functions and how culture perpetuates destructive patterns. For Lasch, the modern family produces narcissists, and narcissists maintain a culture that relies on experts in mental well-being to resolve our psychic woes. This very culture further erodes authority, loyalty, and solidarity within the family.

The attitude of inwardness that so worried Lasch echoes Tocqueville's concern about individualism. For Lasch, the 'narcissistic withdrawal of interest from the external world' is behind our pleasure-seeking lack of commitment as well as the 'intolerable anxiety that continually frustrates' the need for satisfaction (Lasch 1995: 183). This withdrawal from public life was precisely what worried Tocqueville as well.

Individualism, as defined by Tocqueville, however, maintained family solidarity. Tocqueville suggested it was possible to retreat from wider society, enjoying a comfortable private life *with* one's family. Tocqueville would have been familiar with the 'haven in a heartless world' conceptualisation of the family that Lasch identified as common in the 19th century. He even stated in the first volume of *Democracy* that '[w]hen, coming from the agitation of the political world, the American returns to the bosom of his family, he immediately encounters the image of order and peace' (Tocqueville 2010, 1:2; 9.474). He referred to the 'pleasures' and 'joys' found in the family (Tocqueville 2010, 1:2; 9.474). Nevertheless, by the second volume of *Democracy*, Tocqueville knew this haven could also be an appealing escape from the duties of public life and civic engagement.

Tocqueville's individualist was also not preoccupied with immediate gratification like Lasch's narcissist. The individualist was motivated by material interest, but his inwardness was a result of poor 'judgement', not the result of indulging passions or soothing pains (Tocqueville 2010, 2:2; 2.882).

Lasch himself compared the narcissist to 'the acquisitive individualist of nineteenth-century political economy' (Lasch 1991: xvi). Lasch said that unlike the 19th-century individualist, the narcissist 'does not accumulate goods and provisions against the future' and 'lives in a state of restless, perpetually unsatisfied desire' (Lasch 1991: xvi). Additionally, the individualist sees the potential in the world around him, whereas the narcissist sees only himself. Lasch concluded: '[f]or the narcissist, the world is a mirror, whereas the rugged individualist saw it as an empty wilderness to be shaped to his own design' (Lasch 1991: 10). Narcissism is individualism without the optimism of the frontier spirit or the security of family loyalty. Narcissism is individualism without hope.

3.4 Equality, freedom, and the family

Having established Tocqueville's and Lasch's portraits of the modern family, we can consider more closely how the equality and freedom of modern democratic life intersect with family life according to both thinkers. As noted previously, Tocqueville identified how the norms and demands of democratic life 'draw' father and son 'closer and force them to communicate with each other at every moment', fostering intimacy (Tocqueville 2010, 2:3; 8.1037). Additionally, Tocqueville thought that equality affected family life by generating a natural intimacy between brothers. Siblings are not tied together by social and material 'interests' as they were in aristocratic societies, so instead, 'the community of memories and the free sympathy of opinions and tastes' unites brothers (Tocqueville 2010, 2:3; 8.1039).

Gender roles are shaped, too, by democracy, according to Tocqueville. He described democratic girlhood as immensely free and girls' education as liberal, and he suggested that equality of conditions affords young women great power over sexual mores. From the freedom brought by democracy, Tocqueville's democratic woman can 'freely' choose 'the yoke' of family life and domestic service (Tocqueville 2010, 2:3; 10.1049). With 'filial love', 'fraternal tenderness', and 'manly' educated women, Tocqueville's portrait of family life suggests that equality and liberty benefit the family, which is shaped by '[t]he sweet pleasure of these democratic mores' (Tocqueville 2010, 2:3; 8.1039, and 2:3; 10.1049).

While equality and liberty introduce new norms to the family that Tocqueville admires, equality and liberty were not limitless within the family. Notably, women, once married, were subject to the authority of husbands, and Tocqueville suggested wives rarely escape 'the small circle of domestic interests and duties' (Tocqueville 2010, 2:3; 10.1049). In Tocqueville's description of democratic family life, women are not free to be 'similar' to men or to work outside the domestic circle (Tocqueville 2010, 2:3; 12.1063). Tocqueville carefully explained that the Americans introduced equality between the sexes without making the sexes 'similar' or giving them 'the same functions', 'duties', or 'rights' (Tocqueville 2010, 2:3; 12.1063).

Though the position of women was limited in Tocqueville's ideal democratic family, he suggested that the family plays a large role in supporting freedom in a democracy. Tocqueville thought that democracies possessed inherent features that could undermine liberty and lead to 'democratic despotism' (Tocqueville 2010, 2:4; 6.1256). Famously, Tocqueville advocated for the building and maintenance of civil associations, free institutions, and intermediary bodies that cultivated traits that could counter the worst side-effects of democracy, like individualism (see Chapter 4). The family was among these elements of democratic life that fostered social mores to support liberty. As noted earlier, Tocqueville stated that women in particular shaped mores and morals. He believed 'free societies' require 'morals', and therefore women were of 'political interest' (Tocqueville 2010, 2:3; 9.1041). The social mores that Tocqueville believed were essential to the preservation of liberty originated in the home. For Tocqueville, the family had the potential to serve the flourishing of freedom in a democracy.

For Lasch, as a critic, the equality and liberty that define modern life offer more worrisome temptations. The commercialism of liberal societies, according to Lasch, usurped traditional modes of 'cultural reproduction' like the family. He thought that the 'propaganda of commodities' eroded 'puritanical morality and patriarchal authority, subtly allying itself with women against men, children against parents' (Lasch 1995: 14). Lasch thought consumerist society encourages 'self-doubt' (Lasch 1991: 180). Advertising, according to Lasch, does not celebrate freedom of choice but rather feeds the anxious restlessness of the narcissistic consumer.

Additionally, sex and relationships featured prominently in Lasch's concern regarding the liberty and equality of the modern epoch. Lasch bemoaned 'the ideology of "nonbinding commitments"' (a phrase coined by the anthropologists Nena and George O'Neill), which ridiculed romantic love as an 'unrealistic expectation' (Lasch 1995: 139). Lasch thought this ideology was pessimistic, betraying a lack of hope in the future and a lack of desire to prepare anything for future generations (Lasch 1995: 139). Lasch also criticised countercultural lifestyles that seek so-called liberation because they primarily offer a 'retreat' from 'strong emotions' and 'passion' (Lasch 1995: 183). The new norms of countercultural lifestyles, which avoid the passionate in favour of the easygoing and undemanding, were complemented by other social changes that disconnected sex from the 'trappings of romance' as well as love and lifelong commitment (Lasch 1991: 191). Sex pursued solely for the sake of sexual gratification is sex dissociated from 'the future', according to Lasch (Lasch 1991: 191). Approaching sex this way offers freedom while perpetuating the narcissistic inability to relate to the future.

In the narcissistic age, freedom becomes equated with a lack of 'restraints' and 'inhibitions' (Lasch 1995: 140). In particular, the peer group, as a party of equals, becomes especially prized because equals demand little of each other (Lasch 1995: 140–141). Cynically, Lasch commented that

> [t]he idealized comradeship of siblings, united not by undying passion or even mutual respect but merely by a common resentment of adult authority, becomes the model of the perfect marriage, the perfect affair, the perfect 'one-to-one relationship', or the for that matter the commune or extended family.
>
> (Lasch 1995: 141)

The precious equality of our democracy becomes valued for making our relationships less and less demanding.

Ever the believer in a common democratic project, Lasch's anxiety about the drawbacks of the equality and liberty of modern life was far more bitter than Tocqueville's, and he worried that the indulgences and liberties afforded by modern life ultimately left citizens dependent on the state and the anonymous apparatus of mass society. Additionally, Lasch noted authority and power themselves have become shrouded in 'the language of psychiatry', appealing not to a 'moral standard' but instead to 'reality' (Lasch 1995: 185–186). Citizens submit to a magnanimous power that offers to resolve their anxiety and insecurity. Amid the riches of equality and freedom, society has taken responsibility for the individual. Society, according to Lash, 'weakened the capacity for self-direction and self-control' and devastated 'social cohesion' to replace it with a more menacing apparatus, including 'the state, the corporation, and other bureaucracies' detrimental to 'personal and political freedom' (Lasch 1995: 189, see also 1991: 10). Where Tocqueville saw the family as a moral stronghold for protecting freedom, Lasch highlighted the new liberties within private life as generators of dependency and the ultimate turn from political freedom.

3.5 Authority, religion, and the family

While equality and liberty are themes essential to understanding both Tocqueville's and Lasch's portraits of the modern family, this analysis is complemented by an additional angle. By examining each thinker's understanding of how authority and religion intersect with family life, we can gain further insight into their understanding of how family relates to wider society. Here, authority refers to the power to influence and direct moral choices and intellectual growth.

Tocqueville's illustration of family life demonstrates that the intimacy brought about by democratic life 'makes authority less absolute' within the family (Tocqueville 2010, 2:3; 8.1037). Importantly, however, Tocqueville's model democratic family maintains some paternal authority, which Tocqueville suggests is natural. For Tocqueville, the family and the authority therein are pre-political. He said that 'remnants' of the 'aristocratic' fatherhood are found when children are very young, and their 'weakness' necessitates 'the domestic dictatorship' of the father to act authoritatively in 'their interest' (Tocqueville 2010, 2:3; 8.). Beyond this, Tocqueville was careful to note that though the democratic father is not 'master' or 'magistrate', 'the father remains', and though less dominant, 'he is spoken to constantly and readily consulted' (Tocqueville 2010, 2:3; 8.1037). The father's authority within the family results from the respectability of the 'experience of an old man' whose 'advice is usually full of power' (Tocqueville 2010, 2:3; 8.). In a variation in the manuscript, which was discarded, Tocqueville noted that 'unnatural equality' can emerge between fathers and sons, when the father acts as a 'vile comrade of debauchery' and 'does not work to elevate the reason of his sons' but rather mimics his sons' 'juvenile passions' (Tocqueville 2010, 2:3; 8.1038).[2] He called this 'anarchy', 'not democracy' (Tocqueville 2010, 2:3; 8.1038).[3] He hoped that mature democracies would retain enough paternal authority to 'elevate' children (Tocqueville 2010, 2:3; 8.1038).[4] Additionally, as noted, Tocqueville favoured the 'natural' authority of husbands over wives. Mothers are not entirely excluded from a role of authority. Tocqueville invested enormous power in the woman as a central conduit of religion. In this softened way, Tocqueville insisted on some degree of authority within the family that allows for the communication of advice, religious dogma, and mores.

The moral and intellectual authority that resides in Tocqueville's democratic family is even more notable when considered in the context of Tocqueville's other discussions of intellectual authority in democracies. In general, Tocqueville thought intellectual authority necessarily breaks down in a democratic society, as all people can think freely for themselves. He identified the 'philosophical method' of the Americans to be individualistic. He found in America that 'in most operations of the mind, each American appeals only to the individual effort of his reason' (Tocqueville 2010, 2:1; 1.699). He described that the former authority of 'traditions', 'the ideas of ancestors', 'class', or even 'one man' is diminished in the context of equality (Tocqueville 2010, 2:1; 1.699–700).

At the same time, he suggested some avenues to accessing knowledge because 'authority must always be found somewhere in the intellectual and moral world' (Tocqueville 2010, 2:1; 2.716). Beyond their own reason, individuals acknowledge the authority of 'dogmatic beliefs' of 'common opinion' and religion (Tocqueville 2010, 2:1; 2.713, 718). Majority opinion and consensus are powerful in democracies because equal status means people 'have no faith in each other', but 'confidence in the judgment of the public', which

2 This variation is not included in all editions. For this variation, see the Liberty Fund edition of *Democracy in America*.

3 This variation is not included in all editions. For this variation, see the Liberty Fund edition of *Democracy in America*.

4 This variation is not included in all editions. For this variation, see the Liberty Fund edition of *Democracy in America*.

is the sum reasoning of many who possess similar abilities and 'enlightenment' (Tocqueville 2010, 2:1; 2.719). Though the democratic mind reasons for itself, the 'ready-made opinions' offered by the majority have some authority (Tocqueville 2010, 2:1; 2.). Tocqueville worried that the power of the consensus could eventually limit the individual, but saw some value in shared beliefs.

Religion also offered 'ready-made beliefs'. In a variation in the manuscript, Tocqueville argued that 'religion' offers 'a clear and precise solution to a great number of metaphysical and moral questions' (Tocqueville 2010, 2:1; 2.716).[5] By endowing the dogmatic beliefs of religion with intellectual authority, democratic citizens are relieved from needing 'to examine everything' (Tocqueville 2010, 2:1; 2.715). Tocqueville diagnosed that democratic societies naturally discard the authorities that helped individuals make sense of the world in aristocratic societies. Instead, each individual reasons independently, while some dogmatic beliefs are widely accepted as true. Individual reason, consensus, and religion offer moral and intellectual authority in democracies (see Chapters 2 and 7).

Considering this, the authority found in Tocqueville's democratic family proves important. Even though paternal authority is moderated by democracy, the authority of parents to pass on practical knowledge and religion remains intact. Though Tocqueville did not explicitly relate the family to 'moral and intellectual authority', he suggested in his description of the family that fathers support the independent reasoning of their sons and share practical knowledge through the sharing of work, while mothers support mores and share religion. Tocqueville hoped to present a form of democratic family life that maintained enough authority to prepare children for the demands of democratic life. For Tocqueville, though democracy softens both paternal and religious authority, authority is not eliminated.

Lasch also observed in his own time the changing nature of authoritative structures. The narcissist, according to Lasch, is fundamentally anti-authoritarian, contemptuous of external standards, and scornful of norms. The narcissist 'does not like to be asked to live up to expectations' (Lasch 1995: 140). Unfortunately, this 'asking' is precisely the work of the family – cultural reproduction. However, this is difficult in the face of 'the ideology of non-binding commitments and open-ended relationships', which 'condemns all expectations, standards, and codes of conduct as "unrealistic"' (Lasch 1995: 140). Culture, religion, and norms – all underwritten by an authority with judgemental and prudential power – are almost an impossibility in the face of this ideology.

For Lasch, the problem of authority within the family related to the changing nature of authority in general. Where religion and law had served in the

5 This variation is not included in all editions. For this variation, see the Liberty Fund edition of *Democracy in America*.

past, 'social therapy' defines the modern epoch, which means that 'governing classes' make no defence of their 'legitimate authority' (Lasch 1995: 23). The powerful rely on the 'authority of fact', that is 'reality itself' (Lasch 1995: 23). As noted earlier, this makes for submissive citizens. With knowledge itself as 'an industry' and 'trained experts' prepared to manage the average citizen, the structures of modern society leave little room for parental authority (Lasch 1995: 19). In a world where parents lack confidence in their skills and doubt the importance of cultivating moral norms based on abstract principles, their authority rests on a weak foundation. Lasch thought that during the 20th century '[p]arental authority came to rest purely on the provision of material services', precisely at the time direct control over 'production' and 'welfare' was escaping the family (Lasch 1995: 35–36). At the same time, relying on 'duty, deference, or filiopiety' to demand compliance from children is out of step in a self-interested culture (Lasch 1995: 35–36). Beyond this, parental authority was continually eroded by '[o]utside advice' (Lasch 1995: 172). Both advertisers and experts insisted on the crucial role parents play in the lives of developing children while eroding parents' trust in themselves (Lasch 1995: 20, 172). These high-stakes circumstances lead parents to eschew 'the work of discipline and character formation' (Lasch 1995: 173). Lasch summarised that when a 'child refuses to eat what his parents think he ought to eat', doctors are called, and when a child 'is unruly', the psychiatrist is called (Lasch 1991: 182). For Lasch, this calling upon experts takes the parent's 'own problem', which he identifies as 'insubordination', and labels it the child's 'problem' (Lasch 1991: 182). Children exploit their parents' uncertainty by exchanging details with their peers; when children can demonstrate parents are operating outside accepted standards, they gain a strategic edge over their already insecure parents (Lasch 1995: 173).

Parental authority is not in service of the enforcement of family preferences or the communication of moral norms. Much like the authority of mass society that appeals to 'reality', parental authority is accepted as legitimate only to the extent that 'it conforms to reason', and this in turn leads to bargaining, similar to negotiation that prevails in wider society (Lasch 1995: 174). In Lasch's estimation, authority within the family is lost. Uncertain and self-indulgent, parents have little to share with their children in terms of practical knowledge or moral principles (Lasch 1991: 167). Lasch thought that where once they led children, 'the older generation now struggles to "keep up with the kids," to master their incomprehensible jargon, and even to imitate their dress and manners in the hope of preserving a youthful appearance and outlook' (Lasch 1991: 169). This may put us in mind of Tocqueville's idea of 'unnatural equality' between fathers and sons, described previously.

In Lasch's estimation, intellectual authority had come to reside with experts, who are minutely interested in every detail of private life. Regarding the realm of sex and marriage, Lasch stated that the '[l]awgiver and priest retired from sexual supervision only to make way for the doctor', who examines everything (Lasch 1995: 21). Though the erosion of erotic life especially worried him, this medical perspective pervaded society more generally, according to Lasch, replacing authorities of 'parents, priests, and lawgivers' (Lasch 1995: 100).

With the authority of religion and parents waning, citizens relate to authority differently in modern society, according to Lasch. Because authority was now so far removed from the development of an internal sense of right conduct or 'conscience', authority has become 'alien' and threatening (Lasch 1995: 140). Lasch separated the fear of 'punishment' from the fear of 'being judged', and he concluded that the modern narcissistic personality fears judgement more than arbitrary punishment (Lasch 1995: 140). Being accountable to 'unrealistic' standards is the worst possible fate (Lasch 1995: 140). At the same time, authorities have become shrouded in 'benevolence', delegating 'direct confrontations' and 'discipline' away (Lasch 1991: 181–182). Amid this opaque apparatus, the citizen relates to authority in a bifurcated way – pleased with permissiveness yet alert to an alien (and exaggerated) possibility of punishment or judgement.

3.6 Tocqueville's hope, Lasch's despair, and the modern democratic family

Both Tocqueville and Lasch observed their eras, and they were confronted with the great changes in modern life. Themes that were important to both thinkers remain relevant today. In the United States and Western Europe, religious practice is in steep decline.[6] Whether we see this as a tragedy or a triumph of secularism, the decline in religious attitudes leaves people bereft of one mode of intellectual and moral authority. This necessarily elevates the significance of other authorities or permits increasingly independent reasoning. While we may value independent reasoning highly, radical independence may have some drawbacks. We may consider Tocqueville's caution that social coherence requires shared beliefs and Lasch's concern for the restless anxiety of the narcissist lacking moral guidance.

Additionally, Lasch did not predict the 'influencer' culture of our social media age, but it appears to reflect both the peer culture and expert encroachment that Lasch diagnosed. What would Lasch make of this odd democratisation of 'outside expertise' on everything from fitness and fashion to personal well-being and parenting? Further, the prominence of youth culture that Lasch observed continues to shape our shared experience of values and meaning, and we must reckon with how, as Lasch said, 'parents represent the useless past' (Lasch 1995: 175). Rapid technological change and a media landscape largely aimed towards younger demographics structure our culture and our expectations about the educative purpose of the family. Young people are prominent in major public conversations in the United States and Europe, from Greta

6 Pew Research Center, 17 October 2019, 'In U.S., Decline of Christianity Continues at Rapid Pace'; Pew Research Center, 29 May 2018, 'Being Christian in Western Europe'.

Thunberg's influence on climate change discourse to *Harry Potter* film actress Emma Watson's prominence in addressing gender equality as a UN Women Goodwill Ambassador. There may be optimism and hope inherent in elevating the young as especially wise, but the role of older generations remains unclear in a culture that values youth and a marketplace that rapidly changes.

Tocqueville presented a hopeful portrait of an ideal family within a democratic society. The extent to which he observed this type of family during his travels in the United States is unclear, but his illustration is one of the important prescriptive components of his writings. In studying democracy, he wanted to understand 'what we must hope or fear from it' (Tocqueville 2010, 1:1; 1.28). He identified much to fear, particularly the threat of democratic despotism and loss of liberty. He hoped, however, that democratic life could also lend itself to structures that countered the negative by-products of democracy, like individualism. Of course, much of Tocqueville's ideal family does not seem relevant today, especially the position of women. His suggestion, however, that families retain parental authority is worth considering, especially if we deem Lasch's diagnosis insightful. To preserve the cultural reproduction, from mores to religion, that undergirds flourishing democratic life, maintaining some degree of authority within the family may be necessary.

Lasch's account, however, is less hopeful, though he suggested that parental authority would be worthwhile if it could be regained. Overall, his critique is despairing, concluding that the cultural problems of his era were deeply ingrained and self-perpetuating. The worst of 'capitalist society' had come to fruition aided by 'bureaucracy', 'the cult of consumption', and 'the severance of the sense of historical continuity' (Lasch 1991: 68). In the previous century, Tocqueville worried that democracy could lend itself to a growing administrative state, passion for material well-being, and historically disconnected individualism, and in Lasch's estimation, these worries have come to pass. According to Lasch, these features support the anxious, restless narcissistic mentality and a culture in which it is 'increasingly difficult for people to lay to rest the terrors of infancy or to enjoy the consolations of adulthood' (Lasch 1991: 232). Tocqueville also identified 'restlessness' as a troubling feature of the democratic experience. Of course, there is much that Tocqueville could not have predicted, but in examining Lasch alongside Tocqueville, we may wonder if narcissism is simply individualism come of age.

The maturation of individualism into narcissism is devasting for individuals, but it is also concerning for the wider democratic project. Clearly, the culture of narcissism breaks down community life, but it also supports a reliance on outside expertise. In summarising her father's work, Elizabeth Lash-Quinn described that her father thought that expert involvement in formerly private matters had damaged 'the common life', which, for Lasch, was 'a prerequisite for and a goal of democratic citizenship' (Lasch-Quinn 1997: xiii).

By updating the terms of this discussion with Lasch's critique, we benefit from Lasch's perspective which highlights how encroaching expert authority crowds out the democratic habits and practices that Tocqueville so admired in 19th-century America. Our 21st-century democracies must consider how to preserve space for family solidarity and authority as well as the democratic cultural flourishing that families foster. Additionally, we should not underestimate how parental authority at home can be embedded in wider civil society. As civil society organisations and local governance wither, the lack of participatory habits of adult citizens outside the home parallels the lack of active parental responsibility within the home.[7] Further, we must reconsider the relationship between parental authority and expert authority, given the cultural erosion resulting from excessive expert involvement. Experts may possess qualifications, bureaucracies may have far-reaching influence, and free markets may be highly motivating, but modern democratic citizens must ask themselves who we want to take the lead in combatting individualism and social decay. Do we trust experts to fix us, bureaucracies to find us, and markets to connect us?

Tocqueville is often called prescient, and his terms are used (sometimes anachronistically) to describe problems in our modern democracies. Tocqueville's predictions were not all accurate, and of course, our modern democracies look very different from the 19th-century American democracy that he studied. However, by examining Tocqueville alongside a 20th-century thinker, we have a more recent touchstone and perhaps updated language to understand the potential threats to democracy that still fascinate and frustrate us today. Although the proximate causes may have changed or even exacerbated our malaise, the deepest roots of our tendency to retreat inwards are found in the transformation of our social state diagnosed most acutely by Tocqueville, and in understanding the origins of our problems, we may be better suited to tackle them. Tocqueville and Lasch suggested that the prospects of the democratic project rely heavily on families with loyalty, parents with authority, and children with hope.

References

Botting, Eileen Hunt (2009), 'A Family Resemblance: Tocqueville and Wollstonecraftian Protofeminism', in Jill Locke and Eileen Hunt Botting (eds.), *Feminist Interpretations of Alexis de Tocqueville*, University Park: Pennsylvania State University Press, 99–124.

Lasch, Christopher (1991), *The Culture of Narcissism: American Life in an Age of Diminishing Expectations*, New York and London: W. W. Norton & Company.

Lasch, Christopher (1995), *Haven in a Heartless World: The Family Besieged*, New York and London: W. W. Norton & Company.

Lasch-Quinn, Elizabeth (1997), 'Introduction', in Elizabeth Lasch-Quinn (ed.), *Women and the Common Life: Love, Marriage, and Feminism*, New York and London: W. W. Norton & Company, ix–xxvii.

7 This relates to important questions about local, federal, and centralised governance. See Chapter 4 in this volume.

Mitchell, Travis. 'In U.S., Decline of Christianity Continues at Rapid Pace.' *Pew Research Center (blog)*, October 17, 2019.https://www.pewresearch.org/religion/2019/10/17/in-u-s-decline-of-christianity-continues-at-rapid-pace/.

Nolan, James L. (2016), *What They Saw in America*, Cambridge: Cambridge University Press.

Pew Research Center. 'Being Christian in Western Europe.' *Pew Research Center (blog)*, May 29, 2018. https://www.pewresearch.org/religion/2018/05/29/being-christian-in-western-europe/.

Tocqueville, Alexis de (2010 (original 1835)), *De La Démocratie En Amérique Vol. 1, Democracy in America: Historical-Critical Edition of De La Démocratie En Amérique: A Bilingual French-English Edition.* Edited by Eduardo Nolla and Translated by James T. Schleifer, Indianapolis: Liberty Fund.

Tocqueville, Alexis de (2010 (original 1840)), *De La Démocratie En Amérique Vol. 2, Democracy in America: Historical-Critical Edition of De La Démocratie En Amérique: A Bilingual French-English Edition.* Edited by Eduardo Nolla and Translated by James T. Schleifer, Indianapolis: Liberty Fund.

Villa, Dana (2005), 'Hegel, Tocqueville, and "Individualism"', *The Review of Politics* 67: 659–686.

4 Associational life and liberty

A critical assessment of Tocqueville's *Democracy in America*

David Thunder[1]

4.1 Introduction

Alexis de Tocqueville (1805–1859) understood the critical importance of associational life for a free and prosperous democratic nation as well as any modern thinker. His masterpiece, *Democracy in America*, is littered with quotations in praise of the salutary contribution of free associations to a prosperous, self-governing society. Free associations of citizens, erected for a multitude of purposes, whether philanthropic, economical, religious, recreational, or cultural, fulfil three purposes in modern democracy, according to Tocqueville: first, they permit citizens to satisfy a wide range of personal and social needs through voluntary cooperation with their fellow citizens; second, associations form civic character by cultivating habits of *independent action, responsibility, and civic participation*; and third, they permit citizens to develop associational bonds and loyalties that give them greater power than they would have as mere individuals to resist the despotic tendencies of democratic governments. Let us call these three advantages of associational life their *problem-solving*, *character-building*, and *anti-despotic* functions respectively.

From Tocqueville's perspective, the right to associate with one's peers in pursuit of purposes not established or tightly regulated by the state and its subsidiary agencies exists in permanent tension with the prerogatives of the 'people', which seem to press ever more aggressively for complete sovereignty over social life. In other words, freedom of association, understood as an effective capacity to build distinctive, coherent social groups with a life that is at least partly independent from that of 'the people', is threatened by the inexorable tendency of democratic governments to expand their jurisdiction over social life in the name of 'the people' and its sovereign prerogatives. In a post-aristocratic era, in which special privileges and prerogatives are viewed with suspicion and distrust, and differentiated legal and social status is viewed as an aberration from the equal rights of all men and women, the independent purposes and associated privileges and immunities of social groups, as corporate

1 The author gratefully acknowledges the financial support of Fundación Ciudadanía y Valores Proeduca Summa S.L.

DOI: 10.4324/9781032641041-4

actors with a life that is not simply created at the behest of the demos, are more difficult to vindicate before the court of public opinion than perhaps in any preceding era.

Given this ineliminable tension between freedom of association and the ever more expansive ambitions of popular governments to shape the social fabric unilaterally in the name of 'the people' and in accordance with popular – or allegedly popular – conceptions of justice and good order, what sorts of mechanisms or principles might prevent a democratic government from overpowering associations or asserting such expansive regulatory prerogatives as to render them putty in the hands of the state? It is this question that I wish to explore in this chapter, starting out from a broadly Tocquevillian perspective on democracy and group life. While I begin by viewing the problem through a Tocquevillian lens, I ultimately seek a solution in an institutional proposal that takes us beyond Tocqueville's predominantly cultural answer to this problem.

I begin by drawing on Tocqueville's *Democracy in America* to unpack the problem-solving, character-building, and anti-despotic functions of free associations in a democratic society. Second, I explain why Tocqueville sees democratic culture and institutions as containing within themselves tendencies that could erode or even destroy the authority and power of free associations. Third, I probe the text of *Democracy in America* in search of clues as to how a democratic society might shore up and defend the rights and prerogatives of associational life against the despotic tendencies of democratic governments, and find that Tocqueville's solution to this dilemma draws our attention predominantly to the critical role of social norms, civic culture, and local political institutions in curbing the despotic tendencies latent within democracy. Fourth, I argue that while Tocqueville is right to underline the critical role of habits of association and self-government, as well as their embodiment in local political institutions, his predominant focus on civic culture and local political institutions as safeguards of liberty does have some pitfalls, most notably his failure to give adequate attention to the protective function of an institutional and legal framework receptive to the non-democratic prerogatives and cultures of civil associations that do not coincide neatly with any territorial demos. Finally, I round out the argument by discussing, in a very preliminary way, how a hybrid form of federalism, incorporating non-territorial associations into the territorial pact or *foedus*, may, combined with the character and habits of a free and independent citizenry, play a critical role in protecting free associations of citizens against the despotic tendencies of democratic governments.

4.2 The three functions of free associations in a democratic society

4.2.1 The problem-solving and character-building function of free associations

I begin by drawing on Tocqueville's *Democracy in America* to unpack the problem-solving, character-building, and anti-despotic functions of free associations in a democratic society. The problem-solving function of free associations is relatively straightforward. In a society deeply imbued by habits of association, citizens instinctively band together to develop solutions – naturally, with varying degrees of success – to a multitude of social needs, from the mitigation of the effects of alcoholism and poverty to the satisfaction of recreational and sporting interests, to the funding of schools and seminaries:

> Americans of all ages, all conditions, all minds constantly unite. Not only do they have commercial and industrial associations in which all take part, but they also have a thousand other kinds: religious, moral, grave, futile, very general and very particular, immense and very small; Americans use associations to give fêtes, to found seminaries, to build inns, to raise churches, to distribute books, to send missionaries to the antipodes; in this manner they create hospitals, prisons, schools. (…) Everywhere that, at the head of a new undertaking, you see the government in France and a great lord in England, count on it that you will perceive an association in the United States.
>
> (Tocqueville 2000, 2:2; 5.489)

Associational life not only provides citizens with tools for solving common problems; it also provides a social context favourable to the development of a character infused with civic spirit.

In a feudal society, citizens are constantly confronted with vivid reminders of their dependence on others and others' dependence on them because of their integration within a complex network of social ties over which they have limited control. In a democratic society, on the other hand, social relations are more contractual, commercial, and voluntaristic, so citizens can more easily lose sight of their intimate dependence upon others and others' dependence upon them, and retreat into an attitude of self-centred complacency, in which the concerns of others become alien or indifferent to them.

Tocqueville uses the term 'individualism' to capture this steady retreat from the public sphere. 'Individualism', he says:

> is a reflective and peaceable sentiment that disposes each citizen to isolate himself from the mass of those like him and to withdraw to one side with his family and his friends, so that after having thus created a little society for his own use, he willingly abandons society at large to itself.
>
> (Tocqueville 2000, 2:2; 2.482)

For Tocqueville, there is a tight relation between democracy and individualism. Democracy, by weakening the visible bonds between social classes and between past, present, and future generations, 'hides (each man's) descendants from him and separates him from his contemporaries; it constantly leads him back toward himself alone and threatens finally to confine him wholly in the solitude of his own heart' (Tocqueville 2000, 2:2; 5.489).

The principal antidote to individualism and the social apathy it induces is the habit of associating with one's peers to achieve one's ends. Whereas habits of cooperation with others are practically inborn in feudal societies, due to the thick web of interdependent relations people are born into, habits of social cooperation have a more *intentional* or *artificial* character in democratic societies. The necessity of cooperation, beyond the sphere of the household, may present itself in certain well-defined contexts, such as economic exchange, but in general, is not thrust upon people in a democratic society by pre-existing social structures of mutual dependency. Democratic citizens can voluntarily unite within associations to further common purposes. These artificial associations provide the context within which habits of association are nurtured. Regular participation in the life of associations draws citizens out of the narrow sphere of the household, broadening their sympathies and liberating them from 'the solitude of (their) own hearts'.

On Tocqueville's account, there are two basic types of artificial association in a democratic society: *political* and *civil.* Tocqueville's paradigmatic example of a political association is a local town hall in which the common affairs of citizens are examined and citizens freely deliberate about how to further common interests. Only one sort of political association can realistically draw citizens out of themselves, namely, political associations operating at a local level. Here, citizens have a clear incentive to participate in common deliberations and raise their sights above their petty concerns, namely, the desire to defend their private interests. For only at the local level, according to Tocqueville, can citizens see, with relative ease, how public decisions tangibly impact their private destinies:

> Only with difficulty does one draw a man out of himself to interest him in the destiny of the whole state, because he understands poorly the influence that the destiny of the state can exert on his lot. But should it be necessary to pass a road through his property, he will see at first glance that he has come across a relation between this small public affair and his greatest private affairs, and he will discover, without anyone's showing it to him, the tight bond that here unites a particular interest to the general interest.
>
> (Tocqueville 2000, 2:2; 4.487)

Civil associations, though directed to narrower, more private ends than political associations, nonetheless broaden a person's horizon and lift him out of the narrow confines of his immediate household concerns. Their ends could be considered intermediate between the purely private ends of the household and the purely public ends of the municipality or town hall assembly. The motor of civil associations is the desire to advance some cause or end that cannot be realised by one or two individuals alone. Nonetheless, this desire seems to translate into associations with more frequency and intensity in the United States than in Europe, according to Tocqueville, so one would infer that there is a significant element of cultural mores or habits at work as well.

Tocqueville does not draw any sharp boundaries between commercial and civil associations for understandable reasons. After all, many commercial associations, such as community-based businesses and cooperatives, do effectively draw citizens out of the inward-looking attitudes of the private sphere. Nor does Tocqueville define civil associations in terms of the level of participation they entail. Presumably, there is a broad plurality of types of civil association, some more participatory in character than others. Nonetheless, a purely passive civil association would probably be of little interest to Tocqueville, given that the advantage he sees in associations is their capacity to motivate citizens to care about goods beyond the sphere of the household.

Tocqueville observes that 'as soon as several of the inhabitants of the United States have conceived a sentiment or an idea that they want to produce in the world, they seek each other out; and when they have found each other, they unite' (Tocqueville 2000, 2:2; 5.492). Like the habit of associating politically, the habit of associating civilly has a *civilising* effect on people, making them less inward-looking or individualistic, and more outward-looking or public-spirited. As Tocqueville puts it:

> Among the laws that rule human societies there is one that seems more precise and clearer than all the others. In order that men remain civilized or become so, the art of associating must be developed and perfected among them in the same ratio as equality of conditions increases.
>
> (Tocqueville 2000, 2:2; 5.492)

4.2.2 The anti-despotic function of free associations

Besides the problem-solving function of free associations of citizens and their salutary influence over the character and dispositions of citizens – in particular, their moderating effects on individualism – Tocqueville sees free associations as a vital counterweight to the despotic tendencies of the democratic state. The rise of the modern democratic state, as Tocqueville observes, has gone hand in hand with the dismantlement of the rights and privileges of rival corporate actors, leaving individual citizens ever more defenceless before the sovereign prerogatives of democratic rulers and administrations:

> (...) all the diverse rights that in our time have been successively taken away from classes, from corporations, from men, have not served to elevate new secondary powers on a more democratic base, but have been concentrated on all sides in the hands of the sovereign. Everywhere the state comes more and more to direct the least citizens by itself and alone to conduct each of them in the least affairs.
>
> (Tocqueville 2000, 2:4; 5.652)

The interposition of independent secondary powers, capable of resisting the centralising impulses of political rule, occurred almost effortlessly in a feudal, aristocratic society because an aristocratic mind automatically recognised a robust plurality of authorities and corporations. In an aristocratic era, no single actor could plausibly secure enough social power and recognition to impose its designs upon all, because secondary powers were ***built into the social landscape*** by long-standing customs and deeply ingrained social and economic relations. In a democratic era, by contrast, in which the social landscape was populated by ***equal citizens*** freed from feudal ties, secondary powers were no longer a natural feature of the social landscape: they had to be constituted ***artificially*** through the consent of citizens:

> The idea of secondary powers, placed between sovereign and subjects, naturally presented itself to the imagination of aristocratic peoples (…) because those powers contained within them individuals or families whom birth, enlightenment, and wealth held up as without peer and who seemed destined to command. For contrary reasons, this same idea is naturally absent from the minds of men in centuries of equality: it can only be introduced ***artificially*** then, and it is retained only with difficulty; whereas they conceive, so to speak without thinking about it, the idea of a lone central power that leads all citizens by itself.
>
> (Tocqueville 2000, 2:4; 2.640, emphasis added).

Free associations, by uniting the power and prestige of many particular individuals, can erect corporate actors capable of standing up to the authority of the state just as aristocratic individuals and bodies could rival the authority of the King:

> when plain citizens associate, they can constitute very opulent, very influential, very strong beings – in a word, aristocratic persons. A political, industrial, commercial, or even scientific and literary association is an enlightened and powerful citizen whom one can neither bend at will nor oppress in the dark and who, in defending its particular rights against the exigencies of power, saves common freedoms.
>
> (Tocqueville 2000, 2:4; 7.668)

4.3 The threat democratic culture and institutions pose to free associations

The relation between democracy and free associations is ambivalent from Tocqueville's perspective. On the one hand, the equal social conditions favoured by democratic culture and institutions free citizens from the bonds of rigid social hierarchies and age-old institutions, leaving them at liberty to form new associations with their equals. On the other hand, Tocqueville perceived serious dangers lurking within democratic culture and institutions for the future of free associations. Democracy provides three conditions that together favour the regulation and control by a centralised administrative state of the most minute details of associational life, even to the point of destroying the independence and reasonable prerogatives of non-state associations: first, a hankering by citizens after equal and uniform conditions for all, making them impatient with the notion that associations may enjoy robust autonomy, privileges, or prerogatives;[2] second, a deeply ingrained narrative of popular sovereignty that resonated with the democratic spirit of the age, elevating the prerogatives of the sovereign above those of rival associations; and third, a suite of powerful taxing and regulatory tools concentrated in the hands of a centralised administrative state. Once the strong prerogatives of princes, priests, and nobles were set aside, the democratic state could freely assert its democratic mandates over society and find a citizenry predisposed by its democratic spirit to view the directives of the State as authorised by 'the will of the people' and thus virtually unquestionable.

Indeed, the State could become a sort of 'soft despot' or gentle Master who looked out for citizens' most minute interests, removing from them either the need or the incentive to associate to satisfy their everyday needs.

> [This] 'immense and tutelary power' 'willingly works for (citizens') happiness; but it wants to be the unique agent and sole arbiter of that; it provides for their security, foresees and secures their needs, facilitates their pleasures, conducts their principal affairs, directs their industry, regulates their estates, divides their inheritances; can it not take away from them entirely the trouble of thinking and the pain of living?'
>
> (Tocqueville 2000, 2:4; 6.663)

The principal instrument of paternalism, in Tocqueville's view, was the administrative, regulatory state, which could extend its regulatory tentacles into every aspect of social life, placing exhausting regulatory obstacles in the path of human intelligence and initiative: 'Subjection in small affairs', he remarks, 'little by little (…) extinguishes (citizens') spirits and enervates their souls' (Tocqueville 2000, 2: 4; 6.665).

All of these dangers can be summed up by the tendency of the democratic spirit to elevate the will, interests, and prerogatives of the demos and its trustees above those of rival actors, whether individual citizens or groups acting in a collective capacity. Citizens of democratic societies, according to Tocqueville:

> willingly enough grant that the power representing society possesses much more enlightenment and wisdom than any of the men who

2 As Tocqueville puts it, 'as each (citizen) sees himself little different from his neighbours, he hardly understands why the rule that is applicable to one man should not be equally so to all others. The least privileges, therefore, are repugnant to his reason. The slightest dissimilarities in the political institutions of the same people wound him, and legislative uniformity appears to him to be the first condition of a good government' (Tocqueville 2000, 2:4; 2.641).

> compose it, and that its duty as well as its right is to take each citizen by the hand and lead him.
>
> (Tocqueville 2000, 2:4; 2.641)

In this sort of democratic culture, those who cannot credibly claim to speak in the name of 'the people' at large, such as the members of free associations and their representatives, would tend to be viewed as subordinate or inferior to representatives of 'the people' such as legislators and government ministers.

This state of affairs puts free associations in a rather precarious position because the authority of 'the people', or a majority thereof, or the authority of anyone who can make a credible claim to speak on behalf of 'the people', can easily exert itself over the social fabric, even to the point of destroying the vibrancy and independence of free associations, or subsuming their privileges and prerogatives within the bosom of its own constitution, to be authorised or de-authorised at its own good pleasure. The first half of the 20th century puts before us especially vivid illustrations of these dangers, with the emergence, within modern democracies, of authoritarian and fascist movements making appeals to the sovereignty and prerogatives of 'the people', prepared to persecute or even kill 'undesirable' minorities.

4.4 How culture and institutions may protect free associations from democratic despotism

So far, we have seen that from Tocqueville's perspective, the democratic spirit, and the democratic state buoyed up by narratives of popular sovereignty, pose a grave threat to the integrity and vibrancy of free associations because democratic citizens are predisposed to place an inordinate amount of faith in the authority of individual and corporate actors that can make a credible claim to act in the name of 'the people'. Furthermore, actors with a democratic mandate are not confronted with powerful rivals with the sort of effective power and public prestige that princes, lords, and bishops enjoyed in a more aristocratic era. On the contrary, many citizens are relatively naked and defenceless before the modern democratic state – and even when they do associate, if they do not manage to gather a very large number of fellow citizens into a common enterprise, their enterprises can be crushed or regulated into compliance with relative ease by those who wield the administrative power and democratic authority of a modern state. Who, after all, may successfully stand their ground before the power and majesty of the 'sovereign people' and the 'people's parliament'?

Under these circumstances, what precisely is it that stands in the way of democratic despotism, the tyranny of the majority, or the tyranny of demagogues who pretend to govern in the name of 'the people'? What resources do citizens have to defend their associations against the threats of administrative colonisation and micromanagement at best, outright aggression at worst, by governmental agencies acting in the name of the people? Tocqueville does not often address this question in a systematic way, and to the best of my knowledge, never quite formulates it in this precise manner.

But by putting the pieces together, we can infer at least *three Tocquevillian convictions* that can help us answer this question. First, the most fundamental driving force of social tendencies, for Tocqueville, is *culture* – that is, social customs, collective narratives, self-understanding, and habits – rather than specific institutions or organisations. Second, even if culture is more fundamental as an explanatory variable than institutions, well-designed institutions can both foment and complement cultural tendencies. Third, two dimensions of a democratic society, in particular, can save it from the despotic drift of democratic power – first, the habit of association, and second, the existence of vibrant and consequential political institutions operating at the local level. These two ingredients of a democratic society can complement and strengthen each other in holding democratic despotism at bay.

The habit of association is not automatic or universal; for as Tocqueville himself remarks, it is much more ingrained in the American culture and way of life than in, say, French culture and way of life. Tocqueville understands that the habit of association is what saves Americans from becoming completely inward-looking and self-absorbed, and what prevents them from becoming so isolated from each other that the state would have to step in to solve the most elementary of social problems. A culture imbued with habits of association geared towards a variety of ends – whether philanthropic, commercial, religious, or political – helps to preserve the sort of character that is less introspective and more independent and public-spirited, and thus less liable to delegate to the state the management of a citizen's day-to-day life.

But whether this habit takes root in a society, or proliferates across it, seems to be partly a function of happenstance or good luck. Presumably, the type of education children receive at home and in school could help to cultivate the art of association; undoubtedly, the inter-generational upkeep of civil associations of various sorts could help to transmit the habit of association to future generations. But Tocqueville restricts himself, for the most part, to remarking upon the force of this habit on the American continent, and its salutary ethical, social, and political benefits. In other words, Tocqueville seems to view the principal support of free associations as a culture in which the art of association *happens to proliferate.*

Having said that, Tocqueville does not restrict himself to a discussion of the cultural basis for free and independent associations. He also considers local political institutions to play a vital role in nourishing the art of association. Tocqueville observes that it is only when citizens can see a clear positive connection between their private interests and their participation in political decision-making that they are motivated to exercise their civic rights in political assemblies. The types of decisions that can vividly interest citizens and draw them into the process of political decision-making are typically decisions that have a visible, tangible impact on the quality of their day-to-day lives, the amount of money in their pockets, or their property rights (Tocqueville 2000, 2:2; 4.487).

These types of locally salient and consequential decisions are made quintessentially in local political assemblies such as town halls. It is in these sorts of assemblies that citizens venture out of their private pursuits to help settle issues of common concern that affect their private pursuits: 'When citizens are forced to be occupied with public affairs, they are necessarily drawn from the midst of their individual interests, and from time to time, torn away from the sight of themselves' (Tocqueville 2000, 2:2; 4.486). The logical conclusion of this argument is that if we want to keep the habit of association and public-spirited attitudes alive and well, we need local political decision-making structures to have real clout or effective power over public affairs and to be genuinely susceptible to the influence of ordinary citizens.[3]

Of course, one might apply a similar logic to civil associations: if they are structured in such a way as to (1) wield effective power to solve citizens' practical problems; and (2) permit citizens to influence their success and outcomes in practical ways, whether through decision-making or some other form of contribution, then civil associations can also offer citizens significant incentives to come out of their private affairs and at least concern themselves with 'semi-public' affairs of a larger social group. Furthermore, the habits of public deliberation and governance exercised in the context of associational life may be readily transferrable to other social contexts. While Tocqueville would surely not deny any of this, curiously he does not spend a lot of time discussing the power, prerogatives, and institutional structures of civil associations, their formal recognition within the political system, and the way their institutional design and context may either strengthen or inhibit the habit of association. Yet this is a matter of great importance for the future of democratic societies and is by no means of secondary importance for citizens' capacity to resist democratic despotism.

4.5 The institutional gap in Tocqueville's analysis of associational freedom

To sum up, there are two principal resources Tocqueville identifies within a democratic society for holding the despotic drift of democratic power at bay: (1) local political institutions that provide citizens with accessible decision-making structures giving them real power over their issues that affect their

3 As luck would have it, local townships in the United States did appear, at least in Tocqueville's time, to enjoy substantive independence and prerogatives in what concerned their inner life. As Tocqueville remarks, 'The townships generally submit to the state only when it is a question of an interest (...) which they share with others. For all that relates to themselves alone, the townships have remained independent bodies' (1:1; 5.62). Having said that, the internal culture and institutional structure of the townships also have a decisive bearing on the extent to which citizens exert a direct influence over local government. For example, Tocqueville is of the opinion that 'the spirit of the township is less awake and less powerful' 'as one descends toward the south (of the United States)' (1:1; 5.76).

day-to-day lives and (2) a culture in which the habit of association is well-engrained, giving birth to lively associations able to respond to citizens' needs as well as, or better, than the state. This is all good, as far as it goes. But it remains unclear why the culturally engrained habit of association, and the associations to which it gives birth, would be powerful enough to resist the credible sovereignty claims of the territorial demos, whether the demos of the municipality or town assembly or the demos that authorises the state, given that local associations would have a hard time claiming to possess a democratic mandate comparable to that of the demos at large.

There are three reasons to doubt that the cultural habit of association would be sufficient to hold back the despotic tendencies of democratic power. First, discrete associations are often populated by small minorities, whose joint political and economic power is easily outweighed both by the voting power of the majority of the political community and the combined resources they place at the disposal of their democratic representatives.

Second, in a culture in which uniform positive law frequently takes precedence over local and varyiable customs, it is relatively easy for a general regulator, equipped with legislative power, to hem in or even destroy the privileges and prerogatives of civilassociations within its ambit, given that particular associations do not usually enjoy public recognition as rival legislators or sources of law in their own right, except in a highly conditional sense, through freedom of contract modified by the sovereign regulations and policies of territorial governments.

Third, when an actor with a democratic mandate comes head-to-head with an association without a comparable democratic mandate, opposing such an actor is widely perceived as opposing the will of 'the people' at large, which is virtually unthinkable in a democratic culture. The will of a democratic parliament or assembly, which claims to serve as a proxy for the general will of the people, is difficult to resist by invoking the prerogatives of local associations, which seem alien to the logic of popular sovereignty and democratic authority. Invoking a generic freedom to lawfully associate can only get one so far, given that the lawful bounds of associational life are fixed, in practice, by the democratic sovereign.

Habits of association can be degraded and eroded over time, particularly in a culture in which the voice and prerogatives of the majority are constantly echoed through every corner of society, and backed up by a deeply ingrained narrative of democratic sovereignty. Local political institutions might be more accommodating towards local associations than a national parliament, but they are still susceptible to co-option by a numerical majority and may have limited sympathy for the claims of associations that find themselves in a voting minority. So neither the habit of association nor the presence of local political institutions are likely to offer sufficient protection to free associations against the risk of democratic despotism. Yet, Tocqueville does not appear to explicitly identify any institutional resources beyond democratic assemblies for fortifying or protecting free associations against democratic despotism. Why might this be?

It can hardly be explained by the notion that the institutional and legal standing of associations was fixed in stone or immune to change. Had Tocqueville put his mind to it, he might have explored potential mechanisms within the law itself, or within the design of representative institutions, for extending greater recognition to the rights and prerogatives of free associations. Given his rich sociological imagination and his careful analysis of the benefits of local political participation, surely he would have had the intellectual capacity and imagination to come up with institutional proposals for shoring up the independent prerogatives of free associations? It is therefore somewhat puzzling that he did not take his analysis of associational life any further than he did. The puzzle could also be framed as follows: Why is there such a remarkable asymmetry between Tocqueville's attention to the institutional basis for *political* associations, and his relative inattention to the institutional basis for *civil* associations?

In reality, we can only speculate about Tocqueville's reasons for not addressing the role of institutional structures beyond local political institutions in protecting free associations from a potentially overbearing demos. Here is one possible explanation: Although Tocqueville has a keen interest in the conditions most conducive to a functional and just democracy, his normative reflections are strongly rooted in his empirical observations, and he does not tend to theorise at much of a distance from what he observes on the ground. He hopes to learn what he can from the great American experiment, not produce a new institutional model of his own. From Tocqueville's own description of associational life in America, it appears that citizens largely developed the life of their associations based on their own initiative, and the relation between territorial political institutions and non-territorial associations was largely informal and spontaneous rather than defined by elaborate legal regimes.

Furthermore, representation in democratic assemblies was typically not drawn from associations as corporate bodies, but from the population at large, which suggests that associations derived their public standing from a combination of customary recognition and voting clout, rather than from their *formal integration* within the democratic process. The lack of formal integration of associations within the democratic process is made clear by Tocqueville's detailed and colourful description of local political institutions, which are formally constituted by a democratic mandate rather than by associational prerogatives. Of course, none of this rules out the capacity of local associations to influence legislative and policy outcomes. But this influence seems to have been part of the 'messy business' of politics, rather than a formal, institutionalised component of democratic life.

In what follows, I will venture tentatively onto the terrain of constructive institutional design, going beyond Tocqueville's tendency to focus predominantly on the description and assessment of existing institutional structures. A close reading of Tocqueville provides some good starting points for (1) identifying a *limitation inherent in modern democratic societies* – namely, their vulnerability to democratic despotism, and (2) identifying the limits of well-established cultural and institutional resources for tackling this limitation, and (3) proposing a direction of reform that might begin to overcome the limitations of these well-established solutions to the problem of democratic depotism. The direction of reform I have in mind concerns the institutional relation between civil (non-territorial) associations and political (territorial) associations. Tocqueville prepares the way nicely for such a proposal insofar as his own description of American democracy highlights the need for a stronger institutional basis for free associations, an institutional basis that cannot be easily swept aside by the prerogatives of 'the people'.

4.6 Filling the institutional gap: How hybrid federalism might provide superior institutional protection to free associations

The asymmetry in Tocqueville's treatment of the institutional dimension of political and civil associations is striking. Specifically, it is remarkable that Tocqueville discusses the importance of local institutions of self-government in the *political* sphere at some length, yet leaves the institutional basis for independent initiative and self-government in *civil associations* rather nebulous from an institutional perspective. If we are to take his warnings to heart concerning the disproportionate prestige and power of democratic governments compared with the civil associations that fall under their sway, and the ease with which the democratic spirit elevates the demos above its parts, then it is unlikely that the *habit* of association, by itself, will be sufficient to protect associational life from democratic despotism. Associations themselves need some form of *institutional protection* that is not easily overcome by the ephemeral passions of a majority or the potentially despotic ambitions of a democratic assembly.

Territorial federalism, with its doctrine of reserved powers – the notion that those powers not explicitly delegated to the federal government are retained by local units of government – offers some important institutional protections against the accumulation of political power at the centre. Furthermore, insofar as the rights and privileges of cities and townships are laid out clearly in charters or state constitutions, this provides additional institutional protection for the autonomy of local political actors. What is a lot less clear is how the rights and prerogatives of civil or *non-territorial* associations are institutionally shielded, within a federal republic, against usurpation or colonisation by territorial political actors, acting in the name of 'the people' or the political community at large, whether the people of the nation, State, or municipality.

In principle, free associations should be protected in their activities and constitutions by freedom of contract, religion, and association. For example, a state would have a hard time dissolving a church or ecclesial community without finding itself sued in a court of law for violating freedom of religion, and states cannot disband voluntary associations willy-nilly without falling foul of the usual constitutional protection afforded to freedom of association. However, there is a lot of grey area between egregious attacks on civil associations on the one hand and unwavering respect for their integrity on the other. Since lawmakers have the right and capacity to regulate associational life, decide what counts as a 'charitable organisation', determine whether and to what extent associations are liable to taxation, and even define the conditions under which an organisation can be recognised as an association for legal purposes, there is always a danger that an association whose goals are not consistent with the ideology or values of the majority or of a democratic government may be harassed, persecuted, or constrained in its activities even if it is not obviously harming any public interest.

The only way to robustly protect against this sort of outcome is to reconceive the relation between democratic power and the power and prerogatives of civil associations, in such a way that civil associations are viewed as *independent stakeholders* in the democratic project, with a standing in the public square that is not easily erased by shifting political coalitions or tyrannical majorities. Free associations must be somehow integrated into the social pact, and their right to self-regulate, within certain limits of public order, must be legally recognised and must enjoy substantial immunity to the efforts of democratic assemblies to remake associational life in their own image and likeness. In short, the territorial pact or *foedus*, which, in a democratic era, integrates territorial political actors and individual citizens, should be reframed in such a way as to integrate *non-territorial* actors as well.

The tradition of federalism, though currently strongly biased towards territorial units of governance, could potentially be rehabilitated in such a way as to render it more sensitive to the standing and rights of *non-territorial* groups. One of the distinguishing features of the federalist tradition, in all of its manifestations, is a special sensitivity to the need for complex governance arrangements to incorporate diverse social groups, while simultaneously permitting them to preserve some independent prerogatives of governance or domains of action.[4] A cooperative arrangement is instituted without radically subordinating the cooperating units to a single, homogeneous logic of decision-making and action. Daniel Elazar captures this spirit of federalism about as well as anyone, describing it as a judicious combination of self-rule and shared rule:

> Federal principles are concerned with the combination of self-rule and shared rule. In the broadest sense, federalism involves the linking of individuals, groups, and polities in lasting but limited union in such a way as to provide for the energetic pursuit of common ends while maintaining the respective integrities of all parties. As a political principle, federalism has to do with the constitutional diffusion of power so that the constituting elements in a federal arrangement share in the processes of common policy making and administration by right, while the activities of the

4 Within the short space of this chapter, I do not pretend to trace out the historical evolution and leading ideas of diverse strands of federalism. For a representative sample of the literature on federalism, I would refer the reader to works like Elazar 1987; King 1982; Frey and Eichenberger 2004; Kriesi and Trechsel 2008; Ostrom 1991; Althusius 1995/1614; Friedrich 1966; Spruyt 1996 (Spruyt's account of the Hanseatic League is particularly instructive); and of course, Hamilton, Madison, and Jay 2015.

> common government are conducted in such a way as to maintain their respective integrities.
>
> (Elazar 1987: 5)

There are two different ways the *foedus* (variously translated as treaty, agreement, or pact) can be unpacked. On the one hand, we can construe the *foedus* as being agreed to by governments acting in the name of *territorial* populations; on the other hand, we can construe the *foedus* as being agreed to by governments or rulers acting in the name of *non-territorial* groups. Although some federalist thinkers, most notably Johannes Althusius (1995 [1614]), understood a federal polity to combine *both territorial and non-territorial* units of governance, the general tendency of modern federalist theory has been to conceive the units to be federated as territorially defined. Thus, federalism is widely understood as a method of territorial or inter-territorial governance, rather than as a method for coordinating *both* territorial *and non-territorial* units of government. The strong territorial bias in many treatments of federalism (including Tocqueville's), which tend to use the term in reference to territorially defined relationships, might be explained by the fact that territorial relationships have become extraordinarily salient with the rise of the modern state, while non-territorial relationships have become comparatively less salient, especially in discussions of politics and power, with the dramatic decline of feudal relationships and the perception of non-territorial relationships as sources of oppression rather than liberation.[5]

It seems to me that the danger of democratic despotism cannot be successfully held at bay unless we remedy this long-standing neglect of the role of non-territorial corporate actors in the constitutional scheme of a modern nation. Ignoring them or treating them as nothing more than accidental by-products of individual choice fails to protect them as independent actors from domination by the demos and its representatives. Because federalism already contains within it the seeds of respect for group life, it seems like a very promising starting point for institutionalising better protections for the life and reasonable rights and prerogatives of free associations. In this section, I wish to gesture towards a form of federalism capable of more successfully integrating the non-territorial dimension of associational life.

It is hard to imagine a functional society bereft of any form of territorial governance. We are embodied beings who inhabit physical spaces. Our neighbours share our physical surroundings. Many of our vital needs depend

5 My point is not that feudal relationships should be resurrected, but that our historical abandonment of feudalism has narrowed our imagination, making territorial relations artificially salient and rendering non-territorial relations artificially marginal. Johannes Althusius (1557–1638) was one of the last prominent theorists of federal governance who showed great sensitivity to the role of non-territorial associations in the constitution of the republic.

on forms of coordination that are naturally tied to specific geographic units – whether planning and zoning laws, policing, city by-laws, rules of public order, or investment in local building projects or road infrastructure. So it makes perfect sense that the jurisdiction or functions of civil authorities would be defined territorially.

So far, so good. But a moment's reflection reveals that there are many coordination needs for which territorial governments are either motivationally or epistemically inadequate. For example, local schools require rulers who are privy to the intimate workings of the school and its operating ethos and are motivated to show special care and concern for its mission. Similarly, local businesses require their own managers who have intimate, inside knowledge of their workings and are both motivated to care for their employees and capable of setting policies and strategies that help the business thrive and expand over time. Similar considerations can be brought to bear on a broad range of other non-territorial associations.

If we assume that the purpose of civil order is to provide a normative and institutional framework within which citizens can pursue their goals in a more or less orderly, functional, and peaceful fashion, then federalism, as an account of civil order, must be capable of accommodating a variety of different layers or forms of social order within it. A purely territorially based political order that is blind to the role of non-territorial or civil associations, or even hostile to their positive contribution to the life of citizens, could easily descend into a dysfunctional tyranny or oligarchy. A territorial political order, however decentralised, that lacks reliable and socially recognised mechanisms for incorporating the needs and interests of non-territorial associations could inadvertently alienate large chunks of the citizenry by imposing policies that are harmful to large groups of citizens – whether accidentally or by design.

Another reason why federalism needs to pay close attention to non-territorial associations is that one of the crucial checks on political despotism is the power of civil associations to erect independent normative orders that can rival that of the municipality or State, or provide a counterweight to regulatory overreach by municipal or State authorities. Checks on power contained *within* territorial governments are not sufficient because majorities within territorial governments can impose their wishes and policies upon non-territorial associations if such associations are numerically weak or do not muster much political power.

I do not want to suggest that territorial accounts of federalism are completely blind to the role of civil society associations in supporting a shared civil order and enabling a rich variety of forms of human flourishing. There is obviously an acknowledgement by many advocates and theorists of federalism that federated governance requires a culture friendly to the principles of federalism, which seems to imply an important role for civil society groups. Furthermore, federalism normally accepts standard liberal principles of freedom of association and limited government, which imply a certain sphere of associational freedom and autonomy and a certain degree of immunity to state regulation in non-state associations.[6] However, until the central account of federalism explicitly integrates non-territorial groups within its conception of governance and civil order, it will remain incomplete and potentially alienating to groups that are excluded from the social compact, inadequately considered by public policies, or regulated in ways that contradict or sabotage their missions and purposes.

A mixed or hybrid account of federalism would conceive the groups to be federated along two dimensions. First, territorial units, such as municipalities or regions, and second, non-territorial units, such as schools, universities, trade guilds, local businesses, churches, and cultural, artistic, and sporting associations. To be *federated*, in this context, means to be (1) articulated into moderately scaled units capable of joining the foedus of the association (for example, the constitution of an athletic federation) and (2) incorporated into the wider social compact, as a party to the *foedus* – the agreement or treaty or constitution that guides and binds the common life of a given territory.

A mixed account of federalism would have some clear advantages over a more narrowly territorial account. First, it would permit social groups to conserve and defend their *internal purposes and logics of action* in their interactions with other parts of society, by recognising their special prerogatives of action and giving them a corporate voice and standing in political life, instead of dissolving them into a cacophony of individual voices, powerless to resist the prerogatives of the 'sovereign people'. Second, by fortifying the standing and prerogatives of non-territorial groups, a mixed account of federalism offers an invaluable resource for combating despotic and oligarchic tendencies in local, regional and national governments, which may exploit fickle popular majorities or achieve partisan ends by cobbling together electoral coalitions that may not even represent a majority of citizens.

4.7 In conclusion

I began this Chapter by highlighting the critical role of free associations of citizens in solving social problems, building public-spirited character, and limiting the despotic tendencies of democratic governments. I then considered in greater detail why modern democracy poses a serious threat to associational life, from Tocqueville's perspective, primarily on account of its tendency to elevate the will of 'the people' above the will and interests of the free associations that make up the fabric of society. I found that Tocqueville's answer to this threat, while paying close attention to the formative role of civil associations and decentralised and participatory democracy in drawing citizens out of their

6 I say 'a certain degree' of immunity and autonomy because it is always understood that civil associations are limited by values like the rule of law and civility, especially within a society whose laws already grant them a reasonable sphere of autonomy.

private concerns, was strangely silent about potential institutional mechanisms for protecting civil associations from domination by territorial political actors.

I proposed to fill this institutional vacuum by outlining some guiding principles for integrating and recognising the standing of *non-territorial* actors within the federal scheme. Admittedly, this constructive proposal needs to be fleshed out in greater detail, and its full implementation would require far-reaching changes to the prevailing civic culture of Western societies.

References

Althusius, Johannes (1995 [1614]), *Politica: An Abridged Translation of Politics Methodically Set Forth and Illustrated with Sacred and Profane Examples.* Translated by S. Carney Frederick, Indianapolis: Liberty Fund.

Elazar, Daniel J. (1987), *Exploring Federalism,* Tuscaloosa, AL: University of Alabama Press.

Frey, Bruno S., and Reiner Eichenberger (2004), *The New Democratic Federalism for Europe: Functional, Overlapping and Competing Jurisdictions*, Cheltenham, UK & Northampton, MA: Edward Elgar Publishing.

Friedrich, Carl Joachim (1966), 'Federalism and Opposition', *Government and Opposition* 1(3): 289–296.

Hamilton, Alexander, James Madison, and John Jay (2015 [1787), *The Federalist Papers,* Dublin, OH: Coventry House Publishing.

King, Preston (1982), *Federalism and Federation*, London: Croom Helm.

Kriesi, Hanspeter, and Alexander H. Trechsel (2008), *The Politics of Switzerland: Continuity and Change in a Consensus Democracy*, Cambridge: Cambridge University Press.

Ostrom, Vincent (1991), *The Meaning of American Federalism: Constituting a Self-Governing Society*, San Francisco: ICS Press.

Spruyt, Hendrik (1996), *The Sovereign State and Its Competitors: An Analysis of Systems Change*, Princeton: Princeton University Press.

Tocqueville, Alexis de (2000 [1835–1840]), *Democracy in America.* Translated, edited, and with an introduction by Harvey C Mansfield and Delba Winthrop, Chicago: University of Chicago Press.

5 Conservatism, enlightened self-interest, and a threatened civilisational order

John D. Wilsey

5.1 Introduction

Citizens in Western democracies are divided over a host of political, social, economic, and religious issues. Americans have historically had the reputation of being greedy and selfish, in pursuit of money instead of the common good. The question of whether or not self-interest can actually contribute to the common good was a live question in 19th and 20th-century American culture. It remains a live question in the 21st century, especially in the context of the waning influence of Protestant Christianity, perceived threats to democracy, the rise of identity politics, fading confidence in institutions, and uncertainty regarding the power of the American democratic example to the rest of the world. Is there a difference between base selfishness and self-interest rightly understood? Can an enlightened self-interest serve democracy in the 21st century, as it has arguably done in past generations? Is the concept of self-interest rightly understood as essentially liberal or conservative? These are important issues, because if citizens can rightly understand and apply self-interest to the advancement of civilisation, then they will have the ability to strike that tenuous, but necessary, balance between private and public interests. The success of any democracy depends on that tenuous balance.

When Alexis de Tocqueville (1805–1859) came to America as a 25-year-old lawyer, he encountered a society so vastly unlike his native France that he was moved to ascribe it to the hand of divine providence. In *Democracy in America*, Tocqueville wrote that equality of conditions was inexorably spreading its influence in human civilisation. Nowhere was this more evident than in America. Upon encountering American society, he observed a number of consequences to the spread of equality of conditions. One was the effect of what he called enlightened self-interest (*l'interêt bien entendu*). While he did not think Americans were all that virtuous, he did find that they had a keen understanding of the effects of ordinary acts of self-sacrifice for the common good. Such quotidian actions benefited the community at large while also being of benefit to the individual. The difficult balance every society must maintain in order for its members to flourish – that balance between public and private interests – Americans had struck that balance through enlightened self-interest. Other

DOI: 10.4324/9781032641041-5

influences converged with enlightened self-interest to achieve that balance, like public spirit, religion, mores, federalism, and equality of women with men in society. Enlightened self-interest was both a product of these influences and a contributor to their development. Unique traits enjoyed by Americans, such as civil and political associations, a robust legal community, checks and balances between government institutions, religious liberty, commercial habits, and patriotism, were all affected in some way by the doctrine of enlightened self-interest. As Wilfred McClay described it in his book, *The Masterless*, Tocqueville observed that Americans were not particularly virtuous, but instead tended to be selfish and materialistic. Still, they were able 'to coax that vice into paying willing tribute to virtue' through enlightened self-interest (McClay 1994: 44).

Tocqueville believed that enlightened self-interest, along with religion, was necessary to prevent the tyranny of the majority in a democratic society. Tocqueville's particular articulation of enlightened self-interest is conservative in at least three ways. First, enlightened self-interest is consistent with the human condition, which should be taken as it is. Second, enlightened self-interest functions as a secular preserver of freedom alongside its spiritual counterpart, religion, which is indispensable to a free society (see Chapter 2). Third, the doctrine of enlightened self-interest has limited value to society because human nature is bounded by limits. Tocqueville's crafting of a conservative understanding of enlightened self-interest reminds contemporary citizens that human nature has not changed since the 1830s and that enlightened self-interest detached from religion is unenlightened and absurd. Furthermore, Tocqueville's conservative understanding of enlightened self-interest is instructive for citizens in contemporary times, if they have ears to hear.

5.2 Relevance of enlightened self-interest

Tocqueville's conservative articulation of enlightened self-interest is important for contemporary times, just as it was in the 1830s. Western societies are dismayed by the partisanship, discord, disorder, incompetence, triviality, and inhumanity that often predominate in public settings. In America, many fear the failure of the democratic experiment, the dissolution of the Union, or even open civil war. They look in desperation for a figure of greatness who can lead them with wisdom, courage, and hope, but they are disappointed again and again in the leaders whom they elect. Those leaders disappoint because they are polarising, incompetent, blindly partisan, and selfish. Most pernicious of all, however, leaders play the role of the despot when they proactively seek to divide the citizenry and isolate people from each other. Tocqueville said, 'a despot readily pardons the governed for not loving him, provided that they do not love each other' (Tocqueville 2000, 2:2; 4.485).

Enlightened self-interest – complemented by religion, expressed through voluntary associations, informed by the mores, animated by public spirit – serves to bring people together. starting at the local level. This is what makes

Tocqueville's articulation of American expressions of enlightened self-interest conservative. Conservatism is not comprised of a set of political positions or ideologies. Conservatism does entail particular political, economic, social, and even religious positions, but it is more than a set of ideologies. Conservatism is a way of life, a disposition towards reality, and a posture towards God, the world, and oneself (in that order). Defined this way, we can see how self-interest relates to conservatism. Self-interest is integral to human nature and is thus pre-political. If conservatism is primarily an attitude, a way of thinking and living, it must be informed by mores before it is informed by politics.

In historian Robert Tracy McKenzie's words, 'It wasn't the mere fact that Americans pursued their self-interest that eventually impressed him the most. It was *how* they did so' (McKenzie 2021: 230). Americans saw that they could channel their love of self into directions that met not only their own goals but the goals of their communities. Enlightened self-interest made its developed appearance in Volume II, Part 2, entitled 'Influence of Democracy on the Sentiments of the Americans'. Tocqueville contextualised enlightened self-interest in a consideration of some harmful tendencies of the heart in democratic societies. He began by arguing that in democratic societies, people love equality more than they love freedom. To illustrate, he attempted to conceive an ideal democracy, whereby freedom and equality were not at odds with one another but came together in unity. Perfect freedom and perfect equality would be entailed in one another in such a state of affairs, and 'this is the ideal toward which democratic peoples tend' (Tocqueville 2000, 2:2; 1.479). Unfortunately, while this was the ideal form of democracy, Tocqueville observed that democracy's effects on the passions of citizens directed them to imperfect forms, but citizens would not recognise their imperfections. He said, 'there are a thousand other [forms of democracy], not as perfect, that are scarcely less dear to these peoples' (Tocqueville 2000, 2:2; 1.479). Tocqueville's thoughts on an ideal democratic society are similar to James Madison's in which he wrote, 'If men were angels, no government would be necessary. If angels were to govern men, neither external nor internal controls on government would be necessary' (Madison 2005: 281). Madison's next statement is in the same spirit as Tocqueville's thoughts on how equality tends towards despotism, and the need for mitigating influences on those tendencies: 'In framing a government which is to be administered by men over men, the great difficulty lies in this: You must first enable the government to control the governed; and in the next place, oblige it to control itself' (Madison 2005: 281). Freedom and equality were easily confused, but while freedom could exist in a monarchy, aristocracy, or democracy, Tocqueville believed that equality could only exist in a democracy. In democratic societies, Tocqueville argued that people are more passionate about equality than freedom. To abolish equality, the people would have to radically alter society from the bottom up, starting with reworking mores, laws, habits, and ideas 'by long and painful efforts' (Tocqueville 2000, 2:2; 1.480). To abolish freedom, all that was necessary was to let it go, 'and it escapes' (Tocqueville 2000, 2:2; 1.481). People loved equality dearly because equality yielded short-term benefits that were easily won. Freedom required sacrifice and patience.

Tocqueville related the people's devotion to equality over freedom to the tendency towards individualism. Individualism was different than mere selfishness, in that selfishness was 'an exaggerated love of self', arising from 'blind instinct' and 'a vice as old as the world' (Tocqueville 2000, 2:2; 2.482–483). Individualism was a new dynamic. Whereas selfishness had always been part of human nature, individualism was an expression of that human nature in the specific context of a democratic society marked by equality. In individualism, citizens withdrew from society at large to their own familiar circles of family and friends. In doing so, the citizen made 'a little society for his own use' and the larger society in which he was an integral part must now make do without him (Tocqueville 2000, 2:2; 2.483). Peter Lawler described individualism as 'a prideless, apathetic, asocial existence without love or hate' and 'a judgment in favor of the brutish self-sufficiency of Rousseau's state of nature where people are like any other animal because they feel neither pride nor love' (Lawler 1995: 219–220). In this way, individualism gave citizens over to the baser instincts of their nature. For Tocqueville, the long-term effect of individualism was selfishness. In aristocracies, families were connected closely because those societies were static and generations were closely joined together by geography and sentiment. In democracies, family ties were broken up by a society marked by geographical, social, and economic movement, so, as Tocqueville wrote, 'not only does democracy make each man forget his ancestors, but it hides his descendants from him and separates him from his contemporaries' (Tocqueville 2000, 2:2; 2.483–484). In short, the person had only himself on which to depend.

One way in which Tocqueville observed that Americans mitigate the deleterious effects of excessive love for equality and its tendency towards individualism was through free institutions. Noting that despotism flourishes when citizens are isolated from each other, in America, Tocqueville saw that despotism was hindered by the dividing up of the national community into states, and states into local jurisdictions. In those local jurisdictions, citizens felt they were contributing to their own private interests when they were looking after those of the public. 'Local freedoms, which make many citizens put value on the affection of their neighbors and those close to them, therefore constantly bring men closer to one another, despite the instincts that separate them, and force them to aid each other' (Tocqueville 2000, 2:2; 4.487). Free institutions reminded citizens in America that they were dependent on each other for their flourishing, and gave citizens practice in exercising their duties towards their fellows. True, individual citizens may have started out thinking only of themselves, but as Tocqueville put it, necessity gave birth to choice, leading to calculation, then instinct, and then 'one finally picks up the habit and taste of serving' the community (Tocqueville 2000, 2:2; 4.488).

From free institutions, Tocqueville moved on to discuss the significance of voluntary associations (see Chapter 4). Tocqueville expressed surprise at how ubiquitous voluntary associations were in America, and how diverse their purposes were. For great ends and for small, there were associations of every imaginable kind in America. They varied in kind by 'religious, moral, grave, futile, very general and very particular, immense and very small' in order 'to give fetes, to found seminaries, to build inns, to raise churches, to distribute books, to send missionaries to the antipodes; in this manner they create hospitals, prisons, schools' (Tocqueville 2000, 2:2; 5.489). At the time of Tocqueville's visit, there were large associations like the American Bible Society, the American Colonization Society, the Sunday School Union, the American Board of Commissioners of Foreign Missions, and the American Temperance Society. William Lloyd Garrison had inaugurated one of the most prominent anti-slavery journals of the antebellum period, *The Liberator*, in the year that Tocqueville arrived in America, and was a co-founder in 1833 of the American Anti-Slavery Society. There were also hundreds of smaller, local societies dedicated to distinct and parochial causes, such as the Society for the Encouragement of Faithful Domestic Servants in New York and the Ladies' Association for the Benefit of Gentlewomen of Good Family, Reduced in Fortune Below the State of Comfort to Which They Have Been Accustomed (Howe 2007: 192). Whereas in France, people relied on the government to solve problems and in England, they relied on a 'great lord' (Tocqueville 2000, 2:2; 5.489), in America, citizens relied on themselves as they associated together. Once they formed an association, the citizens no longer fell to individualism and isolation, but together they became 'a power one sees from afar, whose actions serve as an example; a power that speaks, and to which one listens' (Tocqueville 2000, 2:2; 5.492). While it was easy for a despot to curtail the freedoms of isolated individuals, apathetic and distracted as they were, it was much harder to abuse an association of citizens who had pooled their resources and advanced their cause through newspapers (Tocqueville 2000, 2:2; 4.493–495).

This context which Tocqueville provided in the first seven chapters of Volume II, Part 2 formed the foundation for his articulation of the doctrine of enlightened self-interest. He argued that in an aristocracy, virtue was extolled continually. Virtue, that act by which a person completely forgets himself and his own interests and turns himself wholly to the interests of others 'like God himself' (Tocqueville 2000, 2:2; 8.500) was the ideal of aristocracy. Actually, Tocqueville doubted whether, in practice, virtue held as supreme a place in the way that aristocrats liked to imagine. In the democratic society of America, citizens did not regard virtue in such ideal terms. They did not value it for its own sake. Rather, citizens regarded virtue as strictly for the sake of its usefulness to themselves. 'American moralists', Tocqueville wrote:

> do not claim that one must sacrifice oneself to those like oneself because it is great to do it; but they say boldly that such sacrifices are as necessary to the one who imposes them on himself as to the one who profits from them.
>
> (Tocqueville 2000, 2:2; 8.501)

While the 16th-century thinker Montaigne (1533–1592) mused upon the usefulness of virtue, Tocqueville thought that Americans had 'universally accepted it' and found it 'not less in the mouth of the poor man than in that of the rich' (Tocqueville 2000, 2:2; 8.502). Enlightened self-interest brought citizens together in America, Tocqueville observed, and continually 'disposes them willingly to sacrifice a part of their time and their wealth to the good of the state' (Tocqueville 2000, 2:2; 8.502). This statement from Tocqueville is consistent with John Locke's conception of the profitability of virtue as he expressed it in his *Essay Concerning Human Understanding*. There, Locke argued that morality was grounded in the existence of God, but virtue was not innate to the human creature. It was through a system of reward and punishment that humans knew virtue: A connection between virtue and happiness. According to Locke, this connection between virtue and happiness was joined by God himself, who also 'made the practice thereof necessary to the preservation of society, and visibly beneficial to all with whom the virtuous man has to do' (Locke 1952, 1:2; §6).

5.3 Enlightened self-interest, virtue, and religion

Regarding enlightened self-interest, Tocqueville's overall point was that it indeed was enlightened. By the power of reason, enlightened self-interest directed the passions outwards from the individual towards society. In a similar way as Madison's famous argument that 'ambition must be made to counteract ambition' (Madison 2005: 281), Tocqueville argued that enlightened self-interest 'turns personal interest against itself' (Tocqueville 2000, 2:2; 8.502). In so doing, enlightened self-interest made no great citizens, but it did prevent citizens from tending towards their baser instincts, like individualism. While selfishness remained basic to human nature and was everywhere apparent, Tocqueville was convinced that Americans had put it to use in order to preserve and advance the common good. Compared to his native France, Tocqueville confessed:

> I do not believe that, all in all, there is more selfishness among us than in America; the only difference is that there it is enlightened and here it is not. ... We want to keep everything, and often everything eludes us.
>
> (Tocqueville 2000, 2:2; 8.503)

The beauty of enlightened self-interest, for Tocqueville, was that it opened a middle path between selfishness and altruism in the act of mitigating the influence of individualism in a society that had little permanent structure to keep citizens from becoming isolated. As Norman Campagna described it:

> the aim of social education in a democratic nation is not the eradication of egoism, but its enlightenment. ··· [enlightened self-interest] retains the idea of sacrifice, but rather than to disconnect it completely from personal gain, it tries to bring the two together. The rationale is: Ask what you can do for yourself by doing something for your fatherland.
>
> (Campagna 2007: 179–180)

While enlightened self-interest could not elevate citizens to ideal greatness, it did point them towards a form of greatness in spite of itself. Alan Kahan summarised this point in writing, 'Tocqueville will use whatever means are available to encourage greatness, even means that are not great in themselves' (Kahan 2015a: 61).

What about the relationship between enlightened self-interest and religion? Was religious belief reconcilable to enlightened self-interest according to Tocqueville? It may seem that enlightened self-interest and the Christian religion are irreconcilable since the Christian faith stresses the importance of putting others' interests ahead of one's own interests. The Apostle Paul wrote to the Philippian church, 'Do nothing from selfish ambition or empty conceit, but with humility of mind regard one another as more important than yourselves' (Phil. 2:3). Medieval Western Europe accepted, almost without question, the idea that this world was passing away, that it did not offer hope in itself. Humility before authority, fear of God, and obedience were central to the medieval West's conception of life, particularly for the monks. Benedict of Nursia (480–547) founded the monastery at Monte Cassino in 529, and from there, he wrote his *Rule* in which he laid out 12 stages of humility (the fear of God, self-denial, submission to authority, perseverance, confession and repentance, contentment with poverty, self-abasement, prudence, silence, solemnity, slowness of speech, and devotion). Benedict's *Rule* provided the template for the life of the monk, but it also helps contemporary audiences make sense of the medieval mind (Lane 2006: 99).

The stress medieval thinkers like Benedict placed on the ephemeral nature of this world and the eternality of the next world is in contrast with the world stamped with Enlightenment and Romantic thought. Reason and feeling were regarded as more certain tests for truth in Enlightenment and Romantic thought respectively than in the medieval period, dominated as it was by Augustinian dualism. Tocqueville perceived this contrast, by observing that:

> In the Middle Ages, priests spoke only about the other life: they scarcely worried about proving that a sincere Christian can be a happy man here below. American preachers constantly come back to earth and only with great trouble can they take their eyes off it.
>
> (Tocqueville 2000, 2:2; 9.505)

One benchmark thinker to influence Tocqueville on the role of faith and reason in enlightened self-interest was Blaise Pascal (1623–1662), an Enlightenment figure who appealed to pragmatic reason in the human heart with regard to religion. While Pascal did not favour reason over revelation, as Locke did, he did find a place for reason as a complement to faith. Consistent with Augustine (354–430) and Anselm (1033–1109), Pascal thought that humans by nature are repelled by God and his ways, despise religion, and fear it because they knew deep down that God is real. Pascal believed that reason, built upon faith, was the key to mitigating this powerful tendency of human nature.

> We must begin by showing that religion is not contrary to reason; that it is venerable, to inspire respect for it; then we must make it lovable, to make good men hope it is true; finally, we must prove it is true.
>
> (Pascal 1952, 3.§187)

From this starting point, Pascal built his famous Wager. In the Wager, he contrasted the believer in God with the unbeliever, the one who had faith and the other who demanded certainty concerning the incomprehensible God based on reason alone. The believer wagered earthly pleasure for eternal happiness, fleeting glory for everlasting life. The unbeliever sought to avoid any wager of that sort. Pascal insisted that everyone was faced with an inevitable wager. Every person was obliged to bet their eternal destiny on the truth or the falsehood of God's existence. Because human beings were finite, and God was infinite, every human being was compelled to wager on the one eternal truth that mattered most, and this wager was inescapable. Pascal wrote:

> Let us now speak according to natural lights. … Do not, then, reprove for error those who have made a choice; for you know nothing about it. 'No, but I blame them for having made, not this choice, but a choice; for again both he who chooses heads and he who chooses tails are equally at fault, they are both in the wrong. The true course is not to wager at all'. Yes; but you must wager. It is not optional. You are embarked. Which will you choose then? Let us see. Since you must choose, let us see which interests you least. You have two things to lose, the true and the good; and two things to stake, your reason and your will, your knowledge and your happiness; and your nature has two things to shun, error and misery. Your reason is no more shocked in choosing one rather than the other, since you must of necessity choose. This is one point settled. But your happiness? Let us weigh the gain and the loss in wagering that God is. Let us estimate these two chances. If you gain, you gain all; if you lose, you lose nothing. Wager, then, without hesitation that He is.
>
> (Pascal 1952, 3.§233)

Tocqueville was deeply influenced by Pascal and thought that Americans employed pragmatic reason as they mixed their self-interest with their religion.

Americans found wisdom in sacrificing some of the temporary pleasures of the temporal world in order to attain assurance of eternal peace and felicity in the next. And, following Pascal, Tocqueville did not believe it was faith alone that led Americans to the making of these sacrifices, but reason also. He wrote, 'one ordinarily sees even in the midst of their zeal something so tranquil, so methodical, so calculated, that it seems to be reason, much more than heart that leads them to the foot of the altar' (Tocqueville 2000, 2:2; 9.505). So, for Tocqueville, enlightened self-interest and religion were not only reconcilable to one another. Religion was necessary for self-interest to be rightly understood.

5.4 Tocqueville's conservative articulation of enlightened self-interest

We have seen that the doctrine of enlightened self-interest is not original to Tocqueville. Tocqueville himself cited Montaigne directly in the pages of *Democracy in America*. Kahan proposed that Tocqueville's primary source for his understanding of enlightened self-interest was the 17th-century Jansenist theologian Pierre Nicole (1625–1695) (Kahan 2015a: 23). Harvey Mansfield traced the first modern usage of the idea of interest in the writings of Giovanni Botero (1540–1617) and Trajano Boccalini (1556–1613), and they were influenced by Machiavelli (1469–1527) (Mansfield 1995: 51). Locke and Madison each appealed to the idea. Tocqueville gave enlightened self-interest a particular expression as it related to the American context of the Jacksonian period, and that expression is distinctly conservative. For example, Tocqueville's analysis of enlightened self-interest accepted human nature as commonly and unchangeably selfish. At the same time, Tocqueville situated enlightened self-interest alongside religion as necessary for human liberty. Like all ideas and actions originating in the mind and heart of limited creatures, Tocqueville knew that enlightened self-interest by itself was limited in what it could achieve. While it may mitigate the worst tendencies of human nature, it cannot cure them. This is evident, not only in American history but also in the history of the Western democracies more broadly since the French Revolution.

Modern conservatism was inaugurated by Edmund Burke's 1790 work, *Reflections on the Revolution in France*. Burkean conservatism emerged as an answer to Jeffersonian republicanism and Francophilia through the Federalist party of Washington, Hamilton, and Adams. American conservatism is ironic because the United States was born out of an effort to turn away from the traditions of old Europe and open a *novus ordo seclorum*. Still, as George Nash observed, American conservatives have combined their modern taste for equality with a premodern taste for what Russell Kirk has called the 'permanent things', spiritual things and the institutions that sustain them. American conservatism has historically begun with belief in God and the stress on the necessity of religion and religious institutions for a rightly ordered society (Nash 2009: 12).

Russell Kirk, the prolific and archetypical traditionalist post-war conservative, identified six principles of conservatism in his classic 1953 book, *The Conservative Mind*. Kirk's six principles included, first, 'belief in a transcendent order' (Kirk 2001: 8). For Kirk, conservatives have faith in God as sovereign, and believe that the order he established in Creation is a moral one. Thus, all human problems are essentially challenges to the moral order established by God. Conservatives are realists, in that they understand that there are limits of human ability to knowledge. Second, conservatives cultivate an 'affection for the proliferating variety and mystery of human existence' (Kirk 2001: 8). Conservatives do not reduce humans according to 'uniformity, egalitarianism, and utilitarian aims of most radical systems' (Kirk 2001: 8). In other words, humans are not widgets. Every individual is complex, and mystery in human nature is not to be spurned. Third, conservatives reject the idea of a 'classless society' (Kirk 2001: 8), but desire order. This is not a rejection of equality *per se*, but it is a recognition that absolute equality is not desirable because it disorders society. Absolute equality tends towards despotism and apathy. Fourth, conservatives accept that 'freedom and property are closely linked' (Kirk 2001: 9). In other words, private property is necessary for freedom, and socialistic tendencies to distribute wealth evenly by government coercion are, by definition, tyrannical and unnatural. Fifth, 'custom, convention, and old prescription are checks upon man's anarchic impulse and upon the innovator's lust for power' (Kirk 2001: 9). Conservatives value tradition because tradition demonstrates that certain ideas, habits, and values have been tried and proven. Every essential problem that human societies face in contemporary times has been faced in the past. Our forebears have provided us with resources for addressing those essential problems in tradition and custom. Sixth, conservatives maintain a particular attitude concerning change. Change is inevitable, but change is not an inherent good. As Kirk put it, 'hasty innovation may be a devouring conflagration, rather than a torch of progress' (Kirk 2001: 9). Change should be guided along by prudence, procedure, deliberation, and patience.

One of the effects produced by these principles is realism about human nature and human potential. While the progressive impulse is to perfect human nature, conservatives know that human nature is fixed. Kirk wrote, 'Radicals believe that education, positive legislation, and alteration of environment can produce men like gods; they deny that humanity has a natural proclivity toward violence and sin' (Kirk 2001: 10). Frank Meyer pointed to the connection between belief in God and the fallibility of human nature. God created a moral order, but that moral order has limits that are prescribed by nature. Because human nature is fallen, there will always be corruption, vice, selfishness, war, poverty, and injustice. Conservatives are, in Meyer's description, 'antiutopian' (Meyer 2020: 33). Conservatism 'recognizes that continuing historical certainty of change … and while it strives always for the improvement of human institutions and the human condition, it rejects absolutely the idea that society or men generally are perfectable' (Meyer 2020: 34). Conservatives find hope in free institutions and free citizens, rightly ordered by just law, in the pursuit of private and public human flourishing.

In expressing his doctrine of enlightened self-interest, Tocqueville embraced conservative realism about the human condition. Especially in his chapter entitled, 'On the Taste for Material Well-Being in America', Tocqueville observed that in aristocratic societies, the poor and rich were accustomed to poverty and riches, respectively. In democratic societies, the poor got a taste for wealth, and they became insatiable. Furthermore, the rich became insecure in their wealth, and they also grew greedy for more in order to preserve their way of life. 'Love of well-being has become the national and dominant taste; the great current of human passions bears from this distinction; it carries everything along in its course' (Tocqueville 2000, 2:2; 10.507–508).

Tocqueville saw that this insatiable passion for material well-being conflicts with humans' desire for immaterial well-being. Tocqueville built on the idea that while human nature is focused on the body, it is also orientated towards eternity through 'belief in an immaterial and immortal principle' (Tocqueville 2000, 2:2; 16.520). The human condition was found, according to Tocqueville, between angel and beast. Humans have the same corporeal existence and needs as beasts, and perpetually seek satisfaction of bodily needs. Still, Tocqueville wrote:

> man is capable of elevating himself above the goods of the body and of scorning even life – of which beasts do not have any idea – that he knows how to multiply these same goods to a degree that they cannot conceive of.
>
> (Tocqueville 2000, 2:2; 16.521)

Because human nature was between angel and beast, Tocqueville argued that people must inspire the soul to greatness, 'and its greatness in the service of the body' (Tocqueville 2000, 2:2; 16.522).

This tension between angel and beast is clear in considering the differences between aristocratic and democratic societies. Aristocratic societies, by extolling the beauties of virtue, tended towards the idealism of the angel in human nature. Democratic societies, with their orientation towards the material world and satisfaction of temporal ambitions, looked to the materialism of the beast in human nature. Persons expressed the tension between angel and beast in human nature in their miserable self-consciousness, wherein a person 'knows something of himself, but he cannot grasp himself as a whole', as Lawler wrote (Lawler 1992: 3). The human 'knows himself as a doubtful, incoherent, and contingent being who passionately desires to be something else. He wishes to be a beast or an angel, but he is miserable as a man' (Lawler 1992: 3). Enlightened self-interest played a mediating role between the angel and beast in human nature. For Tocqueville, enlightened self-interest sprang from the self-love of the beast and an awareness of the duty towards the common good, emerging from the angel. Still, we should not regard Tocqueville as embracing enlightened self-interest as ideally virtuous. As Roger Boesche argued, Tocqueville did not advocate for enlightened self-interest but recognised its value for finite and fallen human beings, crippled by the discontent resulting from the tension between angel and beast. 'A close reading of … *Democracy in America* reveals that he was merely making a small but necessary bow toward realism' (Boesche 2008: 68). Tocqueville still desired that citizens look to a politics that transcended self-interest. He recognised that enlightened self-interest was a start in the right direction, given the limitations of human nature. The tension between angel and beast was reflected in the tension between selfishness and altruism. Humans aimed towards both wealth and the common good. Enlightened self-interest, counterfeit virtue though it was, lifted the human race out of complete depravity. As Campagna wrote, 'Tocqueville has to take democratic man as he is: aiming at riches and material well-being' (Campagna 2007: 183). Enlightened self-interest provides the 'mask of the antique hero' and 'putting on such a mask and forgetting for a while that one is always acting out of egoistic and particular motives is the most one can expect of democratic man' (Campagna 2007: 184).

Consistent with the conservative acknowledgement of God in preserving order in society, Tocqueville placed religion alongside enlightened self-interest as two distinct, yet complementary and necessary drivers away from despotism and towards freedom. Even though people would be more passionate in their love for equality than freedom because of their love for cheap and immediate gratification, human nature's need for faith in God and transcendent ideals would mitigate base tendencies. In his chapter entitled, 'How the Americans Apply the Doctrine of Self Interest Well Understood in the Matter of Religion', Tocqueville considered that even though Christianity taught self-denial, Christianity also taught that people recognised good deeds on behalf of others by thinking about what the individual would want done to himself. 'I therefore do not believe that the sole motive of religious men is interest; but I think that interest is the principal means religions themselves make use of to guide men' (Tocqueville 2000, 2:2; 9.504). Here again, we see the great influence that Pascal had on Tocqueville. Citing Pascal's *Pensees*, Tocqueville wrote, '"In being deceived by believing the Christian religion to be true", Pascal said, "there is nothing great to lose, but what unhappiness in being wrong about believing it false"' (Tocqueville 2000, 2:2; 9.505). Despite his observation of how worldly American preachers could be, and how difficult to know where the preachers' appeals to earthly interests ended and heavenly interests began, Tocqueville noted that 'they make them see daily how religious beliefs favor freedom and public order' (Tocqueville 2000, 2:2; 9.506). Thus, religion and enlightened self-interest played a necessary role in maintaining the balance between public and private interests, thereby achieving harmony resulting in liberty.

Tocqueville stressed that democratic societies tended towards denying the spiritual altogether in favour of the material. Tocqueville reminded his audience that religion pointed people beyond their selfish interests, and beyond the physical world to virtue, excellence, and eternity. Religion in democratic societies in particular was focused on the practical, not on the abstract. In that way, democratic religion was the greatest advantage to society, and the most necessary. 'Therefore', Tocqueville wrote:

> when any religion whatsoever has cast deep roots within a democracy, guard against shaking it; but rather preserve it carefully … for fear that … the love of material enjoyments will come to spread through it and fill it entirely.
>
> (Tocqueville 2000, 2:2; 15.519)

Because human nature was between angel and beast, it was imperative for leaders to encourage the cultivation of the nobler propensities in citizens in order to prevent society from devolving into despotism or anarchy. 'I think it is only in conforming scrupulously to religious morality in great affairs that [governments] can flatter themselves they are teaching citizens to know it, love it, and respect it in small ones' (Tocqueville 2000, 2:2; 15.521).

In Volume I, Tocqueville observed that religion was essential to American culture, so much so that he described religion as 'the first of their political institutions' (Tocqueville 2000, 1:1; 9.280). Tocqueville proposed that religion served as the source of the mores, which in turn, served to inform the laws. In doing so, religion served the same political and civic purpose that enlightened self-interest served, and while religion did so on a spiritual plane, enlightened self-interest did so on a secular plane. Barbara Allen wrote, 'Religion's principal contribution to self government was to secure the individual's mind and soul morally, while leaving political opinions open to deliberation and experimentation' (Allen 1998). Kahan put it this way: 'A religion that can [balance the angel and the beast] is what one might call "religion properly understood", by analogy with Tocqueville's well-known concept of "self-interest properly understood"' (Kahan 2015b: 102). Tocqueville found that enlightened self-interest did not function in American society apart from religion. Religion was a source for enlightened self-interest, and enlightened self-interest was a source for religion. It was impossible for Tocqueville to imagine these two functioning in society isolated from one another.

At this point, we must be reminded that Tocqueville saw the limitations of enlightened self-interest. We see those limits when the doctrine is left to stand on its own as a source of inspiration for citizens to greatness without the necessary synergy with religion. Because Tocqueville understood that democratic citizens were so enamoured of material well-being, enlightened self-interest detached from the ennobling influence of religion could actually cause the citizen to drift towards individualism and selfishness. This is why Tocqueville wrote, 'the soul must remain great and strong, if only to be able from time to time to put its force and its greatness in the service of the body' (Tocqueville 2000, 2:2; 16.522). Once citizens became materialistic, denying the eternal and focusing on the earthly, they would be hardly discernible from animals. Enlightened self-interest fulfilled a good purpose, but Tocqueville admitted that as a doctrine, it was not altogether noble. 'The doctrine of self-interest well understood does not produce great devotion' (Tocqueville 2000, 2:2; 8.502), and furthermore, were enlightened self-interest to become predominant in society, 'extraordinary virtues would without doubt be rarer' (Tocqueville 2000, 2:2; 8.502). Brian Danoff argued that Tocqueville hoped that enlightened self-interest might be left behind and replaced with a virtue-informed political discourse rather than a self-interested one. Danoff wrote, 'Tocqueville hoped for a kind of leadership that could help raise people to their "full height", and like Lincoln, he thus clearly rejected a politics based *solely* on interest' (Danoff 2005: 706).

Slavery and racial prejudice, two blights on American democracy that deeply embarrassed Tocqueville, provide a practical example of the limits of enlightened self-interest, particularly when isolated from religion. When enlightened self-interest directed people to favour the beast over the angel, rather than the angel over the beast, moral outrages such as slavery could be defended as necessary and good for society, as was done in the South. Whereas slavery had been abolished by 1831 north of Maryland, the Southern plantation economy depended on the institution of slavery for its continuation. Sanford Kessler wrote that 'Southern aristocrats rightly concluded that abolition threatened their antique mores, their political power, and their very physical existence' (Kessler 1994: 142). Danoff cited an 1860 speech Abraham Lincoln gave in which he argued that Southern slaveholders would never be able to see abolition as in their interest. Lincoln said,

> The slaveholder does not like to be considered a mean fellow … and hence he has to struggle within himself and sets about arguing himself into the belief that Slavery is right. … Whether the owners of this species of property do really see it as it is, it is not for me to say, but if they do, they see it as it is through 2,000,000,000 of dollars, and that is a pretty thick coating.
>
> (Danoff 2005: 696)

By 1860, slaves represented $2 billion in American wealth, and such a vast number had the effect of blinding American Southerners to the immorality of the institution. Still, one might object by pointing out how pro-slavery advocates often appealed to the Bible to justify slavery. True, but appeals to the Bible were not all the same. One may always attempt to justify a behaviour on Christian morality but do so wrongly. This was exactly the argument Frederick Douglass made in his celebrated speech, 'What to the Slave is the Fourth of July?' Referring to pro-slavery preachers, Douglass said, 'These ministers make religion a cold and flinty-hearted thing, having neither principles of right action, nor bowels of compassion. They strip the love of God of its beauty, and leave the throne of religion a huge, horrible, repulsive form' (Douglass 2011: 517–518). Douglass said that the Christianity argued by the pro-slavery advocates in the South was not Christianity at all, but an abominable twisting of Christianity's teachings in order to justify human selfishness and vice. Such a perversion of Christianity was not compatible with enlightened self-interest, which was a source of uplift for the human spirit, not enslavement.

5.5 Conclusion

If Tocqueville's understanding of enlightened self-interest is, in fact, consistent with conservatism, then enlightened self-interest is important in today's debates on what constitutes a conservative. For example, are libertarians conservative? What about nationalists? Is there such a thing as national conservatism? Where do religious conservatives fit into Western society? A pure conservatism may be evasive, but every category of conservatism can find room for enlightened self-interest. As provocative a claim as that may be, such a claim advances the dialogue and debate that has surrounded the issue of conservative identity since the late 18th century. In America, conservatives have been fighting with each other over the issue of what makes a pure conservative since the Civil War. Feuds over genuine conservative identity will continue, but enlightened self-interest will probably serve as common ground for those engaged in those feuds.

In any event, enlightened self-interest combats the democratic tendency that we have of indifference towards others, a stain that Tocqueville described as a public virtue under despotism. By balancing the angel and beast in our human nature, enlightened self-interest assists in what Tocqueville called 'the apprenticeship of freedom'. The small, quotidian sacrifices we make on behalf of our fellow citizens do not always result in obvious or short-term gains. Freedom is won and preserved through such sacrifices. It is in times like ours that freedom has the potential to spread its benefits. 'Freedom', Tocqueville wrote, 'is ordinarily born in the midst of storms, it is established painfully among civil discords, and only when it is old can one know its benefits' (Tocqueville 2000, 1:2; 5.229).

References

Allen, Barbara (1998), 'Alexis de Tocqueville on Civic Virtue and Self-Interest Rightly Understood in American Democracy', https://dlc.dlib.indiana.edu/dlc/bitstream/handle/10535/599/Allen,_Barbara--Alexis-de-Tocqueville-on-civic-virtue-and-self-interest--american-democracy.pdf.

Boesche, Roger (2008), *Tocqueville's Road Map: Methodology, Liberalism, Revolution, and Despotism*, Lanham, MD: Lexington.

Campagna, Norman (2007), 'Virtue in Tocqueville's America', *Amerikastudien/American Studies* 52, no. 2: 169–186.

Danoff, Brian (2005), 'Lincoln and Tocqueville on Democratic Leadership and Self-Interest Properly Understood', *The Review of Politics* 67, no. 4 (Autumn): 687–719.

Douglass, Frederick (2011), 'What to the Slave is the Fourth of July?', in Hollinger, David A. and Charles Capper (eds.), *The American Intellectual Tradition: Volume I, 1630–1865*, 6th ed., Oxford: Oxford University Press.

Howe, Daniel Walker (2007), *What Hath God Wrought: The Transformation of America, 1815–1848*, Oxford: Oxford University Press.

Kahan, Alan S. (2015a), *Tocqueville, Democracy, and Religion: Checks and Balances for Democratic Souls*, Oxford: Oxford University Press.

Kahan, Alan S. (2015b), 'Checks and Balances for Democratic Souls: Alexis de Tocqueville on Religion and Democratic Societies', *American Political Thought* 4, no. 1 (Winter): 100–119.

Kessler, Sanford (1994), *Tocqueville's Civil Religion: American Christianity and the Prospects for Freedom*, Albany: State University of New York Press.

Kirk, Russell (2001), *The Conservative Mind: From Burke to Eliot*, 7th ed., Washington: Regnery.

Lane, Tony (2006), *A Concise History of Christian Thought*, Grand Rapids: Baker Academic.

Lawler, Peter Augustine (1992), 'The Human Condition: Tocqueville's Debt to Rousseau and Pascal', in Eduardo Nolla (ed.), *Liberty, Equality, Democracy*, New York: New York University Press, 1–20.

Lawler, Peter Augustine (1995), 'Tocqueville on Pride, Interest, and Love', *Polity* 28, no. 2 (Winter): 217–236.

Locke, John (1952), 'Essay Concerning Human Understanding', in Robert Maynard Hutchins (ed.), *The Great Books of the Western World*, no. 35, Chicago: Encyclopedia Britannica.

Madison, J. (2005), 'The Federalist', in Edited by J. R. Pole. Indianapolis: Hackett.

Mansfield, Harvey C. (1995), 'Self-Interest Rightly Understood', *Political Theory* 23, no. 1 (February): 48–66.

McClay, Wilfred (1994), *The Masterless: Self and Society in Modern America*, Chapel Hill: The University of North Carolina Press.

McKenzie, Robert Tracy (2021), *We the Fallen People: The Founders and the Future of American Democracy*, Downers Grove: IVP Academic.

Meyer, Frank S. (2020), 'The Recrudescent American Conservatism', in Bacevich, Andrew (ed.), *American Conservatism: Reclaiming an American Tradition*, New York: Library of America, 28–44.

Nash, George H. (2009), *Reappraising the Right: The Past and Future of American Conservatism,* Wilmington, DE: ISI.

Pascal, Blaise (1952), 'Pensees', in W. F. Trotter (trans.) and Robert Maynard Hutchins (ed.), *The Great Books of the Western World*, no. 33, Chicago: Encyclopedia Britannica.

Tocqueville, Alexis de (2000; original, French edition 1835, 1840), *Democracy in America. Translated*, edited, and introduced by Harvey C. Mansfield and Delba Winthrop, Chicago and London: University Press of Chicago.

6 Building a democratic identity

Self-interest and moral imagination

Stacey Hibbs

6.1 Introduction

Democracy is in peril, or so we may be led to believe. Democratic nations are fractured; their people lack trust in ideas, institutions, and each other. In Harvey Mansfield and Delba Winthrop's translation of *Democracy in America* (2002), Mansfield and Winthrop claim that '*Democracy in America* is at once the best book ever written on democracy and the best book ever written on America' (Tocqueville 2002: xvii). As such, Tocqueville's work lays bare what all democratic nations have to 'hope' or 'fear' from democracy (Tocqueville 2002: 13; 'Introduction'). The story of democracy is a story of two possible futures. One rests in an active, participatory democracy that values human freedom. The other is a centralised government, a 'soft' despotism that reduces its people to sheep in need of a shepherd (Tocqueville 2002, 2:4; 6.663). Tocqueville eerily foretells our own lack of direction:

> Where are we then? Men of religion combat freedom, and the friends of freedom attack religions: noble and generous spirits vaunt slavery, and base and servile souls extol independence; honest and enlightened citizens are enemies of all progress, while men without patriotism and morality make themselves apostles of civilization and enlightenment! Have all centuries, then, resembled ours? Has man, as in our day, always had before his eyes a world where nothing is linked, where virtue is without genius and genius is without honor; where love of order is confused with a taste for tyrants and the holy cult of freedom with a contempt for laws; where conscience casts only a dubious light on human actions; where nothing seems any longer to be forbidden or permitted, or honest or shameful, or true or false?
>
> (Tocqueville 2002: 12; 'Author's Introduction')

Tocqueville is aware of the passions that animate humans in the democratic age, and nothing animates them more than a desire for equality (Tocqueville 2002, 2:2; 1). A real danger is the reductive tendencies found in the pursuit

DOI: 10.4324/9781032641041-6

of equality, particularly when equality is construed as sameness. There is nothing more inimical to human freedom than homogeneity, which simultaneously levels everything to a common denominator and eliminates differences. Tocqueville does not celebrate difference for its own sake. The question he is concerned with is how differences can be maintained and how potential conflict can be mitigated. Identity politics is a case in point. *The Stanford Encyclopedia of Philosophy* defines identity politics as a 'shared experience of injustice' that leads to the formation of a 'specific constituency' that has been 'marginalized' and has a goal of 'self-determination'. In this sense, it leads to a social form of balkanization. While stressing sameness in certain ways (within groups, and within the framework of rights), identity politics also asserts particular and significant differences (differences that are inseparable from the reality of the identity group).

Identity politics often isolates one group from another and places them in opposition. Those within certain 'identity' groups make claims about the rights they have been denied and the ways in which society has excluded them from the promise of democratic governance. These claims may be correct. What happens in the wake of these claims is often inimical to true freedom. By asserting a 'party line' that must be followed, identity groups assert a type of universalism that cuts off rational inquiry (Tocqueville 2002, 1:2; 7.243).

Tocqueville does not deny identity or difference. He demonstrates the ways in which both mutable and immutable characteristics shape us. The American is different from the Frenchman (although the Frenchman can become an American). Americans in the North and the South differ (and their differing ways of life result in civil war). Socioeconomic factors divide us into different classes (although in America class distinctions are not static). Tellingly, Tocqueville writes about how race and gender provide barriers to equality. The three races are distinctive, and their futures are determined by those distinctions, while women, the last group to receive political recognition in America, bear the burden of their 'superiority' (Tocqueville 2002, 2:3; 12.576).

Identity raises certain questions. How can we value liberty yet maintain community? The enforced conformity of the tyranny of the majority erodes human freedom and prepares us for welcoming a new form of despotism. Political power tends to coalesce, and centralisation denies difference. Are identity groups merely forms of the 'factions' that our founders warned of in *The Federalist Papers*? Madison asserts that as factions multiply, they are less dangerous and can only come together to pursue broader, truer, societal goods (Hamilton, Madison, and Jay 1961: 78).

For Tocqueville, identity rests on self-interest – an 'immutable' condition of the human heart. If humans are naturally self-interested, how can they be persuaded to engage in communal life, including politics? Tocqueville advocates for 'self-interest well-understood' (Tocqueville 2002, 2:2; 8.501). In this formulation, self-interest is coupled with a recognition of the common good. It may also be a corrective to the narrow self-interest of identity politics.

6.2 Identity politics: A new name for an old problem

When we look at history, patterns are evident. Tocqueville noted the way in which events in history provided evidence of God's plan regarding the progress of democracy (Tocqueville 2002: 4–5; 'Author's Introduction'). But events in history also provide evidence of identity. In the ancient Greek world, different centres of power reigned supreme and defined themselves in relation to 'others'. In the classical period, Athenians differed from Spartans and Greeks from barbarians, and these differences were encoded in law. In the Hebrew tradition, there were God's chosen people, an identity that entitled them to the fulfilment of the covenant and required their adherence to divine law, and there were others who served inferior, pagan gods. In the Christian narrative, such distinctions become obsolete: 'there is neither Jew nor gentile, slave nor free, male nor female' (Galatians 3:28) – as a result of the 'new covenant' established through the coming of Jesus. Yet the beauty of this passage is not reflected in the reality of life in this world. Distinctions persist. Identities are crafted and are clung to amid assertions of the righteousness of their particular claims. In the realm of religion, what has emerged is a set of identities corresponding to various denominations. To eviscerate particular identities would be to invite the levelling homogeneity that Tocqueville fears.

In *Federalist 10* on faction, Madison acknowledges the existence of

> a number of citizens, whether amounting to a minority or majority of the whole, who are united and actuated by some common impulse of passion, or of interest, adverse to the rights of other citizens, or to the permanent and aggregate interests of the community.
>
> (Hamilton, Madison, and Jay 1961: 72)

The distinctive feature of Madison's definition of faction (as opposed to other forms of association) is that it focuses on self-serving, rather than civil or communal, interests. The threat of identity politics, therefore, has been a persistent problem. The way it has been manifested has differed according to time and place.

6.3 Identity in Tocqueville: The reality of exclusion

America is the 'image' of democracy and presents a unique object of study in which we might discern what we may 'hope' and 'fear' from the democratic age (Tocqueville 2002: 13; 'Author's Introduction'). Tocqueville saw lessons to be learnt that could be applied to democracies everywhere. Tocqueville's narrative of America moves from an idealised account of participatory democracy in the New England townships to a reductive 'sameness' that may arise by means of an expansive, intrusive centralised government. But this narrative is predicated upon a particular identity – an American identity. What does it mean to be an American? To begin, Tocqueville notes that the American identity is shaped by three things – unique circumstances, laws, and mores (Tocqueville 2002, 1:2; 9.265). American identity is consistently contrasted with claims about French identity. The democratic age has very different manifestations depending on 'time and place, men and conditions' (Tocqueville 2002: 7; 'Author's Introduction'). But these manifestations are not so different that they cannot be translated or bridged. Indeed, Tocqueville hopes to use America as a model from which France may learn.

But even this American identity is not what it seems. As Tocqueville delves further into the realities of American life, he sees a nation that is not one but rather is divided in substantive ways. Northerners and Southerners have developed different economic systems, different 'habits' that lead Tocqueville to notice an inherent danger to a unified America. The tensions between North and South that Tocqueville observes revolve around one issue – race (Tocqueville 2002, 1:2; 10.302). Racial identity determines one's fate and is inescapable. It creates social and political ramifications that shape the future. Indeed, Tocqueville's hopefulness about the future of democracy is clouded by the spectre of race.

In Tocqueville's exploration of the three races, a decided shift occurs. The Anglo Americans are no longer the bastions of self-governance and democratic virtue but are rather oppressors. The other two races who occupy the continent are incapable of being part of this 'new world'. The Indigenous peoples, who themselves possess unique linguistic and cultural identities, are reduced to a facile otherness. They are viewed by the Anglos as savages. In turn, the Native Americans view the white men as usurpers, unjustly taking the lands of their ancestors. In observing this dynamic, Tocqueville identifies the Native Americans as presenting an extreme form of liberty – they will not give up their identity (Tocqueville 2002, 1:2; 10.305.

In contrast, the African Americans had lost their identity through racial and generational slavery. They are seen by Tocqueville as shaped by the extreme form of servitude. Race prevents them from ever assimilating into the white man's world, and the habits engendered by slavery leave them unprepared for freedom (Tocqueville 2002, 1:2; 10.305). Slavery is antithetical to the promise of America. It is a cancer eating away at the health of the body politic. As such, it must be excised. Tocqueville's vision here is both prescient and incomplete. Where he sees the danger of war, he views the conflict to come as racial, not sectional. And he sees an identity forged by slavery as a lingering problem for America (Tocqueville 2002, 1:2; 10.326). Tocqueville's assessment of the three races includes a searing critique of America, one that anticipates in many ways the increasingly mainstream critique of America from the perspective of marginalised groups.

6.4 The challenges of identity politics

Ewa Atanassow, in 'Colonization and Democracy', sees Tocqueville's political response to France's own role as a coloniser as indicative of the challenges that await diverse societies. The most stable societies have tended to be homogeneous. (The Fragile States Index 2023 provides a modern data-driven account of this political reality.) Atanassow sees 'integrating racial and civilizational differences both as a decisive factor and the most momentous challenge to democracy's future' (Atanassow 2017: 84–88). Tocqueville sees social and political equalisation as the driving force of the democratic age. Yet he also is faced with the realities of the colonial period, both in America and France. The problematic nature of colonisation is reflected not only in his assessment of the three races that occupy the American continent but also in terms of French involvement in its far-flung colonial holdings. Atanassow notes that 'hatreds born of the iniquities of conquest and sustained by discrepancies in mores and ways of life, raised enormous barriers between settler and native' (2017; 'Tocqueville on Colonization'). Atanassow describes the specific nature of these problems in the context of American history. First, Atanassow notes the realities of colonisation of the American continent – both in its effects on Indigenous peoples and in the reality of slavery. Second, as Atanassow describes the reaction to subsequent waves of immigration in America, certain American myths are laid bare. For example, the myth of the American 'melting pot' obscures pervasive xenophobia.

The equality of conditions that marks the democratic age is thereby an incomplete picture of America. While it may hold true for the Anglo Americans that the rejection of hereditary classes and the almost limitless possibilities found in America create a more equitable society, it is also true that potential dangers arise when particular groups do not have the possibility of achieving equality, as is the case for African Americans, or when particular groups, like the Native Americans, disdain it.

It is precisely because Native Americans hold on to their identity that they do not assimilate. If Atanassow sees identity as self-perception, Joshua Mitchell (2020) sees it as a destructive force that rends the fabric of America. Mitchell sees threats to democracy arising from identity politics, bipolarity, and addiction.

Of these, identity politics is an immediate threat because it demands a 'complete accounting' and the use of emotionally charged language to render interactions as a type of zero-sum game.

Mitchell sees identity politics as part of an 'invisible economy' that divides identities based upon 'transgression' and 'innocence'. In his analysis, the group that is oppressed is seen as 'pure' (2020: xvi). The group that oppresses is guilty. This is a type of moral assessment – a claim that Wendall Berry (1993) also recognises in his writings on American society. So, rather than defining identity as simply different kinds of people, or even as Atanassow does in relating identity to self-understanding, Mitchell asserts that 'identity politics is not about who we are as individuals; it is about the stain and purity associated with who we are as members of a group' (2020: xviii). The consequence of this type of identity politics is, according to Mitchell, a type of 'spiritual eugenics' based upon settling scores. Good must vanquish evil. Rather than 'judge not, lest ye be judged', the whole purpose is to judge, and then to purge: 'Americans have relocated their religion to the realm of politics' (Mitchell 2020: xx).

But here Mitchell downplays two salient points. First, politics has always been infused with religious elements. Second, our ideas regarding sin and purity have often been blurred. To recall, Tocqueville states that the period he is witnessing is one 'where conscience casts only a dubious light on human actions; where nothing seems any longer to be forbidden or permitted, or honest or shameful, or true or false?' (Tocqueville 2002: 12; 'Author's Introduction'). The religious realm was once settled – at least in terms of foundational assessments of right and wrong. The Ten Commandments gave express sanction to those things that must not be done. So, what are we to make of a time where these universal prohibitions (at least in the Judeo-Christian tradition, and which are also found in different formulations in most world religions) are cast into question? Mitchell seems to attribute to the modern age a distinctively charged emotional rhetoric. But again, charged rhetoric has always been a part of political life. Search through the political rhetoric at all points in American history (especially during election cycles and times of social change), and you will see absolute and polarising claims about those who are destroying our country or our way of life. (Philosophically, one has only to look at the work of Rene Girard (1989) on scapegoating to capture the tendency to place blame on a particular individual or group as a way of excising the demons that torment us.) While identity politics may feel different in terms of the demands it makes and the language it uses, perhaps the real difference is that the landscape of social media has made it ubiquitous.

6.5 Equality as sameness

Equality of conditions blurs distinctions if there are not readily observable characteristics, race, language, dress, practices, and so on that make acknowledgement of differences unavoidable. While the homogeneity of the New England townships provided fertile ground for community enterprises, it also provided fodder for the persecution of those who were perceived as different. Differences will always present challenges, but difference alone cannot destroy democracy. Instead, the great fear Tocqueville has for the future of democracy is a reduction to a chilling sameness (Tocqueville 2002, 2:4; 6.663).

There are two significant ways in which Tocqueville addresses strength through difference. The first has to do with Tocqueville's analysis of the status of Catholics in America. Interestingly, Tocqueville places this discussion within his analysis of 'Causes Tending to Maintain a Democratic Republic' (Tocqueville 2002, 1:2; 9.275–277). Tocqueville sees religion as a 'political institution' (although its true power will always be found in its indirect effects on mores). At first glance, Catholicism would seem to be antithetical to the progress of democracy – it is ordered to obedience to a nonpolitical entity, and it is hierarchical. But Tocqueville clearly states that it is 'wrong to regard the Catholic religion as a natural enemy of democracy' (Tocqueville 2002, 1:2;

9.275). Catholicism is linked to the equality of conditions (although there is a hierarchy, all believers are equal under papal authority). More important, the minority status of Catholics leads them to advocate for their rights, and thereby, to become actively engaged in democratic society (Tocqueville 2002, 1:2; 9.276). It is the separation of church and state that allows the various religious groups in America to maintain their differences – to be free – and at the same time, to be equal as American citizens (Tocqueville 2002, 1:2; 9.283).

The second has to do with Tocqueville's analysis of the status of women in America. Women do not have political authority but instead are the makers of 'mores'. In this capacity, they have an impact on democracy that is palpable. It is their ability to sacrifice for the common good, and for the future made manifest in their children, that leads to Tocqueville's remarkable claim that America's success is due to the 'superiority' of American women (Tocqueville 2002, 2:3; 12.576). Women and men are not the same, nor do they wish to be (Tocqueville 2002, 2:3; 12.574). The respect accorded to American women is directly tied to Tocqueville's assessment of 'democratic equality' (Tocqueville 2002, 2:3; 12.574). The different contributions citizens make enable 'the great social work be better done' (Tocqueville 2002, 2:3; 12.574). Because of this:

> Americans constantly display a full confidence in the reason of their mate and a profound respect for her freedom. They judge that her mind is as capable as a man's of discovering the naked truth, and her heart firm enough to follow it; and they have never sought to place the virtue of the one more than the other under the shelter of prejudices, ignorance, or fear.
>
> (Tocqueville 2002, 2:3; 12.575)

Tocqueville clearly glosses over very problematic aspects of religious persecution and gender discrimination in America; it cannot be because he is unaware of these things. He juxtaposes the political and social problems that are found in France because of an incomplete and unnuanced account of religion and gender with the benefits that arise in the freer understanding found in America. He thereby gives a response to two pertinent claims regarding citizenship – that Catholics cannot be good citizens and that women are incapable of exercising the judgement necessary for political life. In his 'retelling' of the history of both American Catholics and American women, he lays bare the falsity of these claims. Both groups make significant contributions to America, contributions that are essential to a healthy democracy.

While the equality of conditions provides fertile ground for American flourishing, a misunderstanding of equality leads to frightening consequences. The desire for sameness inhibits freedom. The relationship between equality and freedom, a relationship that is predicated on inherent human dignity and inalienable rights, may instead decay into an opposition between rival interests.

Human beings simultaneously want to be free and to be led, to believe that no one is better, or worse.

Tocqueville notes the ways in which equality is inimical to freedom. In particular, he focuses on what he calls the 'tyranny of the majority' (Tocqueville 2002, 1:2; 7.239). The democratic principle, that the majority rules, may itself be a form of tyranny. When the majority coalesces around a certain position, it speaks with absolute authority. Because of this, there is no freedom of thought: 'I do not know any country where, in general, less independence of mind and genuine freedom of discussion reign than in America' (Tocqueville 2002, 1:2: 7.244). John Stuart Mill (1978), in *On Liberty*, takes up the torch of freedom searching for protection from the tyranny of the majority and protection for freedom of speech. Indeed, in Mill's critique of *Democracy in America*, he states that the 'greatest defect' of Tocqueville's account is that it is too 'abstract' (Mill 1859: 36). While Tocqueville asserts that the tyranny of the majority ostracises those outside of this fatal circle, Mill cites specific instances of mob violence that are never redressed. It is as if Tocqueville foresees modern 'cancel culture' (and Mill foresees how this might result in more than being 'cancelled'). Perhaps this is because 'cancel culture' has always existed. Viewpoints have always been censored – even to the point of silencing them. This occurs, not just in totalitarian regimes, but even in democratic ones. In a democratic nation, especially one that enshrines 'freedom of speech' in its *Bill of Rights*, the pressure may not be expressly legal but may rest on mores. There are, quite simply, positions one does not express publicly. Sometimes this is the result of an irrational and disproportionate fear; sometimes this is the result of social conditions. But these facets of American life discount another ardently held principle: If the 'marketplace of ideas' truly works, only those ideas that have merit would survive a democratic cage match. Perhaps contemporary cancel culture and identity politics are different in that they do not seek to be part of the conversation, but rather to dominate it; they seem determined to bypass the practices of democratic deliberation, which require the art of persuasion.

6.6 Achieving social cohesion in a free society

Again, the New England township is instructive, both in terms of what is required for social cohesion and what is problematic about it. The township is small and homogeneous. It is white, male, and economically self-sufficient. While the members of the township participate in its governance, decisions are rendered by the majority. Dissenting opinions, as American history demonstrates, may not be tolerated (Tocqueville 2002, 1:2; 7). Roger Williams and Anne Hutchinson are well-known dissenters whose free thought led them to be expelled from their political/religious communities. Hutchinson's trial in 1637 is an example of the way in which differences in thought and religious practice are seen as dangerous to the community, but it is also evidence of Tocqueville's insights regarding the ability of the American woman to exercise her intellect and judgement. When reading the account of Hutchinson's trial, her responses illuminate the limitations and prejudices of her interlocutors.

While the tensions of the early colonial period eventually gave way to a common enterprise, attaining freedom from Great Britain, America continued to struggle with how to achieve unity in a pluralistic nation. Once America was an independent entity, the transition from local, to regional, to national identity gained momentum but was imperfectly realised. The looming threat of civil/racial war permeates Tocqueville's analysis of the Jacksonian era (Tocqueville 2002, 1:2; 10). Sewn into the very fabric of America, the stain of race-based slavery continued to taint the promise of America.

Over time, the expansion of America and the process of inclusion arising from the arrival of different ethnic, religious, and cultural immigrant groups increased the strain on American political and social life. The anti-immigrant rhetoric that dominated, and continues to dominate ('A Historical Context' 2017), certain facets of political discourse ignores the reality that all Americans (unless they are a member of an Indigenous people) came from elsewhere (Cohn, Brown, and Lopez 2021). If we deny our common heritage (as immigrants) and our common destiny (as Americans), how can we hope to move forwards? Again, a fruitful comparison arises in Tocqueville between America and France. It is precisely American constitutional republicanism and American mores that have enabled the country to sustain unity and human flourishing in a nation made up of diverse ethnic and religious groups.

So, it is not simply a centralised national government that threatens freedom; it is also a refusal to see the contributions and importance of all people to the common enterprise that is America. But how do we come to recognise this? The natural affinity we have for those who are like us is not sufficient.

What was natural, that we are meant to exist in social and political relationships with each other, becomes artificial. Because of this, Tocqueville sees that we need to *create* connections between individuals. We can do so by highlighting how individuals unite in pursuit of a common goal. This 'art' of association, as Tocqueville describes it, is also, for Tocqueville, a 'science' (Tocqueville 2002, 2:2; 5.489, 492; see also Chapter 4 in this volume). It requires knowledge of human motivations and the ability to persuade individuals that working together is both beneficial and efficient. And it is the means by which 'the heart is enlarged, and the human mind is developed' (Tocqueville 2002, 2:2; 5.491).

Absent this, the tendency of the democratic age is separation, isolation, and increasing dependence upon a centralised administration. We are no longer a body politic – we are no longer citizens:

> It is easy to foresee that the time is approaching when a man by himself alone will be less and less in a state to produce the things that are the most common and the most necessary to his life. The task of the social power will therefore constantly increase, and its very efforts will make it vaster each day. The more it puts itself in place of associations, the more

> particular persons, losing the idea of associating with each other, will need it to come to their aid: these are the causes and effects that generate each other without rest.
>
> (Tocqueville 2002, 2:491; 2.5)

6.7 Tocqueville's correctives for the excesses of the democratic age

Tocqueville sets forth the conditions under which democracy can be safeguarded from the excesses that plague democracy's innate tendencies. It is necessary, he writes:

> To instruct democracy, if possible to reanimate its beliefs, to purify its mores, to regulate its movements, to substitute little by little the science of affairs for its inexperience, and knowledge of its true interest for its blind instincts; to adapt its government to time and place; to modify it according to circumstances and men; such is the first duty imposed on those who direct society in our day.
>
> (Tocqueville 2002: 7; 'Author's Introduction')

But how do we 'instruct democracy'? How do we become citizens in a tangible way? Being native-born is not enough. An active, knowledgeable citizenry is required for democracy to flourish. Education comes in two forms – reading and comprehending our founding documents as well as accounts of our national history and engaging in the practices and habits that form us as citizens. In addition to actual schools, Tocqueville lauds 'schools of freedom' – such as township governance, deliberative bodies like juries, and associations. Associations, for example, serve real needs – moral, intellectual, civil, and political – and are the arenas in which the individual must work within the framework of communal effort.

Our insistence on the protection of human rights, especially those contained in the *Bill of Rights*, is foundational. As citizens, we have the right to make claims on our government, and the interplay between these claims and the responses of our leaders serves as a bellwether of political health. Tocqueville observes:

> It is therefore above all in the democratic times we are in that the true friends of freedom and human greatness must constantly remain on their feet and ready to prevent the social power from lightly sacrificing the particular rights of some individuals to the general execution of its designs.
>
> (2002, 2:4; 7.670)

Self-interest well-understood connects our claims as individuals to the needs of the society at large. The free press provides for social and political accountability. Forms create limits that rein in democratic excess.

While regimes that are marked by excess have a type of grandeur or decadence that is palpable, Tocqueville aims for a political universe that is both stable and civil. The society Tocqueville envisions is not marked by greatness but rather by a disciplined, reasoned connection between rights and authority:

> I conceive a society, then, with all, regarding the law as their work, would love and submit to without trouble; in which the authority of government is respected as necessary, not divine, and the love one would bear for a head of state would not be a passion, but a reasoned and tranquil sentiment. Each having rights and being assured of preserving his rights, a manly confidence and a sort of reciprocal condescension between the classes would be established, as far from haughtiness as from baseness.
> (Tocqueville 2002: 9; 'Author's Introduction')

6.8 Self-interest rightly understood as the most accessible corrective

How do we achieve a connection between self-interested individuals and the greater society? It is something, Tocqueville argues, that can be done through a type of education that makes this connection both explicit and beneficial:

> The people, instructed in their true interests, would understand that to profit from society's benefits, one must submit to its burdens. The free association of citizens could then replace the individual power of nobles, and the state would be sheltered from both tyranny and license.
> (2002: 9; 'Author's Introduction')

The 'true interests' of a people rest in rightly ordered passions, in an understanding of how one's own good is tied to the common good, and an ability to render assistance to fellow citizens. Tocqueville recognised that appeals to virtue alone are insufficient in an age that focuses narrowly on individual self-interest. Instead of trying to negate individual self-interest, he instead on embracing it. By tying the needs of the individual and the needs of the community, he finds a way for Americans to honour their 'philosophy' – one that is rational, demonstrable, and practical. It is not that Americans lack virtue, but rather that the language of the aristocratic age is foreign to them (Tocqueville 2002, 2:2; 8.501–503; see also Chapter 5 in this volume).

One might extend this concept beyond the individual to encompass disparate groups. For example, in the face of a common challenge, groups that are in all other respects separate, band together because their interests align. Indeed, this is the basic assumption of social contract theory – Hobbes, Locke, and Rousseau all predicate their respective political philosophies on the benefits that arise when individuals give up some degree of autonomy in order to better secure their natural rights. But fear of violent death, as is the case in Hobbes, is not the only factor that gives rise to civil society. Locke's natural reason reveals that all human beings recognise that their individual interests are predicated upon respecting the interests of others. Rousseau's emphasis on pity recognises our innate connection to, and dependence upon, one another (Rousseau 2012). Granted, the 'state of nature' envisioned by each of these theorists is completely hypothetical, but all suggest that there is some type of impetus that moves man from existing in isolation to existing in some sort of civil society. The social contract theory that undergirds the democratic age rests on the same basic principle – our individual good is best safeguarded in a sociopolitical framework.

In recent memory, we can see how significant events may lead us to set aside differences or partisan concerns in ways that involve tangible sacrifices, even laying down one's life for another. The brave actions of first responders during 9/11, the outpouring of assistance in the wake of natural disasters, and the initial reaction to the reality of a global pandemic arise from moments of clarity about the ways in which our lives are intertwined and dependent. But the crux of self-interest rightly understood rests in the everyday. We should NOT require catastrophic events to recognise our shared humanity. It is self-interest rightly understood that protects us from both 'tyranny and license' (Tocqueville 2002: 9; 'Author's Introduction'). It unites us and restrains us.

6.9 How to move from 'me' to 'we'

How, though, do we unite? Identity politics is essentially based on individual identity, what makes 'me', and those who are just like 'me' in a very precise way, unique. It is a perspective that is unyielding in its demands. But it is also a perspective that is inherently limited and fragmentary. Recognition of the problem requires a means to redress it. The answer lies in an embrace of transformative models of citizenship.

In a brief but insightful reflection on the history of America, *The Real American Dream*, Andrew DelBanco (1999) reflects on the importance of narrative, the kinds of stories we hear, and the impact those stories have on us:

> When that story leads somewhere and thereby helps us navigate through life to its inevitable terminus in death, it gives us hope. And if such a sustaining narrative establishes itself over time in the minds of a substantial number of people, we call it culture.
>
> (DelBanco 1999: 1)

The way we perceive our history impacts the way in which we see ourselves. DelBanco divides history into three phases: God, nation, and self. In the first two, Americans are orientated to something transcendent; in the third, Americans are orientated to a truncated, inward-facing concern for the self.

And this last phase is not only problematic but also the antithesis of the American Dream:

> To be really American has always meant to see something beyond America. This is what the Puritans meant in insisting that if we fail to contribute to some good beyond ourselves, we condemn ourselves to the hell of loneliness. It is what Lincoln meant when he insisted that the rights of each person depend on the rights of all persons.
>
> (DelBanco 1999: 117)

Eighteen years later, Mark Lilla notes, in his work *The Once and Future Liberal: After Identity Politics*, the same reductive tendencies. What is lost is a concern for anything beyond the self. He recognises an

> increasingly narrow and exclusionary self-definition that is now cultivated in our colleges and universities. The main result has been to turn young people back onto themselves, rather than turning them outward toward the wider world. It has left them unprepared to think about the common good and what must be done practically to secure it – especially the hard and unglamorous task of persuading people very different from themselves to join a common effort. Every advance of liberal identity consciousness has marked a retreat of liberal political consciousness. Without which no vision of Americans' future can be imagined. (Lilla 2017: 9–10)

In Lilla's examination, there is a corrective to this – citizenship:

> They must offer a vision of our common destiny based on one thing that all Americans, of every background, actually share. And that is citizenship. We must relearn how to speak to citizens as citizens and to frame our appeals – including ones to benefit particular groups – in terms of principles that everyone can affirm.
>
> (Lilla 2017: 14–15)

But how does one inculcate citizenship? Especially when there has been such a seismic shift in our self-understanding? In a very palpable way, there are features of our 'social reality' (Lilla 2017: 23) that cannot be ignored. When John F. Kennedy challenged us to ask 'not what our country can do for us, but what we can do for our country', he acknowledged the innate tendency to be self-concerned (Lilla 2017: 67). The emphasis we place on what our country owes us is a particular sign of our current pathology. Lacking an understanding of democratic foundations, one of which, in the American story, was Christianity, we also lose any sort of purposeful connection. As Lilla notes:

> What Christianity and democracy share is the idea that to live in a purely instrumental relation with other human beings, to exploit and then discard them, is to give in entirely to the predatory instinct and to leave unmet the need for fellowship and reciprocity.
>
> (2017: 91)

Lilla recognises that, unfortunately, our political parties do nothing to address this. The problem of the 'New Left' and the 'New Right' is the lack of a common destiny that is worth the sacrifice: 'The most important lesson is this: that for two generations America has been without a political vision of its destiny' (Lilla 2017: 99).

But, like Tocqueville, Lilla presents correctives to the problem of our age. He emphasises a concern for institutions over movements, democratic persuasion over 'aimless self-expression', citizenship over identity, and civic education. His claims about the importance of citizenship are not new, nor are they innovative. Instead, they rest on wisdom that has been passed down for centuries:

> The old model, with a few tweaks, is worth following: passion and commitment, but also knowledge and argument. Curiosity about the world outside your own head and about people unlike yourself. Care for this country and its citizens, all of them, and a willingness to sacrifice for them. And the ambition to imagine a common future for all of us.
>
> (Lilla 2017: 140–141)

Mitchell too sees citizenship as essential to our future. His emphasis is on what he terms 'liberal competence' (2020: xxvi–xxvii) – that we can, and should be, active, engaged citizens. In language that mirrors Pascal, Mitchell asserts that we live in a bipolar age; we exist between 'extraordinary grandeur and utter incompetence' (2020: xxix). Instead of working hard, we look for shortcuts and are thereby thwarted in achieving even the basic abilities and requirements of citizenship. Mitchell turns to a type of recovery of the past. He acknowledges the profound implications of self-interest properly understood as a way to frame a reclamation of our role as citizens.

Returning to Lilla's analysis, 'What's crucial at this juncture in our history is to concentrate on this shared political status, not on our other manifest differences' (2017: 121). And this requires civic education: 'Citizens are made, not born' (Lilla 2017: 131). But something more is required; we can be educated without actually becoming what we study. For example, as Aristotle (1999) notes in the *Nicomachean Ethics,* it is not enough to know what virtue is; we must become virtuous. Our actions, our habits, define us. If we are to become citizens, we must act as citizens, not as members of insular, self-referential groups. So, how do we renew citizenship today?

6.10 Citizenship and moral imagination

The ability to imagine a common future, to use both our intellect and our creativity, is what separates us from all other life forms. In the realm of political philosophy, an 'imagined republic' began a conversation that continues today. What is the best life for a human being? The answer found in Plato's *Republic* considered human difference in the context of a unity – 'the beautiful city' (Plato 2016, Book II). Aristotle (1999) saw legitimate regimes as those that pursued the common good and saw the life of virtue, both moral and intellectual, as the road to happiness. Over time, the ideas contained in classical philosophy were challenged by Machiavelli's (1995) realism – reason and virtue were supplanted by calculation and virtu. Hobbes' (1994), Locke's (1980), and Rousseau's (2012) justifications of government were based on their hypothetical 'state of nature' and led to very different understandings of effective governance. Utilitarianism proposed to secure the greatest good for the greatest number. Communism posited a transformation of the human person to an extent that government would no longer be necessary – an illusion, to be sure. But these ideas also required a type of moral imagination – what types of leaders or systems would benefit mankind, what types of regimes could be more equitable and, thereby, more just?

What are our options? What practices can lead us forwards and can effectively bridge the divide that separates us?

Thirty years ago, Wendell Berry (1993) published a collection of essays entitled *Sex, Economy, Freedom and Community*. What is remarkable is the way in which he captured the spirit of our present age. His preface begins with the idea of 'sales resistance' (Berry 1993: xi) – how to avoid becoming a mindless consumer, not just in an economic sense, but in the sense of consuming the ideas that a formless and uninstantiated public foists upon us. Berry anticipates Mitchell's claims about purity and transgression when he writes of the way certain groups are accepted by the public domain while others are vilified. Part of this phenomenon is a result of the disintegration of communities. The destruction done to local communities and human souls is akin to the destruction of the natural world by an unchecked industrial economy. What we 'buy' and what we 'buy into' sever us from the true goods of connection to the land and connection to each other. For Berry, we need to return to local communities: Our social, economic, and political lives find their fullest expression in the context of meaningful communal life.

Sociologist Jonathan Haidt (2013) saw the disconnections evident in American life and tied them to a particular premise – that our differences were predicated on differences in moral foundations – not a lack thereof. Haidt sees (contra Berry and Mitchell) that the left and right both try to justify their feelings and reactions through the use of moral appeals. The problem is not a lack of morality but a lack of understanding. Haidt likens our condition to individuals who speak different languages – each individual's language is meaningful but only to those who speak the same language. To those who speak a different language, it is unintelligible. We can converse with each other only if we learn each other's languages. For Haidt, we need to listen and learn from each other.

Alan Jacobs, in his *How to Think*, draws upon Haidt's research and sees that 'people bind themselves into political teams that share moral narratives. Once they accept a particular narrative, they become blind to alternative moral worlds' (Jacobs 2017: 55). His corrective is thought. How we think matters. Thought as a communal exercise – in which both feelings and imagination play a part – results in 'meaningful action' (Jacobs 2017: 43). Rather than separate the rational and the emotional, analysis and feelings must align. True thought is attentive to the whole person and embraces the totality of the human condition. For Jacobs, we need to learn not what to think (which does not require thought at all), but how to engage in civil discourse (which requires that we take seriously the thoughts and feelings of others).

Returning to Berry:

> In order to survive, a plurality of true communities would require not egalitarianism and tolerance but knowledge, an understanding of the necessity of local differences, and respect. Respect, I think, always implies imagination – the ability to see one another, across our inevitable differences, as living souls.
>
> (1993: 173)

In this way, we can do what has been suggested to us throughout the ages – 'do unto others', 'judge not lest ye be judged', 'walk a mile in another's shoes'. The truth of our human condition remains the same.

6.11 Citizenship, political health, virtue, and hopefulness

But how do we allow the 'better angels' of our nature to flourish? What does it mean to be part of a healthy political civilisation?

> Civil people learn to ignore most of the negative externalities that others inflict on them and try to be sensitive to the unintended costs that their own actions impose on others. The first step toward containing the problems created by negative externalities is to cultivate the civic virtues of empathy, courtesy, humility, and tolerance. Civilization will simply be impossible among a people who don't possess substantial amounts of these virtues. If people insist on obtaining absolutely everything to which they think they have a right, civilisation will give way to warfare.
>
> (Heyne, Boettke, and Prychitko 2013: 229)

We have faced problems, significant ones, seemingly insurmountable ones, before. What makes the present different from the past? Have we finally reached the point of no return – the brink of the centralised soft despotism that Tocqueville feared? Have we traded our freedom for material comfort? Have identity politics fragmented us and isolated us into smaller and smaller entities whose sole concern, ironically, is that we are not only equal but alike? Are we incapable of higher aspirations, common action, and self-interest rightly understood?

Tocqueville suggests a response that is echoed in numerous political appeals – hope. Like many political tropes, hope is commonly used but rarely understood. To hope is more than to wish, and it is based on a reasonable, achievable goal. Perhaps the thinker who has best encapsulated both our need for hope and the way in which hope is tied to action is Sarah Stitzlein.

In her recent work, *Learning How to Hope: Reviving Democracy Through Our Schools and Civil Society*, Stitzlein takes up the challenges we face by appealing to the importance of hope: 'When we are hopeless, and especially when we are in despair, not only are our individual lives more difficult but also our social and political lives suffer' (Stitzlein 2020: 1). Stitzlein does not place the responsibility for change on our political leaders, but rather places the responsibility on us. We are responsible for improving our own lives and the lives of others through the habits we learn and the actions that spring forth from them (Stitzlein 2020: 3).

She recognises significant problems: the message of hope has not always aligned with political and social realities, the very existence of inequality and violence in our society, the 'disconnection and distrust' arising from hyperindividualism, and the 'privatized' version of hope we tend to embrace (Stitzlein 2020: 9–15).

Much like Tocqueville, Stitzlein does not adopt a partisan response but rather a philosophical one. For her, American pragmatism holds the key to our future. The pragmatism she heralds focuses on inquiry, growth, truth, meliorism, and hope that involves 'living purposively in the present' (Stitzlein 2020: 29). Habits are the way hope is 'enacted'. 'Habits', notes Stitzlein, 'can be taught and nurtured; they can be revised and improved' (2020: 38). They connect us to the past, are responsive to the realities of the present, and set preconditions for future growth and development. But habits, as Aristotle (1999) notes, are more than just a set of practices, they determine whether we become good or bad. For Tocqueville, they determine whether we become active members of a community or passive recipients who feed from a centralised trough.

Hope, says Stitzlein, is active: 'I contend that hope, as a set of habits and their enactment, is most essentially a disposition toward possibility and change for the betterment of oneself and, typically, others' (Stitzlein 2020: 42). The 'shared work of democracy' is predicated upon trust and the realities of everyday life (Stitzlein 2020: 51).

Moreover, schools and civil society can and *should* teach us to be citizens. They can do so by utilising methods that harken back to our earliest foundational accounts of what it means to be a 'citizen' – imagination and storytelling. While it is easy to view connections with those with whom we share blood ties, something else must occur to bind us to others. As Tocqueville notes, there is only one way to do so, to tie our fate to the fates of others – others who may differ from us in significant ways – self-interest rightly understood. It is a way to imagine the way in which our actions, on behalf of others, may benefit ourselves. As Tocqueville observes, it gives credence to our philosophy rather than our state of virtue, but it is effective. And it is predicated upon hope – the hope that, should we be in need, others will aid us. As Stitzlein rightly states, 'citizenship' is a 'shared fate' (2020: 126). But citizenship is a type of story that can 'save us' if we 'are persuaded by it' (Plato 2016: 303). Our self-interest, rightly understood, requires nothing less.

References

Aristotle (1999), *Nicomachean Ethics*. Translated by Terrence Irwin. 2nd ed. (Indianapolis: Hackett).

Atanassow, Ewa (2017), 'Colonization and Democracy', *The American Political Science Review* 3 (1): 83–96.

Berry, Wendall (1993), *Sex, Economy, Freedom and Community* (New York: Pantheon Books).

Cohn, D'vera, Anna Brown, and Mark Hugo Lopez (2021), 'Americans' Origin and Connections to Their Families' Roots', *Pew Research Center*, 14 May 2021. https://pewresearch.org.

DelBanco, Andrew (1999), *The Real American Dream: A Meditation on Hope* (Cambridge: Harvard University Press).

Fragile States Index (2023), Fragilestatesindex.org.

Girard, Rene (1989), *The Scapegoat*. Translated by Yvonne Freccero (Baltimore: The Johns Hopkins University Press).

Haidt, Jonathan (2013), *The Righteous Mind* (New York: Vintage Books).

Hamilton, Alexander, James Madison, and John Jay (1961), *The Federalist Papers*. Edited by Charles R. Kesler (New York: Signet Classics).

Heyne, Paul, Peter Boettke, and David Prychitko (2013), *The Economic Way of Thinking*. 13th ed. (London: Pearson).

'A Historical Context for Immigration Policy and Sentiment Today: Q & A with Moshik Temkin' (2017), *Ash Center for Democratic Governance and Innovation*, 13 March 2017. https://ash.harvard.edu.

Hobbes, Thomas (1994), *The Leviathan* (Indianapolis: Hackett Publishing).

Jacobs, Alan (2017), *How to Think* (New York: Currency).

Lilla, Mark (2017), *The Once and Future Liberal: After Identity Politics* (New York: Harper Collins).

Locke, John (1980), *The Second Treatise of Government*. Edited by C. B. Macpherson (Indianapolis: Hackett Publishing).

Machiavelli, Niccolò (1995), *The Prince*. Edited and translated by David Wooten (Indianapolis: Hackett Publishing).

Mill, John Stuart (1859), *Dissertations and Discussions, Volume II* (London: John W. Parker and Sons).

Mill, John Stuart (1978). *On Liberty*. Edited by Elizabeth Rapoport (Indianapolis: Hackett Publishing).

Mitchell, Joshua (2020), *American Awakening: Identity Politics and Other Afflictions of Our Time* (New York: Encounter Books).

Plato (2016), *The Republic of Plato*. Translated by Alan Bloom. 3rd ed. (New York: Basic Books).

Rousseau, Jean-Jacques (2012), *Rousseau: The Basic Political Writings*. Edited and translated by Donald A. Cress. 2nd ed. (Indianapolis: Hackett Publishing Company).

Stitzlein, Sarah M. (2020), *Learning How To Hope* (London: Oxford University Press).

Tocqueville, Alexis (2002), *Democracy in America*. Edited by Harvey Mansfield and Delba Winthrop (Chicago: The University of Chicago Press).

7 Why a secularised and pluralistic democracy needs faith

Jonathan Chaplin

7.1 Introduction

This chapter explores how liberal democracies that regard themselves as essentially secularised can nevertheless secure maximum public space for the presence and expression of faith-based political visions – and why they should do so.[1] For Alexis de Tocqueville (1805–1859), religion – notably Christianity, especially Protestantism, and specifically 'Puritanism' – was an indispensable contributor to a widely shared, formative moral code and social vision that facilitated the creation of the civic culture that, he perceived, underpinned the American democracy of the time (see Chapter 2). While the primary presenting concern of *Democracy in America* is not religion as such but the conditions under which liberty might be safeguarded in an egalitarian society, religion is identified as a vital contributor to such conditions. Obviously, our context is radically different to that which Tocqueville addressed. Mid-19th-century America was marked by both a broad consensus on the value of religion and the moral aspirations it was thought to generate, and an optimistic sense that America was a haven of liberty and equality for all comers, especially those fleeing persecution or poverty. Both elements of that consensus have collapsed today – there is deep disagreement both on the public role of religion and on the basic justice of American society. The place of religion in public life has to be rethought in a context of deep dissensus on religion's legitimacy and role.

The chapter takes as its starting point Charles Taylor's account of 'secularity' expounded in *A Secular Age* (Taylor 2007: 1–4). There Taylor distinguishes three expressions of secularity marking the modern West: The differentiation of state from religion occurring in the Reformation and early modern age; the decline of religious belief and practice; and the change in the 'conditions of belief' created by religious pluralism, meaning that religious believers now have to adhere to their faith self-consciously, in the awareness that there are many alternatives. I explore how a differentiated political order that is expected

1 Thanks to the editors and to Paul Billingham for comments on earlier drafts. The usual disclaimer applies.

DOI: 10.4324/9781032641041-7

to adopt a stance of impartiality among them can yet facilitate the legitimate influence of faith-based political claims within democratic processes, without losing the proper gains of differentiation. The first part outlines a model of public faith appropriate for today, adapting Luke Bretherton's term 'faithful secularity' (Bretherton 2019: 227–257). The second illustrates it by exploring what it means for 'faithful speech' (Chaplin 2021a), an application of faithful secularity to the specific possibilities and constraints of political discourse.

7.2 'Faithful secularity'

Notions of 'secularity', 'the secular', 'secularism', and 'secularisation' are vigorously contested today. My focus is on 'political secularism' – a set of formal and informal arrangements whereby political authorities seek to facilitate, frame, regulate, contain, or subdue public religion. There are numerous versions of political secularism.[2] On one side are ideologically driven regimes that seek to wield hegemonic control over religion, instrumentalising it towards some secular state objectives. Examples include the former Soviet Union, Kemalist Turkey, French revolutionary republicanism, and post-independence Egypt. A regime like this, as Bretherton puts it:

> generates specific configurations of divisions between public and private, depends on a monistic and centralized conception of political sovereignty, and looks to the nation-state as both the normative form of polity and the primary focus of identity. At its heart, it seeks the active removal and exclusion of religious considerations from shared moral and political judgments.
>
> (Bretherton 2019: 252)

Such secularism breaches state impartiality and 'reorders and remakes religious life and relations between different religions in accord with norms and procedures alien to the forms of life and the religious communities themselves'. In doing so, rather than domesticating religion, it 'exacerbates religious polarization and inequality as state procedures…inevitably favor some and stigmatize others' (Bretherton 2019: 252). At the extreme, such a hegemonic secular state, as José Casanova observes, 'arrogates for itself [an] absolute, sovereign, quasi-sacred, quasi-transcendent character' and assumes 'the mantle of rationality and universality, while claiming that "religion" is essentially nonrational, particularistic, and intolerant (or illiberal) and, as such, dangerous and a threat to democratic politics once it enters the public sphere' (Casanova 2011: 69).

That variant of political secularism comes in for an abundance of critique from 'postliberal' theologians. Most Western liberal democracies, however,

2 See, for example, Warner, VanAntwerpen, and Calhoun (2010); Calhoun, Jeurgensmeyer, and VanAntwerpen (2011a).

have been shaped by more 'moderate' versions of political secularism which allow, or in some cases encourage, a diverse religious presence in some public spaces while seeking to maintain the broad official religious impartiality of state institutions and the equal standing of all faiths in the public realm (Levy and Modood 2009). Such a religious presence can include extensive participation of religion in the public sector, as in religious schools, hospitals, chaplaincies and other services (Chaplin 2021a). Some 'moderate' secular states even allow forms of weak church establishment or other residues of Christian pre-eminence to persist, more or less reluctantly. None of these are necessary features of moderate secularism (they are far more constrained in France, for example) but they leave these regimes looking very different to the hegemonic forms depicted in the quotation above by Casanova.

However, in several national contexts, the religious presence in the public sector has been under increasing pressure from a classical liberal economic paradigm that has steadily sought to colonise the spaces of civil society and the public sphere, where many religious visions of life are nurtured; and, no less, from a progressive liberal cultural paradigm that has been exerting increasing control over the legitimate autonomy of civil society associations, often in the name of advancing otherwise commendable non-discrimination legislation (see chapter 4; Ten Napel 2017). Even under moderate secularism, it remains necessary to deploy arguments for the legitimate presence and autonomy of faith in both civil society and state.

Such arguments run up against what has for several decades been the dominant liberal secularist view of public religion. This is the view that a neutral state, one capable of offering equal protection to all its citizens' deepest commitments, is only attainable by means of the secularisation of the public realm and the privatisation and depoliticisation of religion. This view was authoritatively declared by the European Court of Human Rights (ECtHR) in 2003 in a case involving the dissolution of an Islamic political party in Turkey. In a controversial and much-contested judgment, the majority declared that 'the principle of secularism' was a necessary presupposition of 'democracy', and that 'sharia is incompatible with the fundamental principles of democracy, as set forth in the Convention' (ECtHR 2003, paras. 93, 123). This pre-emptively – and, as a dissenting judge noted, ignorantly – excluded the possibility that 'sharia' is not a single entity that can straightforwardly be pitted against 'democracy'. Rather it is a richly textured body of texts, practices, mores, norms, and rules that can bear a variety of meanings for Islamic political actors. 'Sharia' is not first a formal legal code, still less primarily a punitive one, but a spiritually motivated way of life informed by often wholesome substantive ethical commitments that can be faithfully retrieved and reinterpreted by Muslims for contemporary plural societies (Hefner 2015). This variant of liberal secularism pre-emptively excludes such a possibility.

The assumption that liberal democracy presupposes this exclusion of faith from the public sphere has been fundamentally challenged from numerous standpoints, including liberal thinkers themselves.[3] I will not rehearse these critical voices here but proceed straight to presenting a constructive view of public faith. A political application of what Bretherton calls 'faithful secularity', I will argue, can help make democracy more inclusive.

For Bretherton, faithful secularity is a quality of openness to diversity that would inform society as a whole: It 'entails the commitment to, and institutional configuration of, a religiously plural and morally diverse common life, the construction and conceptualisation of which vary by historical and cultural context' (Bretherton 2019: 251). It unleashes the possibility of a vigorous plurality of voices seeking 'justice and love':

> As a contingent assemblage, subject to multiple iterations, formations of the secular should be judged good or bad not by whether they are religiously neutral or not, but by the extent to which they enable the possibility of a just and loving common life amid difference, disagreement, and asymmetries of power.
>
> (Bretherton 2019: 229)

While faithful secularity applies to a whole society, at the level of political institutions, it specifically implies that what a 'secular' state should seek to achieve is not the containing or domesticating of religion but the just adjudication of diversity generally. A secular state should be understood not as a 'solution' to the 'problem' of religion, on the assumption that religion displays inherently undemocratic characteristics that secularist worldviews do not. As Bretherton puts it: 'Politically, plurality does present problems, as it makes it harder to form, norm, and sustain a common life. But that is not a problem with religion, nor is religion specifically the problem' (Bretherton 2019: 250–251). Rather, a defensible form of political secularism should be seen as addressing the just response of the state to the wider moral, religious, and cultural plurality of its people.

Both Taylor and Bretherton rightly affirm that such a response must include an official stance of neutrality, or impartiality, or even-handedness, towards diverse ultimate visions of life on the part of the state. This will include securing negative freedom of conscience and religion for the individual citizens and their associations bearing such visions. It will also require, where appropriate, promoting the positive freedom of each to avail themselves of such opportunities and rights. Under an even-handed state, no ultimate vision may receive explicit constitutional preference or endorsement over others, or be invoked by state officials to justify state action. That rules out forms of establishment where the state substantially privileges one or other faiths and seriously disadvantages others. It need not imply a one-size-fits-all relation of the state to all the multiple manifestations of faith-based diversity (Thompson and Modood 2022). The key goal is that the state treats diverse faiths as equitably

3 For example, Laborde (2017), Levy and Modood (2009).

as possible, allowing all adherents who seek to participate in some area of public life the opportunity to do so, within the limits of law.[4] The same must apply to secular beliefs. As Taylor puts it, 'the point of state neutrality is precisely to avoid favoring or disfavoring not just religious positions but any basic position, religious or non-religious' (Taylor 2011: 37). Both merit the same equitable treatment by the state, as far as possible.

This is the element of truth in a much-quoted line from John Rawls: 'politics in a democratic society can never be guided by what we see as the whole truth' (Rawls 1996: 243). But the valid point being made here is poorly formulated, implying that we should set aside our deepest convictions when entering politics. The valid point is that if citizens adhering to incompatible religious commitments seek exclusive control of the state, then we are on the road to serious social conflict or civil war. But states can successfully maintain civil peace, and enhance social trust, among rival believers if they are prepared to scale down the demands they make on the political order. Citizens should learn to look to that order to secure a limited sphere of public order and justice in which plural ultimate visions can flourish. They should not look to the state to embody their religious identity or to advance their version of the ultimate truth.[5] In this specific sense, the state should indeed be officially 'secular'. It should embody what theologian Rowan Williams has termed 'procedural secularism', in which the state oversees and maintains peace among a plurality of 'communities of religious conviction' but refrains from endorsing or conferring legal privilege on any one of them. The result would be a 'crowded and argumentative public square which acknowledged the authority of a legal mediator … whose job is to balance and manage real difference' (Williams 2012: 27).

Political deliberation, then, will confine itself to the content of that 'limited justice' and will not trespass onto the territory of ultimate truth (religious or secular). In the next part, I will argue, nonetheless, that a key purpose of protecting 'faithful speech' is to ensure that such ultimate visions – 'what people see as the whole truth' – can legitimately and substantially inform political debates about justice, yet without imperilling formal state impartiality. But first, let me say some more about the limited justice that the state is responsible for.

A 'secular state' in the sense defended here leaves the task of assessing ultimate truth-claims to other agents – individual citizens, religious and philosophical associations, universities, media, and so forth. As liberal theorist

4 State impartiality means that states must ***not assume the legal competence*** to judge between such visions, as the ECtHR judgment cited above correctly noted: 'the State's duty of neutrality and impartiality is incompatible with any power on the State's part to assess the legitimacy of religious beliefs…and…requires the State to ensure mutual tolerance between opposing groups' (ECtHR 2003, para. 91).

5 The new 'Catholic integralism' refuses this restraint.

Cécile Laborde puts it: 'The state should be secular so that citizens do not have to be secular' (Laborde 2017: 125). A 'secular state' does not imply that the state is committed to the worldview implicit in what Taylor calls 'the immanent frame' (Taylor 2007: ch. 15), nor to a general secularisation of the public realm. Rather, by respecting the restraint of official impartiality, it secures equitable space for plural visions to manifest themselves as fully as they wish to and are able to in the public realm (within the law). This does not amount to moral agnosticism: Every state by its acts and omissions discloses substantive commitments to one or other principle of political morality. A religiously impartial state is not a morally neutral state but only one that refrains from officially and explicitly endorsing ultimate truth-claims, even while protecting the very democratic channels that allow such truth-claims to exercise a bottom-up influence on state acts.

A further consequence is that, instead of seeking to mould everyone into the form of some ideal secular liberal citizen, conversing only in secular languages, a 'faithfully secular' state allows the convictional diversity that actually exists among the citizenry to come to legitimate public expression. It also leaves citizens free to live by what some might see as 'non-liberal' values in their personal lives or private associations. Unlike ideological secularism, it facilitates rather than shuts down these expressions of faith-based pluralism. It allows diverse religious faiths to engage extensively in democratic activity, and to exercise substantial influence over public debate, public policy, and law-making on the same terms as secular faiths.

As Bretherton puts it, faithful secularity calls for a state that will 'uphold a rule-bound, accountable, and equitable arena that enables a just and merciful common life between diverse communities to be negotiated' (Bretherton 2019: 253). The purpose of protecting plural visions is not mere tolerance, but also to release a wider range of perspectives on 'justice and mercy' than might otherwise come to the fore in a more restrictive secularist regime. Thus, a 'faithful and democratic secularity allows for the public recognition and interplay of the myriad obligations and commitments that citizens keep faith with (whether transcendent, immanent, or whatever) and that must be coordinated and negotiated to generate mutual ground' (Bretherton 2019: 255). This seeks to honour the recognition that, as Terry Eagleton puts it, '[i]t is only if reason can draw upon resources and energies deeper, more tenacious and less fragile than itself that it is capable of prevailing'. This is, he claims, 'a truth which liberal rationalism for the most part disastrously overlooks' (Eagleton 2009: 110).

Political secularism primarily concerns institutional arrangements. But, as noted, 'faithful secularity' as a larger societal aspiration summons us to more than this. It also calls for the pursuit of certain cognitive attitudes. Jürgen Habermas, for example, claims that it requires a 'demanding epistemic mind-set' on the part of both religious and secular citizens (2011: 26; see also Habermas 2008). I would express this, not as a strict demand of citizenship – for many will struggle to achieve it and some will conscientiously resist it

– but as a democratically valuable goal towards which those citizens who are able to should aspire as far as possible. It is something that the state itself cannot directly secure, although its actions may be conducive to it. On one side, religious citizens should be encouraged to strive towards what Habermas terms a 'reflexive consciousness'. Such a consciousness would, for example, allow them to treat other religions reasonably, respect the autonomy of 'mundane' sciences, and accommodate their own faith to the requirements of equal human rights. On the other, secular citizens should also seek to meet parallel epistemic demands. They should strive to become aware of the 'limits of a secular or postmetaphysical kind of reasoning'. This might involve acknowledging that 'vibrant world religions may be bearers of "truth contents", in the sense of suppressed or untapped moral intuitions' (Habermas 2011: 27). This requires nothing less than a 'self-reflective transcending of a secularist self-understanding of Modernity' (Habermas 2006a: 15).

I would press this point further. What is called for is not just a recognition that secular reasoning may not already possess all valid moral intuitions. Secular citizens should also be encouraged to see that their own political principles, such as human rights, are grounded in larger moral and philosophical visions that are analogous to religious faiths. Such principles are not simply products of a supposed self-sufficient reason. In brief, secular citizens should work towards an acknowledgement that the religious and the secular are essentially in the same epistemic boat. That is further than Habermas would want to go, but I think it would enhance the prospects for cultivating valuable democratic virtues. The editors of an influential collection, *Rethinking Secularism*, suggest that 'all normative orientations, even those that claim to be entirely rational, in fact depend on some higher-order values'. Even 'being completely rational' can be such a higher value:

> Some higher-order values are very this-worldly, as for example, in economic discourse in which either some indicator of utility or some hedonic principle of human happiness is clearly the utmost good by which the entire analytic framework is organized and which has a standing apart from any merely incremental values. So it is not clear that reference to higher values clearly demarcates religious from secular reasons.
>
> (Calhoun, Jeurgensmeyer and VanAntwerpen 2011b: 19)

As Craig Calhoun puts it in his own contribution to this volume: 'Both religious orientations to the world and secular, "Enlightened" orientations depend on strong epistemic and moral commitments made at least partly pre-rationally' (Calhoun 2011: 83). Or, as Taylor puts it:

> A Kantian will justify the rights to life and freedom by pointing to the dignity of rational agency; a utilitarian will speak of the necessity to treat beings who can experience joy and suffering in such a way as to maximize

> the first and minimize the second. A Christian will speak of humans as 'made in the image of God'. They concur on the principle, but differ on the deeper reasons for holding to this ethics. The state must uphold the ethics, but must refrain from favoring one of the deeper reasons.
>
> (Taylor 2011: 37)

The ability to recognise that fundamental political principles may legitimately be grounded in deeply divergent moral or religious visions is far from easy (and so should not be made a strict requirement of citizenship). It demands an expansion of many citizens' horizons and an enlargement of their natural sympathies. For, Taylor observes, 'we often suspect that those with different basic views can't really subscribe to these principles, not the way we do! (Because, as "we" know, "atheists can't have principles", or as [another] "we" know, "religions are all against liberty and/or equality")' (Taylor 2011: 48). Since we are 'condemned to live in an overlapping consensus' (Taylor 2011: 48), we must all work hard to educate ourselves for, and accommodate ourselves to, the presence of a deepening diversity of politically consequential moral and spiritual visions. This is so even if we cannot positively celebrate all their manifestations, or if we find some such visions repugnant and damaging. Black liberation theologian Cornel West also recognises that this obligation applies to both sides:

> secular thinkers ... must become more religiously musical. ... But religious persons like myself must be secularly musical, because, through empathy and imagination, we must try to get inside other peoples' views of the world, to understand why persons are convinced by this set of arguments. ... It's no small thing.
>
> (West 2011: 93)

Let me now turn to what this epistemic attitude implies for political discourse, for what I call 'faithful speech'.

7.3 'Faithful speech'

One of the conditions for the successful mutual learning process I just outlined is that a democratic regime should intentionally facilitate 'faithful speech', rather than deliberately or inadvertently debilitating it. By 'faithful speech' I mean public reasoning, deliberation, or other modes of communication proceeding from or informed by a particular faith commitment, religious or secular. This includes not only propositional assertions but also public symbols or even ritual performances intended to convey some politically relevant message. A liberal democracy committed to faithful secularity must recognise the legitimacy of, and practically facilitate, the use of faithful speech in many arenas of political deliberation.

It should do so for at least three reasons. First, its commitment to conscientious freedom of speech and expression implies that attempts to curtail the scope of such freedom, if not by law then at least by stigmatising certain manifestations of speech as *inherently* civilly sub-standard, should be avoided at all costs. Second, a liberal democracy should facilitate faithful speech so as to honour the actual plurality of its people. Democracies should recognise that 'the people' embraces all citizens in their territories and not only those conforming to certain dominant or privileged discursive practices. Third, liberal democracies should acknowledge faithful speech as a potential source of dynamic moral energies and political mobilisations behind shared projects of justice. Habermas himself recognises the point:

> as long as religious communities play a vital role in civil society and the public sphere, deliberative politics is as much a product of the public use of reason on the part of *religious* citizens as on that of *nonreligious* citizens.
>
> (Habermas 2011: 24)

Thus: 'Secular and religious citizens must meet in their public use of reason at eye level' (Habermas 2011: 26). Their complementary inputs may then raise the quality of discourse generally: 'The public use of reason by religious and nonreligious citizens alike may well spur deliberative politics in a pluralist civil society and lead to the recovery of semantic potentials from religious traditions for the wider political culture' (Habermas 2011: 8). Such contributions are well-placed to help re-inject rich normative ideas into public debate – to help towards what José Casanova, following Habermas, terms the 'renormativizing' of the public sphere (Casanova 1994: 57–58). This is especially important today given that what Habermas calls the modern 'administrative state' wields such dominance in the sphere of public communication. Here, religion can be a powerful crucible of disruptive critique:

> The only element transcending administrative politics and institutionalized power politics emerges from the anarchic use of communicative freedoms that keeps alive the spring tide of informal flows of public communication from below. Through these channels alone, vital and non-fundamentalist religious communities can become a transformative force in the center of a democratic civil society.
>
> (Habermas 2011: 25)

Religious speech should be part of that 'anarchic' ferment in the public sphere ('anarchic' in the sense of unpredictable because not being under the control of the administrative state). Facilitating such faithful speech may make for a rougher – or at least a less familiar – democratic ride than secular-minded citizens might so far have experienced. It will complicate a democracy's discursive landscape and require citizens to understand (to them) 'alien' political languages. Equally, newcomers to a liberal democracy who bring with them attachments to traditional religions will need to learn (to them) the 'alien' languages of the receiving society. Protecting faithful speech may have the effect of slowing down processes of political consensus-building over deeply disputed questions of justice. But by being more representative of citizens' deeper political motivations, a facilitative stance towards faithful speech may make such consensus wider and more durable, while also enhancing the overall legitimacy of the regime by making it more discursively inclusive.

In the political realm, faithful speech cannot, however, only be the *expression*, still less the mere venting, of one's faith claims. Nor can it be mere identity-assertion, as if it were civically acceptable merely to put one's faith-based identities on display in democratic forums and then walk away satisfied. Habermas rightly notes that, as soon as we enter the public sphere, we inevitably confront a 'pressure for cooperation that we cannot escape'. In this sphere, 'there is upon the minds of citizens a pressure to make contributions to a democratic process which is designed to reach, finally, a decision for collectively binding programs' (Habermas 2011: 115). That quite properly has the effect of concentrating minds on the need for successful communication across convictional and other divides. To put it more precisely – as a form of political speech, faithful speech must be orientated to the specific purpose of the polity, and fitted to the character of and constraints on what political institutions should and can accomplish. Polities are not equipped to create most manifestations of what Bretherton calls 'common life'. As I would sum up the purpose of the polity, faithful speech must be directed to the state's task of securing multifaceted justice in the public realm of society. Faithful political speech must be speech pursuant to the meaning and implications of 'public justice', however that notion may be specifically defined by different faith-orientated communities (Chaplin 2021a, ch. 1).

This proposal evidently challenges what has been the prevailing liberal democratic view of the use of 'religious reasons' in political debates. Like liberal secularism generally, such a view of religious reasons has also been subjected to searching critiques from many quarters (Biggar and Hogan 2009). Summarising, the heart of the debate is over whether religious reasons qualify as the sorts of public reasons that are required by a state committed to liberal principles of freedom and equality. The argument is that such a state must be able, in principle, to rationally justify its coercive decisions to all its citizens.[6] For that to take place, only reasons that are defined as epistemically 'accessible' to all can serve *that specific justificatory role*. Reasons that do not serve such a role are not so constrained (and it is worth noting that a great deal of political speech is not designed to serve that highly specific purpose).

Secular liberals originally applied this 'doctrine of restraint' on religious reasons to the ordinary political reasoning of all citizens, even in the public sphere – in civil society, the realm of free discursive exchange outside of

6 Or, at least, to some suitably idealised subclass of citizens who stand in for all 'reasonable' citizens. I regard such idealisations as harbouring undemocratic implications.

formal political institutions. Recently, many have relaxed this stricture so that it applies only to the reasoning presented in formal institutional settings, such as by political parties, candidates for office, elected politicians, government ministers, or other state officials. One such is Habermas, who, as noted, is appreciative of the democratic potentials borne by certain kinds of religious public reasoning *in the public sphere*. However, he insists that explicitly religious reasoning cannot be invoked as public justifications for laws in the realm of formal institutional politics. The supposed disability is not that religious claims are inherently less 'rational' than secular claims. It is that the use of justifying religious reasons assumes membership of a particular community *narrower than the entire citizenry*, whereas secular reasons do not:

> By using any kind of religious reasons, you are implicitly appealing to membership in a corresponding religious community. Only if one is a member and can speak in the first person from within a particular religious tradition does one share a specific kind of experience on which religious convictions and reasons depend. … [T]he most important experience … arises from participation in cultic practices, in the actual performance of worshipping in which no Kantian or utilitarian has to participate in order to make a good Kantian or utilitarian argument.
> (Habermas 2011: 61)

But is this so? Habermas is clear that the problem is not the literal 'unintelligibility' of religious claims to those outside religious communities. For example, he accepts Taylor's rejoinder that every American, not only members of Christian churches, fully understood Martin Luther King's appeal to religious narratives of liberation (Exodus) to justify his call to America to live up to its constitutional commitment to the equal, inalienable natural rights of all (Habermas 2011: 63).[7] Rather, for Habermas, what 'secular' reasons achieve that religious ones cannot, is that they 'push for mutual perspective taking so that different communities can develop a more inclusive perspective by transcending their own universe of discourse' (Habermas 2011: 66). In that way, they render themselves serviceable for the purpose of public justification.

But, as noted earlier, such an ethos of inclusiveness is precisely what West thinks is eminently possible by at least some religious citizens: by becoming 'secularly musical … through empathy and imagination', they 'try to get inside other peoples' views of the world'. In particular, it is 'prophetic religion' that aspires to a stance of empathetic solidarity with all those who suffer (West 2011: 99). One might add that a wide variety of religious (and nonreligious) traditions and sensibilities, some of whom might not see themselves as

7 Taylor had asked, rhetorically, 'Would more people have got the point had [King] invoked Kant?' (2011, 58n13).

'prophetic', possess a capacity for the inclusiveness that West and Habermas rightly see as vital to the practice of democratic citizenship.[8]

Habermas's worry that membership of a religious community *necessarily* impairs communicative success on matters of public justification thus seems unfounded. There is then a question of whether it is helpful to frame this as amounting to a 'transcending of one's own universe of discourse'. Neither King nor West, nor countless other religiously motivated political actors, can really be said to be 'transcending' their own discursive traditions. Many would claim that it is precisely the particularity of such traditions – specific passages in the Bible or the Quran – that allows them to embrace a radical inclusiveness towards fellow citizens and thus make the effort to understand what are their deepest motivations and to address them in ways that they will find comprehensible and compelling towards shared projects of justice (or, perhaps, complementary or divergent ones).

For Habermas, the key demand facing religious citizens is 'translation'. The basic discursive requirement pursuant to a democratic ethos of inclusiveness is that religious speakers, if they wish to offer justifications of official state decisions and not just participate in open debate in the public sphere, be willing to 'translate' their religious convictions into a secular language, for only such a language can meet the liberal demands of state neutrality (Habermas 2011: 25). If religious citizens decide to invoke religious language *in the public sphere*, they are entirely free to do so, for it would be wrong to 'restrict the polyphonic diversity of public voices at its very source' (Habermas 2011: 26). Thus, Habermas's position does not imply that figures like Martin Luther King must engage in such translation when speaking in that sphere.[9] However, religious citizens must 'accept that the potential truth contents of religious utterances must be translated into a generally accessible language before they can find their way into the agencies of parliaments, courts, or administrative bodies and influence their decisions'. This requires that an 'institutional filter' be established 'between informal communication in the public arena and formal deliberations of political bodies that yield to collectively binding decisions' (Habermas 2011: 26). Such a filter might include a procedural power of a parliamentary house speaker to eliminate religious justifications voiced in parliamentary debates from the official transcript (Habermas 2006a: 10). The filtering process secures the liberal aim of 'ensuring that all legally enforceable and publicly sanctioned decisions can be formulated and justified in a universally accessible language' (Habermas 2011: 26).

By 'translation', Habermas evidently means something more demanding than simply eliminating from proposed public justifications any explicit references to religious ideas such as God, the Bible, or revelation (as a house

8 See Bokenkotter (1998).

9 In fact, one could argue that King was a master at such translation, weaving biblical metaphor, ethical norm, and American constitutional principle into a seamless rhetorical performance.

speaker might do in editing an official transcript). That could be easily, if trivially, achieved: 'God calls us to treat fellow human beings justly' could simply be rendered as 'treat fellow human beings justly'. Translation is not mere excision. Rather, he acknowledges that religion has historically been the bearer of very substantive commitments that now mark the political order of modernity. For example, by assimilating Christian ideas, Western philosophy has articulated 'normative conceptual clusters with a heavy weight of meaning, such as responsibility, autonomy, and justification; or history and remembering, new beginning, innovation, and return; or emancipation and fulfilment; or expropriation, internalisation, and embodiment, individuality and fellowship' (Habermas 2006b: 44–45). Secular philosophy, he claims, has 'transformed the original meaning of these terms, but without emptying them through a process of deflation and exhaustion'. Thus, the Christian idea of humans being made in the image of God has been successfully translated as – transformed into – that of 'the identical dignity of all men that deserves unconditional respect' (Habermas 2006b: 44–45).

Certainly, the idea of 'equal unconditional respect' retains a 'heavy weight of meaning', and religious citizens should be strongly committed to it. But what is 'lost in translation' in this rendition is the much richer and arguably more revolutionary idea that humans as 'images of God' are summoned to the dynamic vocation of being God's 'representatives' within a creation shot through with mandates for justice addressed to all areas of social life. For those 'made in the image of God' to seek justice is much more than showing 'unconditional respect to autonomous individuals'. That would be a substantial 'deflation' of its original meaning. 'Imaging God' constitutively includes resolute opposition to all that frustrates human flourishing, a more comprehensive and demanding idea than the rather arid-sounding Kantian formulation, 'offering unconditional respect'. This is central to the character of West's 'prophetic' stance towards the world, 'an empathetic and imaginative power that confronts hegemonic power always operating' (West 2011: 99).[10] Indeed, the Genesis passage in question was originally composed as a critique of autocratic and hierarchical ancient religions in which ordinary human beings were denied equal dignity.

Habermas's concept of 'translation' is thus problematic, although it reaches for a valid insight. I propose that what he describes as *translation* from religious to secular language be understood rather as a *transposition* of one kind of speech into another, as a musical score is transposed from one key to another. The transposition is from speech addressed to comprehensive matters of ultimate truth and meaning, to speech addressed to the much more limited sphere of political order. It is not that the former is 'religious' and the latter is

10 It includes a readiness to 'keep track of the catastrophic', i.e., to identify and expose the many manifestations of oppression (West 2011: 97). We must not 'deodorize the funk' (West 2011: 97).

'secular'; nor that the former is more important than the latter (since, at least in Christian political theology, the pursuit of political justice is constitutive of true religion); nor that the latter is an inferior analogy of the former. The difference is not of rank or intensity but of depth and extent. Political order is a bounded sphere of human interaction not well-suited to engaging the broadest and deepest questions of truth and meaning. It has its own inherent norms which (as I have formulated it) have to do with the pursuit of public justice through the limited instruments of law and public policy. Such norms include the rule of law, due process, proper jurisdiction, constitutional accountability, democratic representation, human rights, legal equality, distributive justice, and so forth. Speech about politics is speech about such norms. And 'faithful political speech' is not speech *about* faith but about politics viewed through the lens of faith. So it would be misleading to describe such speech as 'thin'; rather it should be *as thick as it needs to be pursuant to that distinctive sphere of discourse*.

Finally, it is necessary to clarify how we may reconcile my robust championing of faithful speech among citizens with the equally affirmed principle that state officials may not deploy explicit references to faith when they engage in public justification of acts of state. What is the rationale for such a contrast and where do we draw the line? These questions can be answered by elaborating a version of the idea of 'role differentiation' emerging from liberal public reason debates.[11]

Within a 'faithfully secular state', citizens, as active agents co-responsible with governmental bodies for the discernment and realisation of public justice, are entitled to be presented by organs of state with intelligible and institutionally pertinent reasons for the laws and policies to which they are to be subject; that is how I shall understand 'public justification'. It is helpful to speak of 'organs' rather than 'officials' of state because, while it is always state officials that actually execute public justification, they never speak as individuals but always as representatives of the state. We are not so much interested in the internal reasoning processes of individual state officials as in the institutional reasoning processes to which they contribute. Such reasoning is expressed in, for example, departmental policy announcements, preambles to pieces of legislation, ministerial statements, and so forth. State officials, acting for state organs, engage in public justification by offering to citizens intelligible and pertinent public justice reasons for state acts.

Here I distinguish two sorts of roles often unhelpfully lumped together as 'state officials'. This will allow me to specify where precisely I differ from Habermas. There are roles whose occupants are acting on behalf of the *executive organs* of the state (ministers, civil servants, etc.) and those acting on behalf of the *representative organs* of the state (elected officials such as Congressmen,

11 The remaining paragraphs in this section utilise material appearing in Chaplin (2021b: 598–600). Thanks to the editors for permission to do so.

MPs, councillors, etc.). Strictly, it is only the former who, when they engage in public justification, speak on behalf of the political community *as a whole*.[12] They are therefore under the most stringent duty to present reasons that the maximum number of citizens will be able to understand and, if possible, acknowledge as politically valid (even if they disagree with them). It also means that, by virtue of their specific office, they will strive to avoid reasons (religious or secular) that will likely risk alienating large numbers of citizens – of leaving them with the justified sense that they are being governed according to ultimate truth-claims they reject. If they do their level best to achieve these goals, they have met the demands of their office – even though they may leave some citizens deeply at odds with the political community's stance on this or that policy. Here, then, what Laborde calls 'justificatory secularism' – state officials recusing themselves from invoking ultimate visions of life to justify state law – is indeed valid (Laborde 2013).

By contrast, the *people's representatives* have a different role, which is to attend to, interpret, interrogate, and then convey (in parliaments, council chambers, etc.) to executive organs of state, the political convictions, aspirations, demands, and interests of the people who have elected them to that role (while testing these against their own and their party's convictions). In this representative role, they do not speak on behalf of the whole political community but only of one of its parts. They 're-present' the concerns of that part of the people that elected them. By virtue of that role, they should enjoy more leeway in selecting the sorts of reasons for laws and policies they choose to present. Otherwise, the people's inputs into the democratic process risk getting vetted by the state for pertinence, whereas it is up to the people themselves in the first instance to determine what is pertinent. Where the people wish to appeal to comprehensive visions (religious or secular) as part of their total package of reasons, their representatives must be left free to convey these (or, indeed, their own). They should be entitled to refer to such visions in settings such as parliamentary debates (although considerations of context and prudence will often counsel against doing so).

An outcome must then be acknowledged that would indeed trouble Habermas. It may turn out that in any process of deliberation on the demands of public justice, there will have been powerfully formative religious or secular comprehensive reasons at work shaping the process and, indirectly at least, impacting on the public justifications that come to be offered for that policy by executive officers. Here, religious reasons are indeed penetrating into the substance of formal state policy-making, not merely being voiced in the 'anarchic' public sphere. I do not see that as a problem for a plural liberal democracy, so long as official public justifications presented explicitly by state organs do indeed confine themselves to public justice reasons. Such justifications may have been shaped by preceding religious arguments, but they must remain

12 It is at this point that Habermas's concern about restricted membership becomes valid.

silent on the role any such reasons might have played in the process leading up to the official declaration of the justification.

In the representative process, *citizens and their associations* remain even freer than their elected representatives to articulate whatever reasons they choose in debates about public justice. They are indeed not directly engaged with the formal institutions of the state, moving rather in the public sphere. As Laborde puts it, to place 'stringent limits on what citizens can say in the public sphere violates basic democratic and liberal rights and, in effect, ask[s] citizens to act, at all times, as if they were agents of the state' (Laborde 2017: 169). Note also that the stipulation that citizens address themselves to the 'requirements of public justice' already serves as a significant steer on what is institutionally pertinent for them to say. The faithful political speech of citizens must address itself to the core purpose, character, and constraints of the polity. This does not imply a call to *censure* citizens who go 'off-piste' in political debate (all democrats have their bad days), but to draw attention to the need to *resource them better* in the skills and disciplines of political deliberation. What is implied, then, is not a 'doctrine of restraint' but an 'injunction towards good citizenship' (of which engagement in the mutual learning processes mentioned earlier is a good example). Capable citizens are not born but made through multiple processes of education, socialisation, and participation that continue throughout their lives. While states should in the first instance engage citizens as they find them, they are not obliged to leave them exactly as they are. They should avoid 'soulcraft' – the intentional moulding of the inner lives of citizens – but they do have an institutional duty to prompt citizens, where possible, to become better equipped at performing the role of citizen. Liberal democracies should worry less about managing the disruptive effects of pluralism and more about how practically to equip citizens to engage in successful democratic deliberation and action in a context of deep diversity.

7.4 Conclusion

This chapter has outlined a model of 'faithful secularity' that embraces deep diversity as an expression of respect for citizens' civic equality and as a resource for the 'renormativization' of the public realm. Such a model facilitates, *inter alia*, the practice of faithful speech, enabling citizens and their associations to bring deep visions of justice to bear in what Habermas calls the public sphere, and beyond it in representative forums of the state sector. While adhering to formal state impartiality towards such visions, and respecting 'justificatory secularism' on the part of those speaking for state organs, faithful secularity seeks to harness the contributions of lawful public religions as constructive democratic resources, rather than to contain them as distracting or disabling burdens.

Faithful secularity offers an approach in which the now-burgeoning plurality of alternative faith-based political visions are guaranteed secure public space, while severally and jointly aspiring to address common issues of public justice, each according to their own lights, but coordinating with others as circumstances permit. That demands three things. The first is a stance of welcome towards such contributions in the public sphere, not only those offering resources for social cohesion but also those advocating 'prophetic' critiques of structural injustices. The second is a vigilant defence of the rights and capacity for self-governance on the part of religious and other 'visionary' associations, including prophetic ones, in the face of constraints imposed by both the administrative state and by colonising markets that would prefer such associations to remain silent and toe the line. The third is an acceptance of the fact that in a vigorous and open democracy, laws and policies will inevitably reflect the influence of one or more plural faith-based visions. That means that, *de facto*, *legislators might end up heeding prophets*, even when, *de jure*, they and other state organs retain a stance of impartiality towards faiths.

A faithfully secular democracy would be committed to rational public deliberation while enabling its citizens and officials to benefit from what Eagleton calls 'resources and energies deeper and more tenacious' than reason itself. We know full well how hazardous an enterprise this can be where public religions lack firm commitment to the principles of constitutional democracy. I submit that it is, all things considered, less hazardous than imposing a restrictive form of secularism that marginalises, belittles, and alienates significant sections of the citizenry. Yet, more importantly, it makes available to a constitutional democracy wellsprings of motivation and wisdom that could prove critical in sustaining and repairing the fragile, fractured democracies we increasingly inhabit.

References

Biggar, Nigel and Linda Hogan (eds.) (2009), *Religious Voices in Public Places*, Oxford: Oxford University Press.

Bokenkotter, Thomas (1998), *Church and Revolution: Catholics in the Struggle for Democracy and Social Justice*, New York: Image Books.

Bretherton, Luke (2019), *Christ and the Common Life: Political Theology and the Case for Democracy*, Grand Rapids: Eerdmans.

Calhoun, Craig (2011), 'Secularism, Citizenship, and the Public Sphere', in Craig Calhoun, Mark Jeurgensmeyer and Jonathan VanAntwerpen (eds.), *Rethinking Secularism*, New York: Oxford University Press, 75–91.

Calhoun, Craig, Mark Jeurgensmeyer and Jonathan VanAntwerpen (eds.) (2011a), *Rethinking Secularism*, New York: Oxford University Press.

Calhoun, Craig, Mark Jeurgensmeyer and Jonathan VanAntwerpen (2011b), 'Introduction', in Craig Calhoun, Mark Jeurgensmeyer and Jonathan VanAntwerpen (eds.), *Rethinking Secularism*, New York: Oxford University Press, 3–30.

Casanova, José (1994), *Public Religions in the Modern World*, Chicago, IL: University of Chicago Press.

Casanova, José (2011), 'The Secular, Secularizations, Secularisms', in Craig Calhoun, Mark Jeurgensmeyer and Jonathan VanAntwerpen (eds.), *Rethinking Secularism*, New York: Oxford University Press, 54–74.

Chaplin, Jonathan (2021a), *Faith in Democracy: Framing a Politics of Deep Diversity*, London: SCM.
Chaplin, Jonathan (2021b), 'An Institutionalist Reframing of the Religion and Public Reason Debate', *Social Theory and Practice* 47.3, 598–600.
Eagleton, Terry (2009), *Reason, Faith, and Revolution: Reflections on the God Debate*, New Haven, CT: Yale University Press.
ECtHR (European Court of Human Rights), *Refah Partisi (Welfare Party) v Turkey* (2003) 37 EHRR I
Habermas, Jürgen (2006a), 'Religion and the Public Sphere', *European Journal of Philosophy* 14.1, 1–25.
Habermas, Jürgen (2006b), 'Prepolitical Foundations of the Democratic Constitutional State', in Jürgen Habermas and Joseph Ratzinger (eds.), *Dialectics of Secularization: On Reason and Religion, ed. Florian Schuller*, San Francisco, CA: Ignatius Press, 19–52.
Habermas, Jürgen (2008), *Naturalism and Religion*, trans. Ciaran Cronin, Cambridge: Polity.
Habermas, Jürgen (2011), '"The Political:" The Rational Meaning of a Questionable Inheritance of Political Theology', in Eduardo Mendieta and Jonathan VanAntwerpen (eds.), *The Power of Religion in the Public Sphere*, New York: Columbia University Press, 15–33.
Hefner, Robert W. (ed.) (2015), *Shari'a Law and Modern Muslim Ethics*, Bloomington, IN: Indiana University Press.
Laborde, Cécile (2013), 'Justificatory Secularism', in Gavin D'Costa et al. (eds.), *Religion in a Liberal State*, Cambridge: Cambridge University Press, 164–186.
Laborde, Cécile (2017), *Liberalism's Religion*, Cambridge, MA: Harvard University Press.
Levy, Geoffrey Brahm and Tariq Modood (eds.) (2009), *Secularism, Religion and Multicultural Citizenship*, Cambridge: Cambridge University Press.
Rawls, John (1996), *Political Liberalism*, New York: Columbia University Press [1993].
Taylor, Charles (2007), *A Secular Age*, Cambridge, MA: Harvard University Press.
Taylor, Charles (2011), 'Why We Need a Radical Redefinition of Secularism', in Eduardo Mendieta and Jonathan VanAntwerpen (eds.), *The Power of Religion in the Public Sphere*, New York: Columbia University Press, 34–59.
Ten Napel, Hans-Martien (2017), *Constitutionalism, Democracy and Religious Freedom*, Abingdon: Routledge.
Thompson, Simon and Tariq Modood (2022), 'The Multidimensional Recognition of Religion', *Critical Review of International Social and Political Philosophy* 26.4, 1–22.
Tocqueville, Alexis de (2000; original, French edition 1835, 1840), *Democracy in America*. Translated, edited and introduced by Harvey C. Mansfield Delba Winthrop, Chicago and London: University Press of Chicago.
Warner, Michael, Jonathan VanAntwerpen and Craig Calhoun (eds.) (2010), *Varieties of Secularism in a Secular Age*, Cambridge, MA: Harvard University Press.
West, Cornel (2011), 'Prophetic Religion and the Future of Capitalist Civilization', in Eduardo Mendieta and Jonathan VanAntwerpen (eds.), *The Power of Religion in the Public Sphere*, New York: Columbia University Press, 92–100.
Williams, Rowan (2012), *Faith in the Public Square*, London: Bloomsbury.

8 Freedom and human rights

Trey Dimsdale

8.1 Introduction

The French Revolution of February 1848 brought the corrupt and incompetent reign of King Louis-Philippe to an ignominious end and with it the end of the not even 30-year-old Bourbon Restoration. The months leading up to the revolution were tense, but not filled with violence and rioting. Rather, a series of partisan banquets among the elite provided a more polite setting for advancing the political debates disguised as dinner speeches. To the great frustration of Alexis de Tocqueville, then serving in the *Chambre des députés*, there was no real concern in the government that these banquets might present a threat to the government. On January 29, 1848, he warned his colleagues in a speech to the *Chambre* that the nation was 'sleeping on a volcano' (Tocqueville 2016: 12). He was right. On February 23, 1848, less than one month later, Prime Minister François Guizot was compelled to resign and the next day saw the abdication of the Citizen King.

The July Monarchy had been a constitutional monarchy with a legislature elected to function accordingly, but the months following the fall of King Louis-Philippe were somewhat chaotic as a new constitution was crafted. It did not take long for what had been crowds of 'curious onlookers and malcontents rather than rebels' (ibid., 21) to begin staging demonstrations and making demands on the new government. In response to previously unaddressed demands for electoral reform, the new constitution would eventually be France's first to provide for universal male suffrage. But other social problems were pressed upon those responsible for the new constitution, including crushing levels of unemployment and the poverty that resulted from it (Agulhon 1983: 36).

With thousands of unemployed men in Paris, loud support for a new Ministry of Work in the new republic gained momentum. Given the distribution of governmental responsibilities among existing ministries, such a new ministry would necessarily be social rather than focused on economic policies impacting employment (ibid.). The mere existence of such a new ministry as proposed by activists would signal 'that the State explicitly recognised social well-being or at least social protection and amelioration among

DOI: 10.4324/9781032641041-8

its responsibilities' (ibid., 37). In the context of contemporary debate, this recognition would mean that the revolution had been a socialist one, so the proposal was understandably controversial.

Tocqueville recognised this and in his impassioned 'Speech to the Constituent Assembly on the proposed constitution, concerning the right to work', delivered in session on September 12, 1848, he argued *against* enshrining a right to work in the constitution of the new republic. The speech is notable for addressing a conflict between two competing conceptions of the meaning of 'human rights'. Tocqueville defended the classical, historical understanding as he opposed the constitutional codification of a right to work against a new, reoriented understanding of rights that was inherent in the socialist[1] proposal for a new Ministry of Work and the state's assumption of responsibility for social well-being, which would represent the first such provision in a French constitution.

Every right granted or recognised for one individual represents a corresponding restraint on the freedom of others by the imposition of a duty or an obligation. As more rights claims are recognised legally or socially, more constraints on the freedom of others necessarily follow. Tocqueville rightly identified in this speech that the creation of a 'general, absolute, irresistible right to work' would impose a duty upon the state to guarantee 'a job to every worker who seeks employment' (Tocqueville 2016: 237). Flowing from this comes, according to Tocqueville, a long chain reaction of unintended consequences both economic and social that are politically and economically destabilising (ibid., 235–236). The creation of this right would impose an obligation on the state that is not within the purview of the state's proper concerns, which Tocqueville never enumerates. He does recognise that in America government is both absent and passive as contrasted with the governments of Europeans who 'believe they are establishing liberty' through governments that assume social powers (Tocqueville 1835: Electronic Edition).

Classical jurisprudence defines a right in relation to just action, which involves an inherent moral claim. Later critics of this definition have objected that the attendant legal duty associated with a rights claim is not, in fact, a moral restraint, but a pragmatic one. It is, in the words of American legal theorist and Supreme Court Justice Oliver Wendell Holmes, Jr., 'nothing but a prediction … [of the] judgement of a court' (Holmes 1897: 459). Rights and duties are not grounded, then, in anything other than the pronouncements of a court, which can be directed by legislatures and constitutions. In this view, rights, duties, and actions associated with each are pragmatic and rational rather than moral in any sense of the word.

1 This does not imply that the new conception of a right is exclusively or uniquely socialist in a technical sense. It is merely the conception advocated by the post-revolutionary socialist faction during the formation of a new government and a new constitution.

The result of the 1848 debates in the French legislature was a compromise. There was no new Ministry of Work, but the legislature did create a new commission to study the issue (Agulhon 1983: 36–37) and in the century and a half since his speech, Tocqueville's position has not prevailed. The classical conception of rights advocated by Tocqueville clearly defines the parameters of a legitimate right that deserves legal recognition and protection. Over time, similar well-meaning efforts across the West have further compromised the integrity of the concept of rights in pursuit of expanding freedom and protections for individuals who are members of narrowly defined groups. This has ultimately created an inflation of rights claims that has paradoxically resulted in a decline of freedom due to competing rights claims and expanded government regulations.

Further, this has all occurred inside a political structure dependent on a classical conception of rights – the modern nation-state. The national form is 'the indispensable instrument for democratic self-government' (Mahoney 2022: 3). It is predicated, at least in part, on the classical conception of rights that clearly defines the parameters of a legitimate rights claim. The well-meaning attempts to address the pressing problem of poverty and the myriad corollary social problems by the socialist faction of 1848 France unintentionally undermined one of the most important underlying assumptions that has allowed the modern nation-state to take shape.

8.2 Human rights

Rights are one of the most important and most basic building blocks of the law and, consequently, the structure of public and private life. It is good to both recognise and respect legitimate rights claims of individuals as the vehicles that create and define the contours of liberty. But there is now a cultural propensity 'to frame nearly every social controversy as a clash of rights' (Glendon 1991: 3). Almost anything related to personal autonomy or the integrity of individual concepts of identity is framed in terms of rights. The language of rights is rigid and absolute. Once a right is recognised, there is no more space for productive dialogue. Any future compromise or accommodation will involve an abrogation or detraction of a once-vested right (ibid., 13). This phenomenon, commonly referred to as 'rights inflation' or 'rights proliferation', has led to conflicting and overlapping rights claims that often make illegitimate demands on others and result, paradoxically, in an overall decline in freedom and intensified social conflict.

There are two primary contributors to rights inflation. One is a lack of technical clarity about the definition of a human right, which leads to laws and judicial decisions that also lack clarity. Some claims are recognised as rights that should be recognised as some other type of legitimate legal claim, but not a right with all the intended and unintended consequences that such recognition entails. The other is a lack of coherent, principled consensus with regard to the philosophical and moral aspects of rightly identifying legitimate rights claims.

8.2.1 What is a human right?

There are three aspects of the classical conception of a right. A single rights claim asserts a 'three-term relation involving a right-holder, a duty bearer, and [a] required action or omission' (MacLeod 2015: 39). Crucially, the right-holder and the duty-bearer are individuals in this scheme, and the required action or omission is imposed upon the duty-bearer. Rights create 'benefits and burdens to the individual' rather than to groups (Scruton 2017). Even when an individual enjoys a legitimate right because of membership in a particular group, it is not the individual's *identity* as a group member that creates the entitlement. The ancient world had no concept of the individual, no concept of groups of individuals, and therefore no concept of individual liberty or human rights (Siedentop 2014: 7–8). This emerged with the rise of Christianity and influenced the evolution of the concept of rights (ibid., 56–61) that is common both to civil law as well as Anglo-American common law.

It is the *fact* of the individual's membership in the group (e.g., the group of descendants with a right to inherit) upon which the basis of the claim of right is formed. The individual has rights among other individuals rather than as an individual with a particular identity. The same is true, too, for duty-bearers. Every individual who is not the right-holder bears an identical duty to act (or not) with regard to the right-holder's right. There is no common feature that binds that group other than the fact that they do not hold the right that creates the duty that they all bear. The difference is, to be certain, a subtle one, but it is crucial for understanding what is entailed in a rights claim. It is, therefore, improper to think of rights as anything but personal and individuated – they attach to persons and not things, ideas, groups, or classes. Even institutional rights spring from the free association of individuals, and the law of corporations (as it is called in the United States) creates the legal fiction that some of these free associations may enjoy the legal status of persons. Those rights are still personal and individual but applicable to an institution via a legal mechanism that makes it possible.

The rise of this concept of rights is traceable to the 15th century (Siedentop 2014: 338). Lawyers and philosophers had already posited that 'fundamental rights ought to protect individual agency … [and] that the final authority of any association (or group) is to be found in its members' (ibid.). The Christian *moral* claim that all souls are equal in dignity eventually translated into a *social* claim for equal *individual* rights (ibid., 339). Those individuals may, from time to time, join groups voluntarily or be a part of them by birth, profession, or operation of law. But even in those contexts, they are individuals among individuals who act to give the group a will and the ability to act.

There are certain types of claims that sail under the flag of 'rights' that are not, in fact, rights. American legal scholar Wesley Hohfeld developed a widely respected and accepted systematisation of these various concepts published as *Fundamental Legal Conceptions as Applied in Judicial Reasoning* in 1917.

Only what Hohfeld calls a 'claim-right' strictly fits the three-term relation definition stated above (Herstein 2023). Other types of claims, like powers, function in some respects like rights and are often colloquially described as a right. An example of a legal power is the power of a property owner to transfer his or her property. There are legal mechanisms that enable the transfer, and there may be legal provisions that limit or define that power. There is no person, however, entitled to receive a transfer[2] of that property, and the property owner has no obligation to transfer it at all.

In Tocqueville's France, the creation of a generalised and individuated right to work would have made every French citizen a right-holder. But who would have become the duty-bearer and what would have been the required action or omission entailed in the creation of this right? Leaving aside the question of whether the content of such a right is legitimate, the framing of this solution to a social problem in terms of a right presents several immediate problems.

First, right-holders and duty-bearers are individuals within the classical definition of rights. But the constitutional articulation of the right would make a non-person, the Republic of France, the duty-bearer regarding this right. Second, recognition of this right imposes an obligation to undertake action to provide employment on the state as duty-bearer. Tocqueville recognised this immediately: 'the state must endeavor to give a job to every worker who seeks employment' (Tocqueville 2016: 235). Groups cannot be duty-bearers because they can only act through the individuals that constitute them. So, in a sense, each French citizen would be both an individual right-holder and a collective duty-bearer regarding the same obligation. They would be, in technical Hohfeldian language, both the object and the subject of the same right.

The same impulse to solve a social conflict or problem has led countries to recognise myriad legal rights in their law or constitutions. In 2001, Greece amended its constitution to create a right to access the internet in language that explicitly obligates the state to facilitate it (Art. 5A Sect. 2). This individuated right then makes each Greek citizen an individual right-holder and, by virtue of being a Greek citizen, a duty-bearer with reference to the same right.

8.2.2 What is the proper content of a right?

Different people have different intuitions about rights due to religious, cultural, and other differences. Anthropological assumptions regarding natural inequality, for example, have driven the relations among persons in unjust social arrangements like the ancient Indian caste system or American chattel slavery. Even within a system like the West today, which is generally orientated towards just social arrangements, different intuitions muddle thinking and discourse about rights. Until very recently, these different intuitions in the

2 Prior to death, a property owner has the power to direct the disposition of his property at death or to allow the property to pass by operation of law.

Western context were primarily prudential ones that resulted from considerations like the role of the state in realising just social relationships. They resulted in category errors like those detailed earlier. Given that Western nations are now home to growing populations of religious minorities, the differences are increasingly attributable to religious and cultural factors, too, which influence perspectives on the proper content of a human right. These differences often present insurmountable impasses to consensus.

Most contemporary human rights work, therefore, is focused on interpreting or expanding enumerated lists of recognised rights irrespective of whether these lists lend themselves to coherent, consistent hermeneutical principles or have a common metaphysical basis rooted in any defensible first principles. The Universal Declaration of Human Rights (UDHR), adopted by the United Nations in 1948, is an example. In many ways, it is a remarkable achievement. But in other ways, it falls far short of being universal in any meaningful sense.

An excellent example is Article 18, Freedom of Thought, Conscience, and Religion. The Article reads in pertinent part that a person's 'freedom to change his religion or belief' is a protected right (UDHR, Art. 18). But this phrase proved controversial in that it conflicts with a particular interpretation of Sharia's prohibition against apostasy from Islam (Morsink 2022: 119). As a result, Saudi Arabia proposed to delete this clause, which was supported by five Muslim-majority member states (ibid., 121). Ultimately, the present form of Article 18 was adopted with only one negative vote and ten abstentions (ibid.).

Further, there was significant controversy regarding how the UDHR would relate to national law. The Soviet Union, for example, insisted that this declaration would have no impact on national sovereignty. Accession to the UDHR, therefore, would not signal an intention on the part of the Soviet Union (or any other state, for that matter) to alter the content or interpretation of its national laws (Glendon 2002: 69). The document would not only need to account for religious plurality but also for philosophical and political plurality, too (ibid.). Again, this observation is not focused on the controversies surrounding any specific article of the UDHR. It is merely illustrative of the fact that different parties from different parts of the world conceive of the proper substance of human rights differently, and at best, statements like the UDHR are best understood to be aspirational statements that can more or less guide the work of the United Nations and other international bodies.

I do not mean, however, to argue that the UDHR itself is incoherent. It does, in fact, have vertical coherence – the articles are mostly conceptually consistent and mirror the US constitutional tradition. What it lacks is horizontal coherence. Nations with constitutional regimes that are common to Western democracies face few challenges in harmonising their national laws with the UDHR. But nations with fundamentally different understandings of law and the role of law in society – namely Islamic nations or Marxist ones, like the former USSR – face challenges in structuring national laws in such a way that they are consistent with the UDHR. Saudi Arabia, for example, likely has no objection to Article 15, which articulates a right to a nationality. Saudi Arabia's historic objection to Article 18's 'freedom to change ... religion or belief' is not easily resolvable with the form of Islam that is reflected in the nation's public life. As a result, the task of integrating the UDHR into national laws is an ad hoc project requiring an article-by-article analysis in some nations and a much more fluid and natural project in others.

There was also no clearly defined telos regarding the UDHR. A notable 1968 assessment of the human rights work undertaken internationally notes that, 'In practice a claim is an international human right if the United Nations General Assembly says it is' (Bilder 1969: 173). There are many different competing and conflicting 'definitional theories' that could underlie the UDHR and similar rights statements (ibid.). The rights claims of the UDHR and other similar statements gain legitimacy, therefore, not from reference to inviolable universal principles but to the authority of a legislative or deliberative organ of a state or governmental body.

Political realities, however, all but guarantee that recognition in this way is problematic and political. Regarding the UN, for example, every member state is entitled to a vote in the General Assembly, where votes are subject to the influence of economic and military pressures. Assent or dissent may come at the end of a gun or through the promise of foreign aid that will, at worst, enrich kleptocratic leaders or create regional military powers capable of controlling often forgotten corners of the world, or, at best, bring food and medical supplies to the impoverished. Much more is at stake in the deliberative process of defining human rights by these means than systematic philosophical consistency or finding common moral ground among the world's great religions.

There are those who do not see the phenomenon of rights inflation to be problematic. In fact, they argue that the recognition of ever-increasing numbers of human rights is a positive development in the quest to secure just conditions and freedom for all people. The expansion of the 'human rights framework continues to prove appealing to new struggles for justice; indeed, "rights inflation" is not a sign of a movement going off-track, but rather of its continuing relevance and attraction' (Petrasek 2020). Still, this sentiment does not address the very real tension between and among various factions involved in human rights work, whether they are found in the governmental, non-governmental, or business sectors.

8.3 The state and human rights

Rights inflation translates into practical challenges because the political and social architecture for understanding, describing, and protecting rights has remained unchanged even as what constitutes a right has evolved and expanded. To press a metaphor, the hardware was built with a different software in mind. To understand how a shift in an understanding of the nature of rights impacts the stability and effectiveness of the national form, it is important to understand the evolution of the nation-state, especially against other alternatives for organising political life.

8.3.1 The origins of the modern state and modern citizenship

It is quite easy for us to take for granted the existence of 'the state'. In fact, Article 15 of the UDHR incorporates a right to nationality as a basic human right. This would have been a confusing assertion just a few hundred years ago. But the existence of the nation-state as the primary, if not the exclusive, modern political form gives rise to the reality that a stateless person lacking citizenship under the laws of any nation has no real prospects for flourishing or even survival. The drafters of the UDHR recognised that 'nationality brings with it not just essential [political] protection but also connections to history and culture' (Morsink 2022: 100).

The concept of citizenship and the state took a rudimentary form in ancient times. The Roman ideal of citizenship, which did not encompass all inhabitants and classes in Rome, was a man 'committed to peace and decency' and 'expected to live in equality with … fellow citizens' (Manent 2013: 138). It was the civil magistrate who was to be the object of a citizens' trust as the one who would 'defend the dignity of the republic and uphold the laws … [as well as] dispense to each his rights' (ibid., 138–139). Of course, these concepts evolved over time, especially with the rise and acceptance of the Christian religion and the Christian church corresponding with the reign of Constantine the Great in the 4th century.

St. Augustine's *City of God* is one of the earliest systematic attempts to reflect on how these concepts morphed, considering the new religion of the empire and the existence of the church, a new religious institution within it. He is writing in the wake of the humiliating 'fall of Rome' in 410 AD and defending Christianity against critics who believed that the 'newly established religion had disarmed Rome' (ibid., 230). So, whatever shifts in the concepts of 'the state' and 'the citizen' that could be attributable to the Christianisation of Rome were on trial.

The *City of God* is complex and nuanced, so any condensation of its arguments always risks oversimplification. But to understand this important juncture in the evolution of the nation-state and the concept of citizenship, there is one critical shift to consider – the development of a concept of private and public motivations. The ancient ideal did not consider that a citizen was also an individual with *private* motives that primarily served his own interests and not the interests of the state. 'The great citizen … prefers his city to his own life' (ibid., 252). As noted previously, it was the Christian moral claim of the dignity and equality of souls that influenced the political claim of equality of *persons* and not merely citizens. The implications of this distinction between public and private realms of life are dramatic and pervasive, but a fuller discussion is beyond the present scope. It is sufficient to say that the rise of Christianity resulted in a new concept of citizenship that incorporated the pursuit of both private, personal flourishing with public, collective flourishing. We now understand a citizen to be a right-bearer rather than a mere servant of the state fixated narrowly on the state's survival and flourishing.

3.3.2 'The majestic portal' of Westphalia[3]

In the Middle Ages, 'Europe itself [was] fragmented into hundreds of political units' (Strayer 2005: viii). These political units had overlapping jurisdictions, disputed borders, and very complex networks of connection through familial and political alliances. In short, 'Europe had little coherence ... and social organisation varied enormously from one region to another' (ibid., ix). Europeans understood themselves not as members of a body politic attached to a state but as lying somewhere along a 'great chain of being, extending from the lowest peasant ... up through the local lord, then perhaps a prince or king, then through to the emperor, the pope, and finally God' (Philpott 2001: 97). A person's existence and subsistence were dependent upon this chain with no reference to citizenship, nationality, or ethnicity other than at the higher strata.

Of course, this is, again, a generalisation with various parts of Europe experiencing different types of political and religious changes. However, it is the Protestant Reformation of 1517 that serves as a significant marker on the timeline of the further evolution of the nation-state. The Reformation fragmented the Christian church as both a spiritual institution and a political one, and eventually, Protestant and Roman Catholic powers went to war (ibid., 97–99). A series of inter-confessional wars known as the Thirty Years' War came to an end in 1648 through various treaties commonly and collectively known as the Peace of Westphalia.

The Peace of Westphalia is commonly cited as the event that ushered in the modern system of nation-states (ibid., 76–77). Historical controversies about whether this is *the* event that established this system are not particularly relevant to this chapter. The reality is that the elemental substance of the rise of the modern nation-state, including an enlightened understanding of the individual, had begun to emerge over the course of several centuries. 'Westphalia', then, is useful shorthand for the metamorphosis of conditions and the resultant state of affairs rather than a particular moment in history.

What Westphalia represents is a moment in history when sovereign states emerged as the 'sole legitimate form of polity within a society' (Philpott 2001: 30). It was no longer the Holy Roman Empire that was sovereign over Christendom with the power to intervene in local affairs. The Westphalian order, then, consisted of (1) sovereign states with (2) viable governments with control inside of their borders and the ability to enter treaties, and (3)

3 This is a reference to Leo Gross, who described the Peace of Westphalia as 'the majestic portal which leads from the old world into the new'.

committed to non-intervention outside of their own territory (ibid., 31–32). In 1648, there was also a requirement that the states be Christian, but as the Westphalian order began to dominate the wider global system over the following centuries, this was no longer a viable criterion for defining a state.

8.3.3 Modern citizenship, human rights, and the nation-state

How exactly is the emergence of the Westphalian order significant to a consideration of the nature of human rights and the modern phenomenon of rights inflation? It is only within the context of the nation-state that the modern concept of citizenship – the concept that recognises both the private and public aspects of an individual's life and motivations – can be realised in any meaningful way. Other forms of political and social organisation have weak or non-existent notions of citizenship.

This conception of citizenship allows the state and the individual full, mutual accountability and 'consists in a web of reciprocal rights and duties, upheld by a rule of law which stands higher than any party' (Scruton 2019: 5). This reality is powerful and scalable across the entire jurisdiction of the nation-state where 'every citizen becomes linked to every other … by relations … which presuppose no personal tie' (ibid., 7). Citizenship cannot exist, however, outside of this context of mutual accountability. The inhabitants of totalitarian nation-states with an unaccountable government do not truly enjoy citizenship, although they may be labelled as such by law. They are more properly classified as subjects of a state that 'need not account to the individual, when the rights and duties of the individual are undefined …, and when there is no rule of law that stands higher than the State that enforces it' (ibid., 6).

Citizenship and the rights that attend it do not necessarily exist in every nation-state, but the only place where citizenship exists is in the context of the nation-state. The reality is that no perfect system exists and that even within the freest nations, there are still ready examples of exploitation and subjection. But the crux of the entire analysis turns on rights – who possesses them and how are they protected and enforced?

A nation-state that is accountable to its citizens cultivates a society of trust. Every citizen is bound by the same rules, and each can expect his or her legally recognised rights to be respected and enforced, but also expects consequences if he or she ignores or violates a duty that flows from a legitimate right (ibid., 7). Problems, however, can arise that will destabilise this trust and erode the society that is contained within a nation-state of citizens who are worthy of discussion. Two of these, the presence of non-Christians as Western citizens and a political and social emphasis on individual autonomy, are considered below.

8.3.3.1 Non-Christians in the Christian West

The practice of faith in nearly all Western nations has declined precipitously in the last generations. The United States, once lagging against the rates of

European decline, has been experiencing a steep decline in religious practice according to every measure (Burge 2023; Bullivant 2022). But the notion of the 'Christian West' has not and is not dependent upon religious participation. The West is 'Christian' because of the fundamental ideas that have formed it. The nations of the West bear what Pierre Manent refers to as a 'Christian mark' (Manent 2016: 19). Specifically, Christian mores have shaped the moral, social, cultural, and political institutions of a nation bearing a Christian mark. This mark shows up in myriad ways and not just in the private vs. public distinctions in the life of a citizen or in the equality before the law that flows from Christian teaching on the equality of persons before God, as discussed earlier. A nation in which 'all citizens have equal rights is also a nation of a Christian mark' (ibid., 109).

A native-born but secular European can disavow the practice of faith or even the existence of God. But will still have been born into and formed in a society with firm roots in a Christian tradition. Secularisation does not neutralise society regarding religion (ibid.). This is not the case for a non-Christian immigrant entering a Western nation. At present, he or she is likely a practising Muslim from a majority Muslim nation in North Africa or the Middle East (Pew Research Report 2016). Can Muslims be citizens in more than just the technical legal sense of the word?

The most recent decade of European history suggests that there are significant challenges involved in 'granting a place [in a Christian society] to a form of life with which [Christianity] has never mixed on an equal footing' (Manent 2016, 108). However, the principles upon which the nation-state is formed do not require a religious test before granting citizens status as right-holders, a status that is inherent in citizenship itself. And these principles also do not exempt any citizen from bearing the duties imposed by the legitimate rights of fellow citizens. The success of the integration of Muslims and other non-Christians into Western nations depends on the ability of these groups to be free to form 'distinct communit[ies] in a nation in which they are all citizens *like others*' but within a 'surrounding community that [everyone knows and acknowledges] *is not Muslim*' (ibid., 109). This is clearly an ideal more easily articulated than realised.

8.3.3.2 Rights and the 'unlimited sovereignty of the individual'

It is important to note at this point that it is not the fact of citizenship or some other type of membership in a political community that confers rights on the individual. The concept of rights is a legal form that translates a thing about a person into something politically actionable. Rights are, as noted previously, personal and individuated. It is the ontological dignity of the individual from which the legal rights spring. However, individuals are members of communities, which is why the classical conception of rights implies a consideration of other individuals in the community.

The shift that Tocqueville argued against in 1848 was one that involved the state's adoption of concern about social welfare within its purview. This altered the relationship between the individual and the state and made the state the guarantor of a certain social condition rather than the guarantor of the right action associated with the legitimate rights of citizens as right-bearers. This has two important effects.

First, every claim that is treated as a right imposes a duty on others. When the state takes on the obligation of guaranteeing social conditions, then it also takes on the task of guaranteeing that others bear the duties that realising that end requires. There are myriad examples of this about which much ink has been spilt. A recognised right to internet access imposes a duty on others to provide. A recognised right to education imposes a duty on others to provide it. There are more onerous examples, too, that may directly impinge upon the conscience of others and create a duty in conflict with the legitimate rights claims vested in others. A right to procure an abortion can translate into a duty assigned to someone to perform one, and a right to self-determination of one's gender can translate into others being compelled to speak or otherwise act in ways that affirm this.

Second, this shift is one that centres the citizen as an individual and is only concerned with the private aspect of individual life and leaves behind the public aspect that was the sole concern of pre-Christian Roman citizenship. In short, it is predicated upon and advances the fiction of human autonomy (Manent 2020: 64). To be autonomous requires that there be no distinction between 'two qualitatively different actions' – to command and to obey (ibid., 65). Because these are two different but corollary actions, they require 'different agents who stand differently in relation to the action' (ibid.). The one who commands begins an action, and the one who obeys pursues the action (ibid.). One conceives of an action and acts to communicate that conception, while the other acts according to how that conception is communicated (ibid.). No one agent can do both.

More simply, 'human beings live in communities, upon which they depend not only for their specific ambitions and goals, but also for the very language with which to describe and intend them' (Scruton 2016: 42). A command to act, the comprehension of the command, an articulation of self-identity, or even an expression of preferences depend on the existence of a community to make it intelligible even within the mind of an individual.

'The unlimited sovereignty of individual rights' (Manent 2020: 75), as Manent calls the resulting state of affairs that follows from the shift opposed by Tocqueville, has flooded society not only with legally recognised rights but with legally binding duties. It has 'condone[d] acceptance of the benefits … without accepting the corresponding personal and civic obligations' of living in a democratic society (Glendon 1991: 14). Rights come into conflict when the legally recognised duties associated with one right conflict with other legitimate and sometimes recognised rights. Such a situation requires the compromise of one right or the other, and in the case when a legitimate right gives way to a spurious but legally recognised one, the obligatory action may be one that transgresses the moral convictions of the duty-bearer. Compliance with the law, therefore, may require betraying one's conscience.

This state of affairs has also created an 'unanswerable argument for anyone who want[s] to prevail against the rules and meaning of any institution whatsoever' (Manent 2020: 75). The proliferation of rights 'rob[s] essential institutions of their meaning and substance' (ibid., xiii) by subjecting the authority inherent in the institution – whether it be the church, the family, the university, or the state – to the radical autonomy of the individual. These very institutions are the 'little platoons', the smaller communities organised around a lesser common good that is orientated towards the greater common good of the national community, in which citizens can cooperate towards common political, social, or economic ends.

But it also can lead to an arbitrary practical recognition of rights. Some rights are favoured over others, and those are the ones enforced by courts. Citizens in such a society no longer enjoy the social and political benefits that come with a common and consistent scope of the law and their rights under it. Namely, this is a society in which trust erodes between citizens (Scruton 2019: 6). This loss of trust runs through all institutions all the way up to the nation-state itself, and as trust erodes, other means of ensuring social stability are required, and citizens begin to morph into subjects of the state. Paradoxically, the project that began to expand rights to address injustice then leads to a loss of liberty and new injustices.

8.4 In conclusion

Human rights are a fundamental building block of any social and political arrangement because they help to define the relationships between members of a given community. But to do so in a way that contributes to the common good and the stability and flourishing of society, rights claims must be properly understood as individuated and affecting more than just the claimant to a right. When claims that are not rights are legally recognised as such, or when the state recognises rights in the pursuit of ends outside of its proper purview, there is no natural terminus regarding what can be legally recognised as a right and enforced as such. The political form of the nation-state evolved along with and assumed the classical conception of rights as a three-term relation involving more than just the right-holder, and this understanding has been compromised through the rise of individual autonomy and the proliferation of rights that followed. It would be dramatic to say that the survival of civilisation requires a return to a classical understanding of rights and the citizen as not merely an individual but also as a member of a community. But without such a return, the trust that has been cultivated between citizens who are equal under the law, which is only realisable in the context of the political form of the nation-state, will erode and leave space for the necessary rise of other means of maintaining social order and cohesion.

References

Agulhon, Maurice (1983), *The Republican Experiment: 1848-1852.* Cambridge, UK: Cambridge University Press.

Bilder, Richard B. (1969), 'Rethinking International Human Rights: Some Basic Questions,' *Wisconsin Law Review* 171 (1): 551–608.

Bullivant, Stephen (2022), *Nonverts: The Making of Ex-Christian America.* Oxford: Oxford University Press.

Burge, Ryan P. (2023), *The Nones: Where They Came From, Who They Are, and Where They are Going. 2nd ed.* Minneapolis: Fortress Press.

Glendon, Mary Ann (2002), *A World Made New: Eleanor Roosevelt and the Universal Declaration of Human Rights.* New York: Random House.

Glendon, Mary Ann (1991), *Rights Talk: The Impoverishment of Political Discourse.* New York: The Free Press.

Herstein, Ori (2023), 'Legal Rights,' in *Stanford Encyclopedia of Philosophy.* https://plato.stanford.edu/entries/legal-rights/#HohfAnalRigh.

Holmes, Oliver Wendell (1897), 'The Path of the Law,' *Harvard Law Review* 10 (8): 457–478.

MacLeod, Adam (2015), *Property and Practical Reason.* Cambridge, UK: Cambridge University Press.

Mahoney, Daniel J. (2022), *Recovering Politics, Civilization, and the Soul: Essays on Pierre Manent and Roger Scruton.* South Bend: St. Augustine's Press.

Manent, Pierre (2016) (translated by Ralph C. Hancock), *Beyond Radical Secularism: How France and the Christian West Should Respond to the Islamic Challenge.* South Bend: St. Augustine's Press.

Manent, Pierre (2020) (translated by Ralph C. Hancock), *Natural Law and Human Rights: Toward a Recovery of Practical Reason.* Notre Dame, Indiana: University of Notre Dame Press.

Manent, Pierre (2013), *Metamorphoses of the City: On the Western Dynamic.* Cambridge, MA: Harvard University Press.

Morsink, Johannes (2022), *Article by Article: The Universal Declaration of Human Rights for a New Generation.* Philadelphia: University of Pennsylvania Press.

Petrasek, Daniel (2020), 'Human Rights Inflation—What's the Problem?,' *Open Global Rights,* 19 February.

Pew Research Center (2016), 'Number of Refugees to Europe Surges to Record 1.3 Million in 2015,' https://www.pewresearch.org/global/2016/08/02/number-of-refugees-to-europe-surges-to-record-1-3-million-in-2015/ .

Philpott, Daniel (2001), *Revolutions in Sovereignty: How Ideas Shaped Modern International Relations.* Princeton and Oxford: Princeton University Press.

Scruton, Roger (2016), *Philosophy: Principles and Problems.* London: Bloomsbury Academic.

Scruton, Roger (2019), *A Political Philosophy: Arguments for Conservatism.* London: Bloomsbury Continuum.

Scruton, Roger (2017), 'Tradition, Culture, and Citizenship,' *Law and Liberty,* 18 December.

Siedentop, Larry (2014), *Inventing the Individual: The Origins of Western Liberalism.* Cambridge, MA: Harvard University Press.

Strayer, Joseph R. (2005, originally published 1970), *On the Medieval Origins of the Modern State.* Princeton and Oxford: Princeton University Press.

Tocqueville, Alexis de (2016) (edited by Olivier Zunz and translated by Arthur Goldhammer), *Recollections: The French Revolution of 1848 and Its Aftermath.* Charlottesville and London: University of Virginia Press.

Tocqueville, Alexis de (1835), 'Of Administration in New England,' in *Democracy in America: Historical-Critical Edition*, vol. 1. Carmel, Indiana: Liberty Fund.

9 Truth, unity, and pluralism

Hans-Martien ten Napel

9.1 Introduction

The theological conception of the Holy Trinity concerns the central mystery of the Christian faith. It holds that although there is one God, he comprises three persons: Father, Son, and Holy Spirit. Similarly, modern democracy has revolved around the triad of truth, unity, and pluralism since its inception 250 years ago. That, in short, is the thrust of this contribution.

The concept of 'truth' in the political sphere can be associated with natural law. It involves 'a complex and many-sided body of moral and political thought' that nevertheless agrees on the point of 'the natural (as distinguished from conventional or man-made) character of principles of right and wrong, and of justice and injustice'.[1] Thinkers and statesmen who adhere to natural law agree, moreover, 'that the standards that ought to guide the ordering of political and social life are accessible to human reason'.[2]

As long as this body of thought was relatively widespread in Western societies, a high degree of moral unity logically prevailed. That was not only true for the period preceding the dawn of the (Early) Modern Era (1450 to 1800), but for a long time also for modernity itself.

Modern constitutionalism, which emerged from the American Revolution (1765–1791), explicitly assumed that truth, including religious truth (Paulsen 2013), existed. However, it would no longer be up to the state to determine which of the diverse truth claims that could be observed among the population was the correct one. Such formed the constitutional response to the increase in pluralism that had taken place, certainly compared to premodernity. The increase in pluralism was partly due to the 16th-century Reformation.

Nevertheless, at the same time, as mentioned earlier, there remained a relatively high degree of moral unity in the still-developing democracies. This unity resulted from the conviction that truth exists no matter what. Pluralism, therefore, remained within certain limits. Moreover, as a rule, the diverse claims to

1 'Natural Law, Natural Rights, and American Constitutionalism', nlnrac.org/about.
2 Ibid.

DOI: 10.4324/9781032641041-9

truth moved within Christian, or at least theistic, frameworks. Compliance was further promoted through legislation; in the United States, primarily within the states.

These were the conditions under which, from the 19th century onwards, so-called 'natural law liberalism' could flourish. These were also the social and political conditions that Tocqueville (1805–1859) encountered when he travelled through America. He has been called the 'great natural law liberal',[3] though not because he was such a great natural law theorist. One will search in vain for a definitive treatment of the theme in his work. His view on the subject, nevertheless, can be deduced from specific passages discussed below.

Instead, natural law forms the self-evident background, factual and normative, against which Tocqueville treated democracy. That also means his treatment of the threats to, and prospects for, modern democracy tacitly presupposed natural law liberalism. The same applies to modern constitutionalism, of which democracy formed an essential component.

Natural law liberalism would remain in place for some time after Tocqueville. Modernity may already have made its theoretical entry with Niccolò Machiavelli (1469–1527) and Thomas Hobbes (1588–1679) and exerted its influence during the democratic revolutions of the 18th century, especially the French Revolution. However, this does not mean it immediately superseded traditional natural law ideas among the population and the legislatures.

In retrospect, this only happened at the time of the cultural revolution of the 1960s. During the 'long sixties', Western thinking in terms of 'good' and 'evil' became subjectivised not only at the individual level but now also at the level of legislation and – increasingly important – case law. Due to this further abandonment of truth, the cultural revolution initially led to a radical decline in unity in terms of 'mores'.

Meanwhile, a new unity is growing at the expense of the pluralism that is an achievement of constitutional democracy. Paradoxically enough, the situation is beginning to resemble premodern times. After all, value relativism thus develops into a new type of truth, albeit one whose content is the opposite of the traditional concept of truth.

When this chapter observes that truth, unity, and pluralism form the holy trinity of modern democracy, it does so because this has been the case for a considerable time since the inception of modern democracy 250 years ago. This also raises the question of whether it will eventually be able to do without a natural law conception of truth, especially now that liberalism appears to have lost its compass. As a result, the constitutionally guaranteed pluralism is subject to erosion.

In what follows, Section 9.2 first looks back at the tense relationship that has existed over time between the two schools of thought that form the basis

3 Christopher Wolfe, Galbraith Lecture: 'Was American Liberalism Doomed to Fail?' University of Dallas, 15–16 June 2021 (https://www.youtube.com/watch?v=YlC7v5Ktg4c).

of Tocqueville's natural law liberalism. Next, Section 9.3 gives a brief outline of its main principles, partly against the background of the emerging 'postliberalism'. Section 9.4 then discusses why natural law liberalism may still be necessary for the proper functioning of constitutional democracy. Partly in light of the recent increase in tension between natural law liberalism's constituent parts, the chapter concludes with a brief reality check: What is the practical feasibility of natural law liberalism in the 21st century? Furthermore, what concrete, Tocquevillian recommendation arises from the chapter?

9.2 A tense relationship

Since ancient times, man has reflected on how to become 'happy'. Political institutions ideally facilitate this quest for happiness if only because, according to the classical view, the collective dimension is paramount. The American Declaration of Independence (1776) also spoke of 'the pursuit of happiness', which was presented as an inalienable individual human right on that occasion.

There is a second related difference between how happiness was viewed in the (European) Tradition of classical philosophy and Christianity and how it is viewed in modernity, in addition to the contrast between a collective and an individual approach (Kinneging 2020). In short, happiness was previously thought to have objective content. The Ten Commandments from the Bible are perhaps the best-known example of rules of natural law as defined above, although not all Christians will see it this way.

In modernity, however, the concept has become subjectivised. That means that nowadays, the basic principle is that everyone can and must decide for themselves what happiness is and how best to achieve it. Liberalism is the philosophical movement that wants to give free rein to this individualised and subjectivised search for happiness at the political level, albeit that the (sub-)state was initially still allowed and even required to regulate morality (Krabbendam & Ten Napel 2000; West 2017).

For this last reason, and because of the religious views he found among the population, Tocqueville observed that liberalism and natural law were compatible. Although he realised he had irrevocably entered modernity with one leg ('liberalism'), he wanted to remain anchored in the Tradition with the other ('natural law'). As noted, this remains reasonably implicit in his work. That does not alter the fact that in *Democracy in America*, one can find a passage inspired by natural law thinking, such as the following:

> I hold it to be an impious and an execrable maxim that, politically speaking, a people has a right to do whatsoever it pleases, and yet I have asserted that all authority originates in the will of the majority. Am I then, in contradiction with myself? A general law – which bears the name of Justice – has been made and sanctioned, not only by a majority of this

> or that people, but by a majority of mankind. The rights of every people are consequently confined within the limits of what is just.
>
> (Tocqueville 2011 [1835]), 1:1; 7.272. Cf. Van Bijsterveld (2021:86). Translation by Henry Reeve in Tocqueville (2006), 1; 15. Part 2.267)

An article explicitly devoted to the place of natural law in Tocqueville's thought concludes:

> Although Tocqueville does not create a new original concept of natural law, it plays an important role in his thought. His idea of natural law is based mostly on the Catholic rational concept of this law. Natural law constitutes a steady point that enables him to assess social phenomena-inter alia positive law. The importance of natural law is more obvious when we take into consideration the role of freedom and virtue in his thought. The article demonstrates that it is hard to correctly understand those two values without a reference to natural law. Taking all these arguments into consideration, we could conclude that the concept of natural law constitutes one of the most important keys to the proper interpretation of Tocqueville's thought.
>
> (Tracz-Tryniecki 2008: 36)

Stepping into modernity with one leg while remaining anchored in the Tradition with the other is easier said than done. It is not surprising that the literature speaks of Tocqueville's 'strange' or 'aristocratic' liberalism (Boesche 1987; Kahan 1987).

Natural law and liberalism were originally opposites. The rise of liberalism from the 17th century onwards was essentially a reaction to the dominance and content of natural law in the preceding period. This opposition continued to exist afterwards. To use an image of Christopher Wolfe, Professor Emeritus of Political Science at the University of Dallas and former President of the American Public Philosophy Institute, liberalism and natural law are, in the first instance, emphatically 'distinctly unlikely (and uncomfortable) bedfellows' (2006: 1).

Nevertheless, Wolfe, like Tocqueville, believes that it is also possible to characterise the relationship between liberalism and natural law as one of 'good spouses' (ibid.). After all, the two would have become intimately connected under the influence of the classical-liberal philosophy of John Locke (1632–1704).

Indeed, in the early phase of modernity, an attempt was made to embed the then very much alive idea of natural rights in the old natural law, resulting in a conceptual puzzle. Put simply, in the Tradition, the idea of 'virtues' was central. Later, partly under the influence of the Reformation, the notion of 'duties' came to the fore. With the rise of the Enlightenment, it was not immediately evident what place was reserved for 'rights', even though the notion of natural rights also existed in the classical legal tradition, albeit then in the sense of 'goods inherent to man's being' (Hervada 2020: 55). When the latter idea is no longer paramount, the question is what the concept of natural rights is based on? For this reason, someone like the moral theologian Nigel Biggar advocates a return to the discourse of virtues and duties (2020).

Even a far-reaching integration of the idea of natural rights with that of natural law does not mean that friction between liberalism and natural law can no longer occur. In a real marriage, too, periodic frictions between the two partners are part of life. At best, however, a relationship can develop so that they learn to appreciate their complementarity. Both partners will then gradually realise that at the end of the day, they can no longer do without each other.

From the side of natural law thinking, such a rapprochement with liberalism seems to have finally taken place. The Roman Catholic Church provides the clearest institutional example. In the 19th and early 20th centuries, the Roman Catholic Church was still extremely reserved towards modernity and liberalism.

However, at the time of the Second Vatican Council (1962–1965), there were official openings towards democracy and human rights (Tanner, SJ, 2012). The Church has traditionally seen this not as a break, but as a further development of its ideas. There is something to be said for that view in this case, as the origin of a concept like 'freedom' obviously goes back further than the rise of liberalism in the 17th century. Christianity provided an essential source (Siedentop 2014; Holland 2019).

Nevertheless, this acceptance by the Roman Catholic Church of democracy and human rights is increasingly giving rise to discussion. A more conservative current considers the rapprochement going too far and seeks refuge in a so-called 'integralism', which advocates a leading role for the church in the state (Foccroulle Menard & Su 2022).

At first sight, this movement wants to return to the situation before the Second Vatican Council. However, the question is how exactly Vatican II should be interpreted. Indeed, an expert by experience, such as Pope Benedict XVI (2005–2013), repeatedly stressed in his speeches that the Church's rapprochement with liberalism was always conditional (Cartabia & Simoncini 2015). Such rapprochement should, expressed in terms of this chapter, not lead to a form of value relativism, but should continue to respect natural law (Harinck & Ten Napel 2013). In this way, the triad 'truth, unity, pluralism' remains intact, and modern democracy is acceptable.

This involves no small reservation, since precisely when the intended rapprochement of natural law thinking to liberalism took place, liberalism began to abandon its natural law foundation. Indeed, recently, the love on the part of natural law thinking, insofar as it still exists, seems to have been almost entirely unrequited by liberalism.

The cultural revolution in the West during the (long) 1960s plays a decisive role in this. For this reason, this event has been identified as a revolution of world-historical significance (Kinneging 2020: 13). From a synthesis of classical philosophy and Christianity, which is rooted in Judaism, natural law thinking emerged. Plato (429?–347 BC), Aristotle (384–322 BC), Augustine (354–430), and Thomas Aquinas (c. 1225–1274), in all their diversity, can be considered the four great thinkers of the great European Tradition.

With the rise of modernity, Enlightenment thinking emerged as a second source of Western civilisation, which provoked a reaction in the form of Romanticism. At least Enlightenment thinking is not automatically at odds with natural law, as rationality is paramount in both. As a result, natural law thinking remained influential for quite some time (Kinneging 2020: 14).

As a result of the cultural revolution of the 1960s, that period came to a provisional end. It would be entirely wrong to blame liberalism alone for this. Instead, the fragile balance between Christianity and liberalism has also been lost because of the implosion of Christian organisations. In this way, more than four centuries after Machiavelli's *The Prince* (1532) and three centuries after Hobbes' *Leviathan* (1651), modernity can be expressed in full.

This observation raises an important question:

> What could be more fundamental to our sense of meaning and purpose than a conception of whether the strivings of the human race over long stretches of time have left us better or worse off? How, in particular, are we to make sense of modernity – of the erosion of family, tribe, tradition, and religion by the forces of individualism, cosmopolitanism, reason, and science? So much depends on how we understand the legacy of this transition: whether we see our world as a nightmare of crime, terrorism, genocide, and war or as a period that, by the standards of history, is blessed by unprecedented levels of peaceful coexistence.
>
> (Pinker 2011: 14)

Whether peaceful coexistence, in the sense of constitutionally guaranteed pluralism, is still possible in the 21st century appears to be answered differently by the remaining adherents of natural law thinking and those of contemporary liberalism, which has broken away from it. Supporters of natural law also differ in their opinions among themselves. The following sections discuss the main principles of natural law, liberalism, and natural law liberalism, respectively, against the background of the current postliberalism.

9.3 Postliberalism and natural law liberalism

The first decades of the 21st century have thus seen perhaps a more tense relationship between liberalism and natural law than ever before. Wolfe believes that the tensions remain manageable even now. To some extent, all Westerners, including adherents of natural law, are liberal. In his book *Natural Law Liberalism* (2006), he attempts to define what that means. Many will be inclined to think that this makes little sense. The variety of liberal currents, such as those of classical and contemporary liberalism, is too great for that.

At the same time, when people from other parts of the world have to answer the question of what the West stands for, a clear answer usually follows. It may be why they hate the West. It may also be why they envy it. In either case, however, it usually has to do with liberalism, though not specifically with one of its various currents.

Both cases – hate or love – involve the founding ideas of Western constitutionalism. They concern the things that Western constitutional systems have in common, despite the differences between them that they may also exhibit. These principles will be specified further below.[4]

First, however, we must briefly introduce the so-called postliberals. Given the increased mutual tension, the question arises: What do they choose – liberalism or natural law? Like Tocqueville, they feel they have at least one foot in modernity. The passage of time alone makes this even more challenging to deny than in the first half of the 19th century. However, the perceived excesses of contemporary liberalism weigh heavily on them. They no longer allow themselves to be convinced by an author like Wolfe or, before him, Tocqueville.

9.3.1 Postliberalism

Postliberalism can be broadly summarised in three points (Overeem 2021: 182–184). First, the movement is characterised by the thesis that liberalism has become dominant in recent decades in social, cultural, and, for example, economic areas. This thesis is hardly controversial. Neoliberalism is a case in point. The second postliberal idea is that liberalism can be harmful to society. That refers to the fact that it is an 'ism', i.e., an ideology. In the case of liberalism, it is not difficult to see that the central premise of individual autonomy distorts reality, postliberals argue. This idea is understandably more controversial than the first point. Third, postliberalism is characterised by the belief that liberal dominance has ended. Of course, this does not happen overnight, just as no 'successor ideology' is ready to take over immediately (Pabst 2021). Postliberalism does want to stand as a candidate to fill that vacancy.

Within postliberalism, there are then more moderate and radical variants (Overeem & Ten Napel 2021). The radical form, faced with the choice above between liberalism and natural law, opts unconditionally for natural law.[5] For it, liberalism is, at best, a means rather than an end. That goal is realising the 'common good' concept derived from the classical legal tradition. This concept has recently been attracting more attention, partly thanks to several prominent representatives of this school of thought, such as Harvard law professor Adrian Vermeule (2022). In a political sense, he defines it as 'the happiness or flourishing of the community, the well-ordered life in the *polis*' (28).

4 In so doing, I shall overlook that quite a few of the founding ideas of Western constitutionalism have their origins in a period that sometimes far precedes the rise of liberalism.

5 It is not always easy to distinguish the more moderate variant from natural law liberalism, which is yet to be discussed. It will therefore remain largely unmentioned here.

Here again, we touch upon the crucial difference between liberalism and natural law. Earlier, we saw that natural law assumes an objective description of happiness, whereas, in modernity, this concept has become individualised and subjectivised. Liberalism concludes that visions of the good life must also be kept out of the public domain as far as possible. As long as a population predominantly holds natural law views, the triad 'truth, unity, pluralism' is maintained in principle. After all, such views will continue, more or less implicitly, to impact legislation and case law.

In this way, it proved possible for some time to promote the common good in a natural law sense with the help of liberalism. That was, in short, as long as liberalism had not yet assumed an all-pervading role in politics and society and was, as a rule, limited to the institutional design of the constitutional order. The turning point in the 1960s meant that, under the influence of changing public opinion, liberalism also began to influence the content of laws and case law substantially. That should not be seen exclusively due to the change in views among Christian population groups, the so-called 'secularisation'. Views outside Christian circles consistent with classical philosophy also changed (Olsen 2017).

Although theoretically substantive neutrality is maintained, this is different in practice. Liberal views on abortion, euthanasia, gay marriage, and Sunday rest have rapidly undone and replaced natural law views. As a result, according to its postliberal critics, liberalism has developed into an obstacle to realising the common good. Indeed, sometimes liberalism now even leads to active opposition to this ideal. When another means proves more effective, more radical postliberals exchange liberalism for it.

That is true, even if this may be at the expense of constitutionally guaranteed pluralism. Therefore, radical postliberals advocate a partial return to a premodern conception of the political community. In doing so, they draw attention to the growth of a new kind of unity identified above and occurring at the expense of pluralism as an achievement of constitutional democracy. As a result, the situation already resembles premodern times. However, the value relativism underlying this unity is opposite in content to the traditional concept of truth.

9.3.2 Liberalism

Supporters of natural law liberalism, on the other hand, argue that the essential principles of liberalism remain defensible from a natural law perspective and can also be regarded as entirely 'good'. For certain tendencies that liberalism exhibits, however, natural law will express reservations. This requires an explanation.

In his book, Wolfe identifies five liberal principles (144–145). These are, successively: The foundation of human dignity, derived from the principle of equality; the legitimation of political power based on the declaration of consent by the people; the protection of (natural) rights as the goal of the constitutional order; powerful but at the same time limited government; and, finally, binding both the people and the government to the 'rule of law'. Without elaborating further on these principles here, it is thus the case that Wolfe considers them unquestionably compatible with natural law. To deviate from these principles now would mean no, or at least insufficient, evidence of 'true' liberalism. It is conceivable, for example, that 'progressivism' could take its place, which would require separate consideration. In the book under discussion here, however, Wolfe does not get around to doing so.

In addition to these principles, Wolfe observes certain liberal tendencies (145–147). These are, successively: A penchant for rationalism; a reformism; a tendency towards individualism; a predilection for rational religion or secularism; and a self-evident universalism in the sense that liberalism assumes its principles can, at least theoretically, be shared by everyone everywhere. It is not necessary to elaborate on these tendencies here. Earlier, it became clear that there is an inherently tense relationship between liberalism and natural law. It is also plausible that this has to do with several of these tendencies. Whether this means that liberalism 'degenerates' by definition, as radical postliberals believe (Deneen 2018), or whether, for example, the disappearance of the natural law counterweight is necessary for this to happen is open to debate.

9.3.3 Natural law

When we shift our attention to natural law, at least self-evident universalism is a conviction that liberalism and natural law share to some extent. The content of natural law is less massive than is usually assumed by critics. However, it depends on which view of natural law is taken. As with liberalism, there are various currents within this school of thought.[6]

A common feature of all natural law thinking, however, is that in a general sense, it is possible and also desirable to distinguish between 'good' and 'evil'.[7] How exactly this should be concretised is another matter. To some extent, this can differ according to time and place, which contrasts with liberal universalism.

However, some things are fixed, at least within the mainstream of natural law. These principles form the 'substructure', as it were, on which the 'superstructure' can vary in content. Fortunately, a concrete example of elaborating the 'superstructure' is available, if only because it shows that a natural law approach is still feasible today. This elaboration can be found in Catholic social teaching, as it has gradually developed since Pope Leo XIII's encyclical Rerum Novarum (1891) (Pontifical Council for Justice and Peace 2004).

6 Wolfe (2006: 174–175) also gives an attempt to formulate a common core of natural law thinking in 13 points, but I do not follow it here. That is partly because of lack of space and partly because the points reflect rather strongly the so-called 'new natural law theory'.

7 Inspired by Larry P. Arnn, President of Hillsdale College, in an online lecture on C.S. Lewis.

The substructure includes questions of micro-ethics. Thus, the use of 'correct' anthropology is paramount. By this, we mean the view of the human person traditionally associated with classical philosophy and Christianity. In current affairs, this plays a role, for example, in discussions on gender. Macro-ethical issues such as climate change and migration belong to the 'superstructure'.

These examples show, at the same time, that an approach that wants to lay claim to the qualification 'natural law' is not entirely free in the design of its 'superstructure' either, also because the same anthropology figures in both sub- and superstructure. Indeed, in recent years, Catholic social teaching has emphasised the close relationship between human and natural ecology. At most, the approach to the latter is more time-bound.

What is at stake in discussions about this is a second central concept in natural law, besides the common good we encountered earlier in the context of postliberalism. That is the concept of human dignity. Although virtually all currents in natural and non-natural law use the idea of human dignity, they do so in widely divergent ways. The crux, again, is whether the concept is given an objective or a subjective interpretation.

It will be apparent that the definition of human dignity used here is objective, certainly regarding its micro-ethical aspects. That contrasts with the contemporary liberal approach, which defines the concept so that individual autonomy is central. The more autonomy people have in micro-ethics, the more justice is done to human dignity. In the natural law view, the very meaning of the concept of human dignity stands in the way of maximising freedom of choice in micro-ethics.

9.3.4 Natural law liberalism

As stated, Wolfe (2006: 185–195) considers a synthesis between natural law and liberalism still possible even in the present day, pointing in particular to the following points of agreement: The fact that every human being deserves 'equal concern and respect'; popular consent, despite certain reservations, as a legitimate and valuable part of the political exercise of power; rights occupy a central place, but related to duties, and directed towards the good and the true; an important, but at the same time limited and frequently indirect role of the state in the realisation of the common good; and respect for the 'rule of law'.

Even with most of the tendencies of liberalism, natural law can go a long way, despite the tensions it raises (2006: 195–205). These include in particular those mentioned above, namely, its rationalist tradition, in which reason and 'enlightenment' are central; its reformist tendencies; its recognition of the importance of the individual and, to some extent, his autonomy; its preference for rationalist over revealed religion, insofar as the compatibility of faith and reason is also crucial in natural law; and, as already shown above, liberalism's universalist tendency, given the anchoring of natural law in human nature.

This fascinating attempt at synthesising natural law and liberalism deserves at least two comments. First, even those who favour such natural law liberalism should remain aware that the synthesis is imperfect. It does chafe, and Wolfe himself adduces this superfluously based on liberalism's relation to the concept of truth, revealed religion, and the family (2006: 208–214). Indeed, with the developments within liberalism in recent decades, a 'separation' and thus a more moderate or radical form of postliberalism undoubtedly remains the 'reasonable alternative' for a possibly growing number of adherents of natural law. That is partly because natural law liberalism and moderate postliberalism are positions on a scale rather than each other's absolute opposites.

A concrete example of where there is friction in practice between liberalism and natural law, or where the opposition seems almost unbridgeable, is that of abortion. This applies more to the United States than to Western Europe. In Western Europe, at least, there is a strong tendency to regard it as an issue on which political decisions have been taken at some point, which is said to be 'irreversible'. In the United States, on the other hand, as is well known, even 50 years after the liberalising decision of the American Supreme Court in the case of Roe *v.* Wade (1973), no social and political consensus has emerged that this should be the last word. As a result, this decision was 'overruled' by the Supreme Court in 2022.[8] Due to the ruling, the debate in the political institutions within the states will continue in renewed intensity for the foreseeable future unless Congress takes up the case.

Literature on natural law has also argued on the cutting edge that the 'overruling' of Roe *v.* Wade and renewed discussion in the political institutions would be necessary. After all, what is at stake, according to the authors concerned, is little less than the rule of law in the American political system:

> Abortion presents the gravest question about justice that a society can face: whether an entire class of human individuals is to be stripped of that equal protection of the law against killing which protects every other human individual, and thus exposed to unfettered disposal by those who have the will and legal authority to do so. For the unborn are surely human individuals – biology and the other sciences establish that much beyond doubt.
>
> (Bradley 2017: 426).

In Roe *v.* Wade, the latter was nevertheless left in the middle, which leads the same author to a sharp judgement:

> A polity which aims at the truth about persons is likely to get it right, and can self-correct if it does not. A polity which does not even aim at the truth, and which instead decides to suppress the truth about the unborn

8 Dobbs *v.* Jackson Women's Health Organization, 597 U.S. ___ (2022).

> for the sake of others' (chiefly, but not only, women's) interests, is not only going to get it wrong. At least in one decisive respect, such a polity is nothing less than barbaric.
>
> (ibid., 427).

With the transfer of the issue to the political institutions, it is still unclear whether the unborn child possesses 'personhood'. Hence the discussions will also focus on this issue.

The second comment on Wolfe's attempt to synthesise natural law and liberalism is that, as the earlier example illustrates, from the point of view of natural law, the choice of ideological allies and institutional design ultimately remains pragmatic. Followers of this tradition will therefore choose the constellation in which the substantive principles of natural law thinking can best be promoted at a given time and place.

This has already been shown to be the case for radical postliberals. However, when it comes down to it, it also applies to liberals orientated towards natural law. Institutions have hardly been discussed above, although, in the latter case, they are partly implied by liberal principles. Followers of natural law will therefore agree in principle with these institutions. Incidentally, their principles somewhat fuel this (Wolfe 2006: 178–180). Nevertheless, such questions of institutional design ultimately remain of secondary importance to natural law liberals. The primary issue is that justice can continue to be done to both truth and unity, and pluralism. In this respect, liberalism can play a vital role under the right circumstances.

9.4 Possible contemporary relevance of natural law liberalism for democracy

Why, against the background of the trite concepts of truth, unity, and pluralism, can natural law liberalism still be of importance for the proper functioning of democracy today? As indicated above, the cultural revolution of the 1960s initially led to an increase in pluralism. This resulted from the loss of unity in terms of 'mores', and is also to be expected when the concept of truth makes way for value relativism.

It is also the development that many have experienced as a 'liberation' and therefore welcomed. Initially, this also seemed to benefit democracy. In a country like the Netherlands, for example, the rule by elites made way for more direct political participation by the population (Lijphart 2022). In some Protestant political theologies, 'pluralism' also occupies an important place (Chaplin 2016). Naturally, 'freedom' also increases when truth becomes relativised, and freedom is undoubtedly likewise an underlying ideal of liberal democracy, albeit its precise meaning is not agreed upon. Nevertheless, improving social and political freedom can hardly be considered a disadvantage.

However, at some point, a switch was thrown. Further research is needed to establish precisely when and why this happened. In anticipation of this, it seems

Table 9.1 Truth, unity, and pluralism over time

	Truth	Unity	Pluralism
Premodern period	+	+	-
Modernity	+	+	+
Currently	-	+	-

reasonable to assume that a new kind of unity is developing at the expense of pluralism. The so-called 'cancel culture' is a striking illustration of this. More generally, intolerance increases when, in the name of tolerance, 'intolerant' views gradually become less constitutionally safeguarded (cf. Ratzinger 2004). Thus, as indicated, the situation resembles premodern configurations to some extent. Table 9.1 can clarify this.

The contemporary situation is thus one that would also seem undesirable to Tocqueville, for example, given his preference for social and political pluralism, which he shared with his contemporary John Stuart Mill (1806–1873) (Berlin 2002).

Illustrative of the increasing unity of 'mores' is the comparison that is sometimes made between the past communist influence and the liberal influence today (Legutko 2016; cf. Dreher 2020).[9] There remains a world of difference between the two situations, as the authors involved also acknowledge. Nevertheless, today's 'soft' totalitarianism resembles the 'hard' one of the past in some respects. Indeed, in both cases, there is such pressure on personal views, and sometimes even consciences, that they can no longer be called liberal. The revival of integralism can be explained against this background.

Convinced liberal democrats see things differently. They point out that freedom in the modern sense of the term still needs to be sufficiently realised and disseminated and that, if necessary, the latter must be achieved using some coercion. This coercion is, in any case, in the service of a good cause. After all, liberal democracy can be further perfected in this way. Although presenting it as if citizens are there for the regime in this vision is overly firm, there is at least an element of truth to that thesis. According to an authoritative contemporary interpreter of Tocqueville's message, 'to love democracy well, one must love it moderately' (cf. Manent 1996). That is an adage that has been forgotten in modern times. Democracy in general, and liberal democracy in particular, are now unconditionally loved.

This is understandable insofar as liberal democracy is the form of government ideally suited to modernity (Kinneging 2020: 140). Modernity can be characterised by two ideals – freedom and equality. In a liberal democracy, liberalism represents freedom, while democracy represents equality. In

9 I choose this type of substantiation rather than an empirical one, although the latter could also be provided.

combination, this leads to a form of social or progressive liberalism, which in turn fuels a love of liberal democracy. Although there need not be any objections to this in itself, it should be noted that, in principle, there are few limits to this freedom and equality. Democracy entails the rule that the majority decides. In principle, this majority is not obliged to aim for decisions in harmony with objective truth. The idea, however, is that the pillar of modern democracy based on the rule of law will steer democratic decision-making in the right direction.

Indeed, constitutional and human rights are still considered the 'hardest' element for the desired framing of democratic decision-making. In recent decades, however, there has been a proliferation of these rights. As a result, fundamental rights as a whole are subject to inflation. This tendency is reinforced by the fact that rights tend to be interpreted 'dynamically' by democratic majorities and courts. As a result, constitutional and human rights also become part of positive law, which may be different tomorrow than it is today. Therefore, it is an open question whether the classic, 'natural' rights such as freedom of religion, freedom of expression, and freedom of assembly and association will guarantee pluralism by mitigating the urge for unity within the democratic pillar.

That does carry a risk. Following the initial optimism after the fall of the Wall in 1989, the world has witnessed a 'democratic recession' (Diamond 2015). The question is how many postliberals, the relatively small number of only 24 remaining liberal democracies worldwide, can afford (Economist Intelligence Unit 2023). Indeed, more radical postliberals are turning away from liberalism entirely, putting further pressure on this form of government, even internally in the West. The resurgence of populism meant that this was already happening, albeit partly for different reasons than why natural law liberals have reservations about contemporary democracy and with no, or at least other, solutions (cf. Loughlin 2022: 191–202).

Therefore, whoever has a good heart for democracy must do almost the same for natural law. After all, the moderation of modern democracy Tocqueville refers to was historically brought about by that same natural law tradition. This tradition only, paradoxically enough, seems capable of setting limits to the pressure on constitutionally guaranteed pluralism, as it can be observed. Natural law does not exclude democracy, and especially not the rule of law, but it does make both less 'immoderate'. The continued relevance of natural law liberalism thus consists in the fact that truth, unity, and pluralism effectively form the holy triad of modern democracy (cf. Pera 2011).

9.5 In conclusion

Finally, regarding the practical feasibility of natural law liberalism in the 21st century, the following can be observed. It could be expected that, despite the trend in recent decades, there will continue to be the necessary support for at least its natural law component. This follows from its pretension to connect realistically to what is known scientifically and otherwise about the human condition. Even if faith is on the wane in the Western world, reason will remain the source of knowledge about that condition. This is evident from the natural law definition given at the beginning of this contribution.

Suppose reason equally came under pressure due to the 'second secularisation' the West has undergone since the 1960s, i.e., the loss of knowledge of classical philosophy. In that case, it is to be expected, for the same reason, that the ship will turn back at some point. Although it would go too far to elaborate on this here, history teaches us that natural law regularly revives after a storm hits. The last time was after the Second World War.

Followers of other religions, particularly Islam, as well as non-religious people, can also be receptive to the idea that the triad of truth, unity, and pluralism forms the holy trinity of modern democracy. The perceived loss of the relationship to 'truth' is a significant source of non-Western democratic criticism. As the Catholic social teaching puts it, especially in natural law thought, it is ultimately a question of an integral humanism which, in principle, can be shared by all people of 'good will'.

It may well be, therefore, that the other component of natural law liberalism, liberalism itself, faces a more uncertain future. In the end, someone like Fukuyama (2022) remains optimistic about its prospects. The publication of the book titled *Liberalism and Its Discontents*, however, already serves as a warning sign. It makes it abundantly clear that liberalism has come under pressure from the 'right' and the 'left' (due to 'progressivism').

This chapter's main recommendation is that renewed attention to the relevance of natural law for democracy is no luxury. It is a thoroughly Tocquevillian recommendation because he favoured educating people to prevent despotism. His concern was 'acquainting people with a rich cultural heritage from which they would learn the freedom of thought and personal discipline of desires as well as the habits of political participation' (Boesche 1987: 262). The particularly desired political education had to be 'education directed at the individual's relationship with society more than at the individual's self-cultivation in so far as these are distinguishable in the Aristocratic Liberal "system"' (Kahan 1987: 305).

References

Berlin, Isaiah (2002), 'John Stuart Mill and the Ends of Life', in: H. Hardy (ed.), *Liberty*, 2nd ed. Oxford: Oxford University Press, 218–251.

Bradley, Gerald V. (2017), 'Natural Law Theory and Constitutionalism', in: George Duke & Robert P. George (eds.), *The Cambridge Companion to Natural Law Jurisprudence*. Cambridge: Cambridge University Press, 397–427.

Biggar, Nigel (2020), *What's Wrong with Rights*. Oxford: Oxford University Press.

Bijsterveld, Sophie van (2021), 'Postliberalisme volgens Deneen: Aanvaarding of afwijzing van de moderne samenleving', in: Patrick Overeem & Hans-Martien ten Napel (eds.), *Het radicale midden overzee. Verkenningen van het postliberalisme*. Delft: Eburon, 83–102.

Boesche, Roger (1987), *The Strange Liberalism of Alexis de Tocqueville. Ithaca and London:* Cornell University Press.

Cartabia, M. & A. Simoncini (eds.) (2015), *Pope Benedict XVI's Legal Thought a Dialogue on the Foundation of Law*. Cambridge: Cambridge University Press.

Chaplin, Jonathan (2016), 'Liberté, Laïcité, Pluralité: Towards a Theology of Principled Pluraism', *International Journal of Public Theology* 10 (3), 354–380.

Deneen, Patrick J. (2018), *Why Liberalism Failed*. New Haven, CT: Yale University Press.

Diamond, L. (2015), 'Facing up to the Democratic Recession', *Journal of Democracy* 26 (1), 141–155.

Dreher, Rod (2020), *Live not by Lies. A Manual for Christian Dissidents.* New York City: Sentinel.

Economist Intelligence Unit (2023), *Democracy Index 2022. Frontline Democracy and the Battle for Ukraine*. London & New York: Economist Intelligence.

Foccroulle Menard, Xavier & Anna Su (2022), 'Liberalism, Catholic Integralism, and the Question of Religious Freedom', *Brigham Young University Law Review* 47 (4), 1171–1219.

Fukuyama, Francis (2022), *Liberalism and Its Discontents.* New York: MacMillan.

Harinck, George & Hans-Martien ten Napel (2013), 'Democracy: Instrument for or Expression of a Christian Political Order?', *Journal of Inter-Religious Dialogue* (11), 42–49.

Hervada, Javier (2020), *Critical Introduction to Natural Right.* 2nd English ed. Montréal: Librairie Wilson & Lafleur.

Holland, Tom (2019), *Dominion. The Making of the Western Mind.* London: Little, Brown.

Kahan, Alan S. (1987), *Aristocratic Liberalism. The Social and Political Thought of Jacob Burckhardt, John Stuart Mill, and Alexis de Tocqueville.* Chicago, Illinois: The University of Chicago ProQuest Disserations Publishing.

Kinneging, Andreas (2020), *De onzichtbare maat. Archeologie van goed en kwaad.* Amsterdam: Prometheus.

Krabbendam, Hans & Hans-Martien ten Napel (eds.) (2000), *Regulating Morality: A Comparison of the Role of the State in Mastering the Mores in the Netherlands and the United States.* Antwerp: Maklu Publishers.

Legutko, Ryszard (2016), *The Demon in Democracy. Totalitarian Temptations in Free Societies.* New York & London: Encounter Books.

Lijphart, Arend (2022; originally published in 1968), *The Politics of Accommodation Pluralism and Democracy in the Netherlands.* Berkeley Los Angeles, CA: University of California Press.

Loughlin, Martin (2022), *Against Constitutionalism.* Cambridge, MA & London, England: Harvard University Press.

Manent, P. (1996), *Tocqueville and the Nature of Democracy.* Translated by John Waggoner. Contributor Harvey Mansfield. Lanham, MD: Rowman & Littlefield.

Olsen, Glenn (2017), 'The Death of Liberal Education: Its Implications for the University, Democracy and the American Polity', *VoegelinView*, 17 November

Overeem, Patrick (2021), 'Vuurtorens en veldhospitalen: Het postliberale alternatief', in: Patrick Overeem & Hans-Martien ten Napel (eds.), *Het radicale midden overzee. Verkenningen van het postliberalisme. Delft: Eburon*, 181–197.

Overeem, Patrick & Hans-Martien ten Napel (eds.) (2021), *Het radicale midden overzee. Verkenningen van het postliberalisme.* Utrecht: Eburon.

Pabst, Adrian (2021), *Postliberal Politics. The Coming Era of Renewal.* Cambridge & Medford, MA: Polity.

Paulsen, Michael Stokes. (2013), 'The Priority of God: A Theory of Religious Liberty', Pepperdine *Law Review* 39 (5), 1159–1222.

Pera, Marcello (2011), *Why We Should Call Ourselves Christians: The Religious Roots of Free Societies.* New York & London: Encounter Books.

Pinker, Steven (2011), *The Better Angels of our Nature. Why Violence has Declined.* London: Allen Lane.

Pontifical Council for Justice and Peace (2004), 'Compendium of the Social Doctrine of the Church', https://www.vatican.va/roman_curia/pontifical_councils/justpeace/documents/rc_pc_justpeace_doc_20060526_compendio-dott-soc_en.html.

Ratzinger, Joseph Cardinal (2004), *Truth and Tolerance. Christian Belief and World Religions.* San Francisco: Ignatius Press.

Siedentop, L. (2014), *Inventing the Individual. The Origins of Western Liberalism.* London: Allen Lane.

Tanner, S.J. (2012), Norman, *Vatican II. The Essential Texts.* New York: Image.

Tocqueville, Alexis de (2006; last updated 2013) (translated by Henry Reeve) (original edition 1835-1840), *Democracy in America. The Project Gutenberg EBook:* Penguin Classics.

Tocqueville, Alexis de (2011; original edition 1835-1840), *Over de democratie in Amerika. Integrale editie met alle tekstvarianten. Vertaling door Hessel Daalder en Steven Van Luchene, bewerkt door Andreas Kinneging.* Rotterdam: Lemniscaat.

Tracz-Tryniecki, Marek (2008), 'Natural Law in Tocqueville's Thought', *Journal of Markets & Morality* 11 (1), 27–40.

Vermeule, Adrian (2022), *Common Good Constitutionalism. Recovering the Classical Legal Tradition.* Cambridge Medford, MA: Polity.

West, T.G. (2017), *The Political Theory of the American Founding: Natural Rights, Public Policy, and the Moral Conditions of Freedom.* Cambridge: Cambridge University Press.

Wolfe, Christopher (2006), *Natural Law Liberalism.* Cambridge: Cambridge University Press.

10 Tocqueville's legal spirit as a force of hope for presentist democracy

Carinne Elion-Valter

10.1 Introduction

In *Democracy in America,* Tocqueville (1805–1859) expresses his concern for democracy's future. Although it is the regime of hope for realising freedom for all, democracy might fall prey to a rush to the future or, due to a focus on petty interests, regress into a certain form of stasis, or immobilism without hope or enthusiasm. To counter these risks, Tocqueville presented inter alia the 'esprit des légistes', or the way of thinking of lawyers and the judiciary. With their conservative mind, they would have a moderating effect on democracy's desire for change and control. Tocqueville thus proposes a professional ethic and 'savoir faire' as a countertemporal balance to democracy's risk of speed and stasis. What did he mean by this esprit des légistes? To what extent was it meant as 'conservateur'? And what is its value for today's democracy? Might current democracy not ask for a more progressive way of legal thinking to bring us out of its focus on the here and now?

Today's liberal democracy resembles Tocqueville's premonition on certain points (see Section 10.4 of this chapter). It is generally considered as 'presentist', i.e., focused on the near present, with legislative and policy changes occurring at an ever higher speed. At the same time, democracy is beset by discontent because the law (or the state) does not seem able to offer hope for future challenges or even to meet expectations of legal certainty and decent administration. Legal institutions and legal thinking have come to the centre of attention of questions regarding the legitimacy of the democratic constitutional state and what it may achieve or not.

As law seems to be part of many problems of today's democracy, it might be naive to put the legal profession as a counterbalance to current democracy and its legislation. Still, I think that Tocqueville's idea of the legal mind as a counterbalance continues to be relevant, not because it is 'conservateur', but because legal thinking may be a progressive force that urges democracy to take a distance to its presentism.

This chapter critically examines the relevance of Tocqueville's ideas about the importance of legal thinking as a counterbalance to democracy from a temporal perspective. To this end, the chapter first sets out Tocqueville's ideas regarding

DOI: 10.4324/9781032641041-10

the temporal dimension of democracy and 'l'esprit des légistes' (Sections 10.1 and 10.2). Then it will turn to the temporal dimension of liberal democracy of today and to what extent legal thinking is implied in this (Sections 10.3 and 10.4). Finally, it will show how legal thinking nowadays acts as a counterbalance to democracy in response to calls for legal hope (Section 10.5).

My reflections will be theoretical and take an external critical perspective on the temporal aspects of law and democracy. The chapter makes use of ideas developed by K. Mannheim's utopian temporalities (Mannheim 1954), the regimes of historicity as developed by the French historian François Hartog (Hartog 2003), and François Ost's analysis of Time and Law (Ost 1999).

10.2 Tocqueville, antimodern or postmodern?

10.2.1 Tocqueville's pessimism about democracy

Tocqueville wrote his *Democracy in America* over a period of several years. The second part was published five years after the first part. Between those two parts, there is a notable change of tone. In the first part, the tone is one of rather cool analysis. Tocqueville acknowledges that democracy, as the regime of equality (in the sense of the absence of classes), can endanger individual liberty. Democracy hurries to the future where the promise of progress beckons. He points to several societal forces that should slow down this hurry to the future. They should protect democratic man against the 'unreasonable pretense to know and to change everything' (Tocqueville 1981: 37 [my translation, CEV]; 'Foreword').

The second part of *Democracy in America* is marked by overtones of concern, if not a feeling of the tragic condition of democracy. 'A more detailed examination of the subject and five years of new meditations have not diminished my fears, but have changed my focus' (Tocqueville 2004, 2:4; 6.816). Democracy will not disappear anymore, Tocqueville predicts, but may turn into a benevolent despotism of the administrative state. The administrative state will cover society with a dense network of rules. People will accept these rules since they are foremost occupied by their petty interests and daily concerns. With this despotism of rules, the futuristic orientation of democracy will change into a certain stasis or immobilism. It is a rather permanent situation of instability in which change has no direction and the spirit gets tired (Tocqueville 2004, 2:3; 13.626) and there reigns a certain indifference (Tocqueville 2004, 2:3; 17.639). Nevertheless, the longing for freedom will not disappear but will find its way in a tendency to popular sovereignty, prone to irresponsible decisions in which new leaders pretend to speak in the name of an absent and inattentive crowd.

10.2.2 **L'esprit conservateur des légistes**

To prevent this downward slide of democracy from liberty to equality without a future, Tocqueville proposes several counterforces. Among these are civil associations, participation in local government, a free press, a wise legislator who will respect citizens' rights, and the 'conservative mind of the legal profession', *l'esprit conservateur des légistes.* By their love of forms, of chains of reasoning, and of a certain practical wisdom, the *légistes* are naturally opposed to the *esprit révolutionnaire* and the 'unreflected passions of democracy', to both the 'hard and soft despotism' that democracy may turn into (Tocqueville 2004, 1:2; 8.308; see Yellott 1993: 105).

By these traits, the legal spirit may purify democracy's morality and temper its passions and activism. It may offer the blind instincts of an inexperienced democracy some practical knowledge and temper the will of its government by drawing attention to concrete circumstances and time and place (cf. Coutel 2004: 131). Due to their temperance and insight, the *légistes* can protect democracy against its extremes. On one hand, the feverish democratic revolutionary spirit that, guided by abstract and mathematical principles, repeatedly wants to redesign society from scratch without paying attention to the right moment. On the other hand, the legal mind may protect democracy against the bureaucratic obsession with the regulation of private interests and administrative execution. The legal spirit will remind democracy of the revolutionary principles of freedom and equality with which democracy all started.

Sharing an *esprit de corps* the *légistes* may form a 'hardly noticeable power' (Wolin 2001: 223) and fulfil a function comparable to that of the aristocracy under the *Ancien Régime.* As a result of the jury system and participation in local government, this spirit would even extend to the whole of society. Civil participation in legal affairs may contribute to a broadly shared application of legal habits and turns of mind related to public affairs.

10.2.3 Two approaches to legal thinking

How should we qualify Tocqueville's *esprit des légistes?* Superficially read, Tocqueville's ideas might call into mind the famous court drawings of Honoré Daumier of lawyers and judges gesticulating in court and fighting over textual and procedural details. Indeed, at first sight, Tocqueville's *esprit des légistes* more or less corresponds to what today is called legal thinking or legal method. This rather formal way of thinking is featured by a procedural outlook (Tocqueville's 'love of forms'), respect for legal and authoritative sources, argumentation from rules, well-defined concepts, and facts (the *légistes* love of chains of reasoning) and practical knowledge. According to Schauer, legal thinking distinguishes itself from other professional thought by counterintuitively persisting in these matters (Schauer 2009: 7). It is generally seen as a way of thinking that stresses a methodical approach, supported by clear and logical argumentation and sound method. Below it will appear that the understanding of legal thinking as logical argumentation fits well with the approach of law as an object of legal science and an instrument of utilitarianist policy.

However, read into the historical context, Tocqueville's vision on legal thinking does not so much correspond to this formalist and rationalist vision. It should be understood as having a broader meaning with more fundamental implications drawing upon legal thinking as an epistemology and a body of thought. Call it legal thought, as in *la pensée juridique*. More than argumentation, it is the ability to deal with incompletely theorised concepts and the gap between general rules and concrete facts supported by concrete legal experience. More than pure knowledge of legal sources (case law, statutes, royal edicts, and so forth), it comprises an epistemology of interpretation, informed by social experience, a sense of institutional and political sensibility and rhetorical prowess. It is conservative by being able to integrate tradition and development. The roots of this critical and interpretivist tradition of legal thought go back to the *scientia juris* developed in the Middle Ages (see Baranger 2018: 263–290). *La pensée juridique* allowed law to be the specific expression of Western culture, the central nervous system of a civilisation that considered itself as supported by law (Grossi 1988: 426). In other words, legal thinking was crucial for law as the legal scaffolding or *échafaudage* by which man instituted himself (Legendre 2017: 145 ff.), the core *Texte normatif* of a *civilisation en marche*.

A short review of the historical context of *l'esprit des légistes* shows that Tocqueville's legal spirit stands more in this interpretivist tradition than in the formal tradition of legal thinking. It is primarily as such that it could be relevant for today's democracy.

10.2.4 Search for a new aristocracy and an understanding of history

This interpretivist understanding of Tocqueville's legal mind is supported by the historical context of his thoughts and his own 'method' of developing ideas. First, his légistes are not just about reigning in democracy by clear method and love of rules, but by a certain mentality. Tocqueville's 'aristocracy of the bench and the bar' (Wolin 2001: 230) very much reflects the 19th-century debate on the position of aristocracy in the new democracy. Tocqueville's *légistes* were his answer to the search for *la nouvelle aristocratie*. The question he and his contemporaries were struggling with was whether democracy needs an intermediary class that would guarantee proper government and prevent egalitarian democracy from making bad decisions and be able to appease the lower classes. Other than the liberal Guizot, Tocqueville did not believe in reinstalling a constitutional aristocracy constituted by a property-based census (Jaume 2006: 974) but sought the solution in a translation of functions formerly fulfilled by the aristocracy. In *L'Ancien Régime et la Révolution*, he praised the energetic love of freedom of the French 'noblesse' of feudal times (Tocqueville 1866: Chapter 11, 115 & Chapter 12, 124 ff.; cf. Compagnon 2005: 33), their respect for tradition, rules, hierarchy, and norms of propriety, and dislike of popular actions (*les actions de la multitude*) and popular government (Jaume 2006: 971). Thus, Tocqueville's own aristocracy functioned as a model for the professional ethic of America's *noblesse de robe*.

Second, Tocqueville's doubts about the future of democracy reflect the 19th-century philosophical debate in society and literature over the sense of history after the French Revolution. In line with this, the conservatism of the legal mind comes forward as a matter of historical awareness, not as nostalgia for times past. Tocqueville and his contemporaries were in search of new ways of understanding the relation between past, present, and future, or in historiographic terms, a regime of historicity (Hartog 2003). A 'regime of historicity' refers to how a society relates to the past, present, and future, in short, what historical frame or orientation is dominant in a certain time. These frames of temporal understanding shift depending on the experience of the present and the changing, sometimes receding, then again nearing horizon of expectation, a horizon that is laden with hope, fear, wish, and desire (Koselleck 2004; see also Bantigny 2013: Parts IV and V). In the 19th century, the past as the primal guide for action (*Historia magistra*) was overruled by the future. This shift of temporal horizon left those doubting about the boons of the future in search of new anchors. Take, for instance, Flaubert's novel *L'Éducation Sentimentale*. It analyses the loss of hope to realise ideals, even the loss of ideals themselves (cf. Calvino 2002: 45). This emptiness or lack of purpose also concerns the law. Frédéric, Flaubert's protagonist, is a lawyer who excels in an empty use of words. He is a walking warning sign against the potential wordiness and emptiness of law and legal thinking, which have lost touch with their tradition (Weisberg 1984).

Tocqueville stands out by his specific contribution to this debate. Other than Chateaubriand, who in *Atala* presented the American *sauvages* as having wisdom comparable to that of the Greek and Roman Ancients, Tocqueville lucidly accepted times have changed. The examples of the *Ancien Régime* will not illuminate the present and the future anymore. The light will inevitably have to come from the future, although this future is still unknown (Hartog 2003: 96). Instead of reaching back to the past or reaching over to some idealised future, Tocqueville seeks to reinterpret the past and the present. He distils democratic elements in the *Ancien Régime* and feudal elements in democracy (Wolin 2001: 230). By this functional translation of aristocratic values into those of the legal profession, Tocqueville constructs not a historical, nor futuristic, but a transhistorical account of the passing of time. Similarly, the lawyer's conservative mindset is not *passéiste* nor futurist or presentist, but transhistorical.

Transhistoricity essentially means that some phenomenon, for instance, a myth, retains its persuasive force through different historical periods. In the context of art theory and literary theory, the concept refers to the fact that artworks and literary works have different meanings in different times while retaining their value (Setari 2018: 27) thanks to an intertemporal dialogue (Bal 2018). This guarantees their subsistence and continued value over time. Likewise, Tocqueville does not present the former aristocratic values as 'classic' ones that everybody should hold on to forever but stresses their continuous relevance for future times accepting they will need a retranslation. In fact, he assigned his *légistes* the noble task of safeguarding law as the nervous system of a now democratic civilisation.

10.2.5 A precursor of postmodernity

Because of Tocqueville's scepticism about the promises of democracy, he is frequently taken to be a conservative or an *Antimoderne* in the tradition of Burke (cf. Compagnon 2005: 64). In that line, *l'esprit des légistes* can be easily taken as a love of method and moderation serving conservatism. However, considering Tocqueville's functionalist translation of aristocratic values into legal values, it is defensible to qualify him as a precursor of postmodern attempts to rephrase the supposedly linear progression from the past to the future. The esprit conservateur des légistes indicates the countertemporal function of legal thinking in relation to the temporality of democracy. Consequently, the *esprit des légistes* may also be progressive in order to safeguard the civilising function of law.

10.2.6 A call for retranslation

Can legal thinking still act as a countertemporal force against current democracy's propensity for rush or immobilism? What does it entail if legal thinking is taken as a potentially progressive force to safeguard law as the Normative Text that it always was? In other words, can we again make a translation of Tocqueville's ideas to our era just as he did with his noble tradition? For this, we must analyse current democracy's relation to time and see how legal thinking has been involved in this.

I will proceed by briefly reviewing the time horizons of present democracy (Section 10.3) and how these relate to law and legal thinking (Section 10.4). It will appear that law and the legal mind have been instrumental to current democracy's relation to time. Law has provided hope for justice to come but also contributed to the presentism of today's democracy. At the same time, presentist democracy has instrumentalised law in such a way as to make it almost unrecognisable as law (Section 10.4). After exploring the temporality of present democracy and the role of legal thinking, Section 10.5 will review some current demands made upon the legal mind for providing some legal hope and explore what conception of legal thinking is implied by this call to legal thinking to provide justice.

10.3 Temporalities of democracy

10.3.1 Democracy as the regime of hope

From a political perspective, democracy is generally taken as the government by men for men. From a cultural and temporal perspective, however, democracy is primarily the regime of the forward-looking gaze, of hope and human desire. It is not willed by some external power, as Tocqueville's reference to Providence sometimes seems to suggest, nor the result of an emulation of times past as was the regime of historicity of the *Ancien Régime*. Instead, democracy is a human and willed invention. Democracy implies a future-orientated perspective intent on realising human will (*voluntas*) by men. This forward-looking thrust is part of human time. It is not a matter of prophecy that 'transgresses the bounds of calculable experience', but of prognosis (Koselleck 2004: 18). Democracy is not a matter of revealed truth. It does not position itself outside time, like a theocracy. Democracy believes that truth is something to be reached by rational means and discovered while 'doing' democracy inside human time.

As government *for* men, democracy is trusted to bring some good to men in general, not the gods or one class or one ruler. What this 'good' is, depends on the horizon taken. Below I will expand on the main horizons or utopian mentalities of democracy. Democracy is therefore a carrier of hope and expectations. However, as a government *by* men and as a regime of the human will within limited possibilities, democracy is also very much a regime of disappointment. As the future will forever recede before the present and the past cannot be brought back, democracy can also turn into a regime of despair when this temporal situation is not accepted, and time is experienced as closed (cf. Marcel 1951: 61). Due to this inbuilt disappointment and despair, democracy is the regime of change, if not instability.

10.3.2 Utopian hopes and expectations

The various versions of democratic hope are manifest in the temporal horizons connected to visions of what kind of 'good' a democracy should provide. The German sociologist K. Mannheim grouped these temporal orientations into various utopian mentalities (Mannheim 1954). In *Ideology and Utopia,* he distinguishes four orientations – chiliast, liberal, socialist, and conservatist. It is important to note that the terms 'conservative', 'socialist', and 'liberal' must be taken as ideal types, not as political categories that correspond to some political party.

The chiliastic millennialist mentality is intent on realising a revealed truth attainable by way of extreme devotion. The mentality can be present in spiritual communities or in groups promoting revolutionary action intent on realising an unmediated truth, such as anarchism. The liberal mentality reacts to the disappointment of unworldly ideals that tend to neglect individual value. The liberal mentality is guided by the hope to realise the principles and ideals of liberty and individual autonomy in the future. It appeals to the faith that one day these principles will be realised, thereby embracing a temporality of the *longue durée* and a historicity of the future. Since these liberal principles are abstract and cannot be realised as they seem to promise, disappointment or despair will arise. This may lead to a change in temporal focus and a new utopia. The socialist mentality translates these liberal principles of freedom and equality into material and concrete expectations to be met within a foreseeable time span. The socialist mentality embraces the *courte durée* and the historicity of the present. Since the future will continue to recede and expectations can still not be met as forecasted (even less than principles), this 'socialist' utopia almost certainly leads to disappointment and frustration, inviting a cycle of new promises and enhanced control, supported by technocratic and/ or authoritarian means.

Another reaction to the disappointment about liberalist abstract hopes or socialist unfulfilled expectations is delivered by the conservative mentality. Weary of lofty principles or unkept technological promises, this fourth mentality may be present in attitudes that promote moderation and organic change and may call to religion for further legitimacy, since religion may fulfil a mediating role between utopianism, fatalism, or millennialism in reaction to secular mentalities that were not able to hold up to their utopian promises (see Chapter 2). In its extreme, conservatism may be sourced by anti-intellectualist and activist desires to revive the past, sometimes imagined as a Golden Age (Mannheim 1954: 197–236). A final escape from democracy's disappointments may be offered by stepping out of democratic time altogether and fleeing into dreams of an unmediated future in the hands of technology and artificial intelligence (such as promoted by transhumanism), dreams that may be chiliast in a new cloak.

10.3.3 To conclude

This brief overview of utopian mentalities shows that liberal and 'socialist' democracy is closely connected to various kinds of hope and despair: Hope as faith in some abstract promises for the future, hope as expectation in reaching some nearby goals, and hope as a rather unreflective desire for escape towards something thought perfect, be it the Golden Past or some spiritual or technological heaven. It is important to notice that like each of these 'utopias', democratic and liberal ideals may turn into a self-legitimising ideology. Although societies need ideologies or doxa for direction, empty ideologies turn into mere myths, replacing hope with wordiness that leads to closure and, at the end, unfounded because of undisputable and arbitrary power (Ricoeur 1986: 426). In Section 10.5, it will appear that legal thinking is crucial to prevent democratic promises of justice from becoming empty words.

10.4 Presentism of today's democracy

10.4.1 Time compressed

After this general picture of the temporalities of democracy, it is time to cast an eye on the temporality of today's democracy. After this, we can explore the question of what role legal thinking has played in this temporality and whether it may still be able to function as a counterforce to democracy's time.

As premonished by Tocqueville, present democracy is primarily focused on the here and now. Mannheim's dynamic of utopian mentalities helps to understand why. Stimulated by the wish to realise popular demands and ideals of social justice and influenced by modern scientific thinking, democracy has changed from the regime of possibility to a regime of continuous legislative and policy change supported by technocratic and procedural control. This regime of control is turned into itself and hides the long-term future and past from sight. In society, progress has been replaced by speed, for which the purpose is contingent (Sutherland 2014). In its economic aspects, current democracy stands out by its reproducibility and availability (Cantor 2000: 114). Uneven accessibility raises new expectations for social-economic compensation, thereby enhancing the need for control.

Current time is regulated by measurable clock time and closely regulated procedural steps. However, although the past and the future are compressed into a present without clear direction, and science has shown the relativity of time, democracy still holds on to ideas of linear development. It continues to follow a conception of time as an arrow (Tanake 2019: 43 ff.). Time is supposed to advance in a purified way, without there being a narrative space to understand the meaning of this arrow of time (Latour 1997: 40–41). Continuous change without any narrative to direct it leads to a closure of perspective. So, present democracy seems to live in a continuous present with uncertain borders. It has lost connection with its past and its future, while not being able to think itself clear from the future.

Meanwhile, our present time is very fond of the past. Museums, places of remembrance, and the wish to protect patrimony are witnesses to that. In fact, these places of remembrance and museums are foremost citations. Compared to their active symbolic life of before, the paintings, churches, and cenotaphs are like copies of what they stood for when still in function. They are, as Hartog says, signs of a past that is set apart from the present and has lost its power to provide meaning to the present (Hartog 2003: 141–142, 146). There is a 'presentism of the past'.

All in all, modern democracy is more presentist and less synchronised than Tocqueville might ever have imagined. As explained in Section 10.1, he proposed the conservative spirit of the legal profession's way of thinking as a counterbalance to the downward slide of democratic liberty. The question to address now is whether legal thinking met his expectation (or hope)? How are law and legal thinking involved in today's presentism?

10.4.2 Role of law and legal thinking in democracy's temporalities

Law and ideals of justice have been instrumental in formulating as well as in frustrating these liberal hopes and 'socialist' expectations. The liberal temporality of the future is rooted in ideals of justice and equality. They found their way in fundamental rights and basic principles of law, intent on protecting the individual against the power of the collective and the authority of the state. Social rights and the extended regulation of the welfare state aim to translate the liberal hopes into tangible 'socialist' safeguards of freedom and equality for all. Law has thus been deeply involved in creating and entertaining liberal hopes and 'socialist' expectations. Law provided the future-orientated gaze of democracy a sense and meaning but also changed it into a myopic obsession with rules and results.

The legal involvement in these hopes and expectations is backed up by philosophical and theoretical stances. Modern philosophy and modern science have presented these promises of law and justice as eternal truths, although these hopes and expectations are infused with historicity. Legal positivism and formalist visions on the legitimacy of legal institutions and legal thinking tend to deny the temporal modality of law (cf. Longo 2021: 4). Legal realist visions on law (in shorthand, law is valid once it is considered as such) tend to put law into time as a neutral and inert object that can be instrumentalised at will. In short, in their search for indubitable reason, philosophy, science, and doctrinal legal thinking have set law *outside* time, first by imagining it being universal and eternal, and later, with the onset of positivist science, as something utterly neutral.

10.4.3 Instrumentalisation of law

So, as supposedly eternal or neutral, law has been instrumental in the various utopias of democracy. At the same time, the positivist and scientific approach of law and legal thinking have contributed to the 'de-temporalisation' and instrumentalisation of law for utilitarian and voluntarist purposes. Law has thus been deeply involved in as well as affected by the current presentist state of democracy, in such a way that the hope for justice, redress, and tangible equality is frustrated or even becomes meaningless.

As to legal thinking, under the influence of presentist democracy, it has been restricted to a utilitarian rationality. Legislation and regulation are for an important part instrumental in realising goals tied to social rights. The regulatory state we live in features a dense network of rules, including soft law, issued by overlapping legal orders (international regulatory bodies, national, and regional regulatory bodies). Besides being layered, this regulation is intensely procedural. Regulating bodies set out the steps lower regulating bodies must take in order to realise preset policy goals (Westerman 2018). Enforcement is frequently reached by seducing citizens to follow the law based on utilitarian and rationalist considerations to follow the law for profit. Finally, as legislation is tied to societal needs, legislation changes frequently. There is an acceleration of law and the legislative process that affects the rule of law guarantees of legality, consistency, and demands of proper legislation in a negative way (Rosa 2018: 73; Van Klink 2018: 33). In sum, in the context of current presentist democracy, law and legislation have turned procedural, utilitarian, and rationalist and focused on providing the practical needs of today's society. Disengaged from liberal hopes and principles, legislation falls short of providing democracy a temporal self-understanding. Law's time becomes just an accident without connection to the unconditional character of time as well to change (cf Nancy 2019: 30). It has turned ahistorical, leaving the present without sense and the future without hope (see also Chapter 9).

Referring to Tocqueville, we can conclude that current law stresses and enlarges primarily the logical and systematic aspects of legal thinking that Tocqueville presented as valuable. Legal thinking has been instrumental and instrumentalised in cutting the present loose from the future. It threatens to make the promise of law meaningless. Is it then still possible for legal thinking to function as a temporal counterforce to presentist democracy? Below, it will appear that the answer is positive but not in the conservative direction as Tocqueville imagined it.

10.5 Calls for hope

We are now in the rather absurd situation that democracy still believes in development, following some arrow of time mythology, while it is directed by a rather fixed structure and subject to utilitarian considerations. In other words: blind development is guided by ahistorical principles. How could Tocqueville's idea of legal thinking as a counterforce to democratic rush or inertia be realistic? Still, some current developments show that law and legal thinking are able to help democratic society step outside this presentism without perspective. I provide three examples of legal thinking as a temporal counterforce to current democratic presentism and utilitarianism. I can only sketch these developments roughly.

10.5.1 A plea for re-integration of the past, the long term, and a slower pace

My first example regards the relation between *the present and the past.* Debates about slavery and colonialism challenge the experience and meaning of historical events that happened centuries ago and invite reflection upon law's role in the scaffolding of Western civilisation. Recognition of the legal relevance of past events such as slavery invites reflection on a divided past. Redefinition of shared history (Immler 2021: 3 ff.) calls legal categories such as statutes of limitations (5, 10, or 20 years) into question. Reparatory justice (material compensation of damage and harm) and restorative justice (restoration of the dignity of both offenders and victims) address a long-term past. The enhancement of civic justice through participation and inclusion in society and socioeconomic justice ask for a long-term vision of the future (Immler 2021: 4, referring to Laplante 2013). These calls for transformative justice cannot be met by a positivist and materialist perspective of monetary expectations but ask for a perspective intent on providing hope. In other words, this transformative justice breaks through the walls of presentism by calling into question the fixed time limits and the fixed order between past, present, and future. By reconsidering existing legal concepts and inventing new ones, legal thinking is actively acting as a counterforce to a presentist mentality.

A second instance of legal thinking as a counterforce to presentist temporality relates to *time scales.* Due to a heightened awareness of the long-term consequences of our present economic system, legal thinking has to integrate nature's time in human time. The development in thinking about economic value asks for a fundamental reflection on fixed legal categories such as property, the division between private and public, the responsibility of private companies, legal subjectivity, and the legal person. The concept of rights of nature (see rightsofnaturetribunal.org) illustrates this. A country like Ecuador has codified such a right in its constitution, which allows for claims made by the Indigenous population against threats of environmental damage (cf. Knauss 2018). In other cases, specific parts of nature are allowed legal personhood, which makes it possible for the population to act on behalf of it. New Zealand Maori managed to get their river recognised as a legal person (Kramm 2020). Dutch case law such as the Urgenda climate case[1] and Vereniging Milieudefensie *v* Royal Dutch Shell[2] demonstrate the capacity of judicial legal thought to mediate existing law and new demands for justice, thereby extending existing understandings of tort and responsibility.

A third instance of reconsidering legal temporality regards *tempo and timing* and relates to concepts of slow democracy and slow law. Slow democracy focuses on participatory democracy and the improvement of local government and democratic legitimacy (see, e.g., Clark & Teachout 2012). Slow law focuses on the right pace of legislative change and on deregulation. In a certain way, legislation must be slow to be legitimate because it has to be coherent, congruent with societal developments, and feasible (Van Klink 2018). Slowness, however, is not a matter of lagging behind societal developments. It is foremost a matter of adequate temporal tuning and finding the right pace for legislative change. As the examples regarding the reconsideration of the past and the human time scale show, it can be necessary that law is ahead of society. In this way, it can stimulate the development of future social norms or reinforce emerging social norms as in the rights of nature that I just mentioned. This implies the ability of legal thinking to distil and formulate norms that are implicit in the current interaction (Van Klink 2018: 49).[3]

10.5.2 The need for legal countertemporality

These examples show how legal thinking is involved in inventing new legal concepts that allow us to transcend presentism. Legal thinking is involved in relating past, present, and future, integrating nature's time in human law and tuning into societal development. By this transhistorical and transtemporal activity, the legal mind acts as a countertemporal force against current democracy's presentism and law's purported ahistoricity. With this, legal thinking allows law to continue to fulfil its function of 'scaffolding' societal development and to provide hope.

1 Dutch Supreme Court, dd December 20, 2019, ECLI:NL:HR:2019:2006; version in English: ECLI:NL:HR:2019:2007.

2 Court of Justice, The Hague, dd May 26, 2021, ECLI:NL:RBDHA:2021:5337; version in English: ECLI:NL:RBDHA:2021:5339.

3 An example is also the regulation of parenthood by creating overlapping forms of parental authority that meet societal developments.

To give form to this forward-looking inventivity, legal thinking draws upon features that are part of the tradition of legal thought and the *scientia juris* as I set out before with regard to Tocqueville's *esprit des légistes*. To mediate written law and calls for justice, the legal mind has to deal with incompletely theorised concepts, manage the gap between general rules and concrete facts, and draw up concrete legal experience and case law. Since existing legal categories do not offer solutions, legal thinking must resort to interpretation and show rhetorical prowess to handle institutional and political sensibility. Daumier's jurists are definitely in tune with modern times and demonstrate how legal thinking is still able to act as a counterforce to democracy's presentism and, even stronger, to revitalise hope and faith in ideals of justice.

10.6 The transhistoricity of legal thinking

10.6.1 Integration of past, present, and future

How to envision this countertemporality from a theoretical perspective? Ost's analysis *Le temps du droit* is of value to see how these examples fit into the inherent transhistoricity of legal thought (Ost 1999). First, law binds the future by legitimising promises and instituting trust (Ost 1999: 157). In this way, law makes time productive and provides sense and meaning to legal relationships. As we saw, law is not merely a cure for short-term problems, but a reflection of a promise for the long-term future. In other words, the bindingness of law is meant to keep the future open for future generations, not closing it off from hope. Likewise, legal thinking does not think backwards but forwards. The calls for, for example, rights of nature, illustrate the relevance of this.

Law also works in other temporal directions than the future. It allows the present to relate to the past (Ost 1999: 39), allowing the past to be freed from the present. For instance, law activates memory by codifying custom and tradition, allows a revindication of lost property, or legitimises a fine or sanction for torts or crimes committed in the past. Interpretation prevents the law from becoming a frozen memory, set apart from society's present. The relevance of this liberation of the past is demonstrated by the calls for a reconsideration of colonialism or slavery. Restorative and transformative justice opens up the past for revision and creates hope for a new future. Still, law also frees the present *from* the past by offering the possibility of forgiveness and pardon (Ost 1999: 111). Forgiveness prevents the present from staying in the grips of the past and provides hope for reinterpreting the past.

10.6.2 Themis, Nomos, *and* Dikè, *straddling different temporal dimensions of law*

The above shows the capacity of law and legal thinking to straddle past, present, and future and its ability to mediate the several time scales of law, their transhistoricity and transtemporality. With this, it might be better to replace the Daumier-like figures of Tocqueville's *esprit des légistes* with a more transhistorical imagery. In fact, Greek thought attributed these temporal dimensions of law to different goddesses: *Themis*, *Eunomia*, and *Dikè*,[4] and shows they are interrelated.

Themis symbolises the long range of presumably untouchable laws, given by the gods, nature, or some other source not subject to human voluntarism. Themis' law is in a certain way 'impresent' and outside time. It is a hidden law. In today's world, we find aspects of Themis' law in legal ideals and principles, institutional arrangements, and constitutional law. They are open to interpretation and may conflict with each other.

As 'impresent' and outside time, Themis' law has to be instantiated and revealed by a more concrete manifestation of law. *Nomos* (cf. *Eunomia)* refers to manmade law as part of custom and legislation. Related to the actual world, nomos refers to legislation and regulation, but also to customs and social practices. Cover's treatment of the laws of traditional religious communities shows that *nomoi* have always been negotiations with the purported immutable laws of the past (Cover 1982). They stand in a symbolic relation to Themis' law and make these principles present, although never in a finite or perfect form. So, the ideal dimension of law does not imply that it is immutable, only that its meaning is hidden and awaits translation (cf White 1999). This demands legislative imagination, not only reference to existing legal framework. The 'rights of nature' are instances of this legislative imagination.

For this translation of Themis into Eunomia, however, active judicial interpretation and legislative imagination are necessary. Hidden and manmade law still consists of general rules that have to be interpreted in light of specific circumstances. *Dikè* refers to legal thinking in action and the art of judgment. *Dikè* may take the cloak of a judge, but in fact also the role of the legislative. As conscientious legislator, she will refrain from enacting laws that are not feasible, or normatively or politically incongruent with higher law, thereby preventing legitimacy from turning into an empty myth. As honest judge, she is able to withstand unfounded expectations to uphold laws she does not think fair in order to entertain hope for justice. In both cases, she is alert at the right moment. It is where legal thinking as analysed previously, is working most visibly. It is inside time and connects Themis' law with changing *nomos*. *Dikè* is very much aware of the fact that law only gets meaning when it is interpreted and enacted. *Dikè* or the art of judgment is crucial for entertaining hope in the legal system. She is capable of explaining her judgments in such a way that even when one does not have one's day in court, one stills keeps faith that one day justice will be done. So *Dikè* also represents the hope of procedural justice.

In short, legal thinking is much more than rationality and formality, argumentation, and procedural awareness. When we reconnect legal thinking with

4 *Eunomia* and *Dikè* are, together with *Eirene* (peace), the daughters of Zeus and Themis.

its tradition of legal thought, it appears as transhistorical and transtemporal. It is of the past without being *passéiste*, of the present without being presentist, and of the future without being futurist. This transhistoricity and transtemporality of legal thinking are essential for legal thinking to function as a countertemporal force against the presentism of current democracy and its short-term result-orientated regulation. The examples provided earlier show how important this countertemporality of legal thinking is in order to uphold hope and trust in legal institutions. As the concepts of transformative justice, rights of nature, and slow law show, legal thinking can invent new words to give footing to new hopes and thereby safeguard the belief in law, since, in the end, law is like time. Just as with time, we have to live with law as being there and change at the same time (cf. Nancy 2021: 30). The Greek goddesses witness this congruence of change and stability.

10.7 Conclusion

So, Tocqueville's idea of the legal mind as a counterbalance to democracy's inertia or rush to the future is still of value. However, just as Tocqueville did with his own aristocratic tradition, his ideas also ask for translation into a form that fits present circumstances. As premonished by Tocqueville, current democracy suffers from a combination of speed and stasis. Other than he thought (hoped), current democracy is not focused on the future but is thoroughly presentist. Obsessed with meeting socioeconomic expectations, it cannot provide hope. Law has been instrumental in this presentism, allowing it to be subsequently instrumentalised. Sourced by belief in its supposedly universal and perennial validity, law founded the liberal and socialist hopes for freedom and equality. However, under the influence of positivism and utilitarianism, it has been thought of as a neutral inert instrument to serve presentist democracy's utilitarianism and need for technocratic control.

New calls for transformative law, broadening of rights, and finetuning the tempo of law and legislation challenge this presentism of current law and democracy. They call for an integration of the past into the future and a reframing of principles of law. Hopes that formerly were projected upon some ideal future, subjecting everything in its wake, or on the near present, legitimating every means of control, or on the past, ignoring even the passing of time, must now be set in an adaptation of law to new time scales. Legal thinking is called to act as a countertemporal force and to support and strengthen these signs of hope. It is called to historicise and futurise the present.

For this, legal thinking can fall back on its tradition of legal thought, an epistemology that is proper to law, the *pensée juridique*. As *scientia juris*, legal thinking acted as the scaffolding of a *civilisation en marche* supported by insight into legal experience, the art of interpretation, and practical wisdom. It is upon legal thinking to pick up this venerable tradition again. *L'esprit des légistes* needed today is not *conservateur* but progressive in dialogue with time.

References

Bal, M. (2018), 'Towards a Relational Inter-Temporality', in: E. Wittocx et al. (eds.), *The Transhistorical Museum* (Amsterdam: Valiz; co-production of Frans Hals Museum Haarlem & M-Museum Leuven) 48–63.

Bantigny, L. (2013), 'Historicities of the Twentieth Century', *Vingtième Siècle, Revue d'histoire* 117 (1), 13–25.

Baranger, D. (2018), *Penser la loi, Essai sur le législateur des temps modernes* (Paris: Gallimard).

Calvino, I. (2002), 'Nature et histoire dans le roman', in: Idem, *Tourner* la page (Paris: Gallimard) 35–63.

Cantor, P. (2000), 'Postmodern Prophet: Tocqueville Visits Vegas', *Journal of Democracy* 11 (1), 111–118.

Clark, S. & W. Teachout (2012), *Slow Democracy: Rediscovering Community, Bringing Decisions Making Back Home* (White River Junction, VT: Chelsea Green Publishing). See also: slowdemocracy.org.

Compagnon, A. (2005), *Les Antimodernes, de Joseph de Maistre à Roland Bartes* (Paris: Gallimard).

Cover, R. (1982), 'Nomos and Narrative, the Supreme Court 1982 Term', *Harvard Law Review* 94 (3), 4–68.

Coutel, C. (2004), '"L'esprit légiste" chez Alexis de Tocqueville', *The Tocqueville Review* 25 (2), 127–137.

Grossi, P. (1988), 'Pensée juridique', in: A.J. Arnaud (ed.), *Dictionnaire encyclopédique de théorie et de sociologie du droit* (Paris: LGDJ & Story Scientia) 426–428.

Hartog, F. (2003), *Régimes d'historicité, Présentisme et expérience du temps* (Paris: Éditions du Seuil).

Immler, N.L. (2021), 'What is meant by "Repair" when Claiming Reparations for Colonial Wrongs? Transformative Justice for the Dutch Slavery Past', *Esclavages & Post-esclavages* 5, 1–25.

Jaume, L. (2006), 'Tocqueville face au thème de la 'nouvelle aristocratie', *Revue française de science politique* 56 (6), 969–983.

Klink, B. Van (2018), 'Law at the Right Time: A Plea for Slow Law in Hasty Times', in: L. Corrias & L. Francot (eds.), *Temporal Boundaries of Law and Politics* (London & New York: Routledge) 33–53.

Koselleck, Reinhart (2004), 'Modernity and the Planes of Historicity', in: R. Koselleck (ed.), *Futures Past. On the Semantics of Historical Time* (New York: Columbia University Press) 9–25.

Knauss, S. (2018), 'Conceptualizing Human Stewardship in the Anthropocene: The Rights of Nature in Ecuador, New Zealand and India', *Journal of Agricultural and Environmental Ethics* 31, 703–722.

Kramm, M. (2020), 'When a River Becomes a Person', *Journal of Human Development and Capabilities* 21 (4), 307–319.

Laplante, L.J. (2013), 'The Plural Justice Aims of Reparations', in: S. Buckley-Zistel et al. (eds.), *Transitional Justice Theories* (London: Routledge) 67–84.

Latour, B. (1997), *Nous n'avons jamais été moderne, Essai d'anthropologie symétrique* (Paris: La Découverte).

Legendre, P. (2017), *Leçons X, Dogma: Instituer l'animal humain, Chemins réitérés de questionnement* (Paris: Fayard).

Longo, E. (2021), 'Time and Law in the Post-COVID-19 Era: The Usefulness of Experimental Law', *Law and Method*, September, 1–21.

Mannheim, K. (1954), *Ideology and Utopia* (New York: Harcourt, Brace & Co).

Marcel, G. (1951), *Homo Viator, Introduction to a Metaphysic of Hope* (Chicago: Henry Regnery Company).

Nancy, J.L. (2021), 'L'accident et la saison', in: J-Chr. Bailly (ed.), *Voir le temps venir* (Paris: Bayard) 27–55.

Ost, Fr. (1999), *Le temps du droit* (Paris: Odile Jacob).

Rosa, H. (2018), 'Airports Built on Shifting Grounds? Social acceleration and the Temporal Dimension of Law', in: L. Corrias & L. Francot (eds.), *Temporal Boundaries of Law and Politics* (London & New York: Routledge) 73–88.

Ricoeur, P. (1986), 'L'Idéal et l'utopie: deux expressions de l'imaginaire social', in: Idem., *Du Texte à l'Action* (Paris: Seuil) 417–433.

Schauer, F. (2009), *Thinking Like a Lawyer, A New Introduction to Legal Reasoning* (Cambridge, MA: Harvard University Press).

Setari, N. (2018), 'Notes on Transhistoricity', in: E. Wittocx et al. (eds.), *The Transhistorical Museum* (Amsterdam: Valiz co-production of Frans Hals Museum Haarlem & M-Museum Leuven) 22–37.

Sutherland, Th. (2014), 'Getting Nowhere Fast: A Teleological Conception of Socio-technical Acceleration', *Time and Society* 23 (1), 49–68.

Tanake, S. (2019), *History without Chronology* (Ann Arbor, MI: Leverpress in Cooperation with Amherst College Press and Michigan Publishing).

Tocqueville, A. De (1866) *L'Ancien Régime et la Révolution* (Paris: Michel Lévy Frères).

Tocqueville, A. de (1981), *De la démocratie en Amérique, Transl.* by Fr Furet (Biographie, préface et bibliographie) (Paris: GF Flammarion).

Tocqueville, A. de (2004), *Democracy in America, Transl.* by Arthur Goldhammer (New York: The Library of America).

Weisberg, R. (1984), 'Lawyers and Liars: L'Éducation Sentimentale', in: Idem, *The Failure of the Word, the Protagonist as Lawyer in Modern Fiction* (New Haven: Yale University Press) 104–114.

Westerman, P. (2018), *Outsourcing the Law: A Philosophical Perspective on Regulation* (Cheltenham: Edward Elgar Publishing).

White, James B. (1999), *Justice as Translation, An Essay in Cultural and Legal Criticism* (Chicago: University of Chicago Press).

Wolin, Sheldon S. (2001), *Tocqueville between Two Worlds: The Making of a Political and Theoretical Life* (Princeton: Princeton University Press).

Yellott, J. (1993), 'Tocqueville, Judge Hand, and the American Legal Mind', *South Dakota Law Review* 38 (1), 100–129.

Other sources*:*

On transhistoricity, see Fabula Littérature, Histoire, Théorie, no 23 (déc. 2019), www.fabula.org/lht/23/ [accessed 14 February 2022]

Rosellini, M. (2019), 'Pour une pratique de la transhistoricité dans la transmission pédagogique de la littérature', in: Fabula Littérature, Histoire, Théorie, (Trans-)historicité de la littérature, https://www.fabula.org/lht/23/rosellini.html [accessed 9 August 2021]

Seixas, P. (2021), 'Review of François Hartog, Regimes of Historicity: Presentism and experiences of Time', in: International Network for Theory of History, inth.ugent.be [accessed 4 August 2021]

Index

www.ingramcontent.com/pod-product-compliance
Lightning Source LLC
LaVergne TN
LVHW021129300926
849160LV00010B/931
* 9 7 8 1 0 3 2 6 4 0 9 7 6 *